HIGHER LEARNING

READING AND WRITING ABOUT COLLEGE

THIRD EDITION

EDITED BY

Patti See

UNIVERSITY OF WISCONSIN–EAU CLAIRE

Bruce Taylor

UNIVERSITY OF WISCONSIN–EAU CLAIRE

Boston   Columbus   Indianapolis   New York   San Francisco   Upper Saddle River
Amsterdam   Cape Town   Dubai   London   Madrid   Milan   Munich   Paris   Montreal   Toronto
Delhi   Mexico City   São Paulo   Sydney   Hong Kong   Seoul   Singapore   Taipei   Tokyo

Editor-in-Chief: Jodi McPherson
Editorial Assistant: Clara Ciminelli
Marketing Manager: Amy Judd
Managing Editor: Central Publishing
Project Manager: Laura Messerly
Art Director: Jayne Conte
Editorial Production Service: Saraswathi Muralidhar/PreMediaGlobal
Manufacturing Buyer: Laura Messerly
Composition: PreMediaGlobal
Cover Designer: Linda Knowles
Cover Image: Fotolia

Credits and permissions are listed on pages xvi–xviii, constituting an extension of the copyright page.

Library of Congress Cataloging-in-Publication Data

Higher learning: reading and writing about college / edited by Patti See,
Bruce Taylor.—3rd ed.
    p. cm.
  ISBN-13: 978-0-13-231801-3
  ISBN-10: 0-13-231801-6
  1. Readers—Education, Higher.   2. Universities and colleges—Problems, exercises, etc.   3. Education, Higher—Problems, exercises, etc.   4. Readers—Universities and colleges.   5. English language—Rhetoric.   6. Academic writing.   7. College readers.
I. See, Patti.   II. Taylor, Bruce
  PE1127.E37H54 2012
  428.6—dc22

                                                                2010048800

10 9 8 7 6 5 4 3 2 1 RRD-VA 14 13 12 11 10

Allyn & Bacon
is an imprint of

www.pearsonhighered.com

ISBN-10:   0-13-231800-8
ISBN-13: 978-0-13-231800-6

Contents

CHAPTER ONE

Where We're Coming From   1

LEAVING OTHER LIVES

From *Up from Slavery* • *Booker T. Washington**   2

MEMOIR (1901)   Prejudices in 1872 force the author to sleep outside during his journey to college. When he finally reaches what he calls his "promised land," he must pass an unconventional test before he is admitted.

Incurring My Mother's Displeasure • *Zitkala-Sa**   7

MEMOIR (1900)   Recounts the author's difficulty balancing her Native American childhood with learning the "white man's ways" at college and living with the pain of disobeying her mother by continuing her education.

From *One Writer's Beginnings* • *Eudora Welty**   10

MEMOIR (1983)   Chronicles this Pulitzer prize–winning author's earliest memories in a household that valued books.

From *The Latehomecomer: A Hmong Family Memoir* • *Kao Kalia Yang**   15

MEMOIR (2008)   An immigrant family follows the American dream: education for the children and a house of their own.

Saved • *Malcolm X*   21

MEMOIR (1965)   Malcolm X uses his time in jail to hone his reading and writing skills.

Student Response to "Saved"   24

Miss Rinehart's Paddle • *Jeri McCormick*   25

POEM (1991)   Depicts the loss of power for students who always follow the rules and for those who can't help themselves.

---

*First-generation authors.

CHAPTER TWO

School Daze   65

LIFE IN THE FIRST YEAR

CHAPTER THREE
Student Relations   121

FAMILY, FRIENDS, AND LOVERS

CHAPTER FOUR

Teacher, Teacher   187

WILL THIS BE ON THE TEST?

CHAPTER FIVE

Been There, Done That   227

LOOKING FORWARD, LOOKING BACK

Appendix   277

THINKING AND WRITING ABOUT FILM

Preface

I magine entering a foreign country where you understand just enough of the language to communicate, but where you cannot quite grasp the customs or the etiquette of the land. Imagine that you have to learn the culture of that country without anyone showing or telling you how. This is what going to college is like for many first-year students. *Higher Learning: Reading and Writing About College, third edition,* appeals to students and teachers because it is written from their point of view. The fiction, poetry, essays, creative nonfiction, lists, journal entries, and articles included here allow students to see how their individual experiences fit into the culturally and historically diverse traditions and perspectives of university life.

Avid readers—students, teachers, and lifelong learners—know that literature is the one place a person is never alone. This collection allows readers to discover people just like themselves, as well as people sometimes so different from themselves as to be almost, at least at first, unimaginable. Students can watch these people struggle with problems and challenges, most of which never appear in any college catalogue or on any class syllabus. Although universities provide an array of student support systems, new students must work through some aspects of university life mostly on their own. Character, maturity, and experience will be as essential to success as high school class rank or ACT scores. Alienation, isolation, and loneliness will be as much of a challenge as English composition or college algebra.

Many college-success textbooks for first-year students focus on time management, critical thinking, active reading, and lecture and text note taking. These survival skills are the nuts and bolts of college success. The collected readings in this textbook display the whole academic machine chugging along in all its imperfect glory. These readings provide good and bad examples, some broader views and alternative takes of individual experiences, parables of the admirable, cautionary tales, and funny stories.

College students, especially first-year students, often feel isolated. The degree to which they feel a sense of place and a way of fitting in, which many teachers and administrators by now take too much for granted, leads to how well the students perform and, in fact, to whether or not they complete a degree. *Higher Learning* offers some of the "inside" stories of college life and university culture, addressing the difficult issues that students face in their transition to college. It also provides students and teachers with a vehicle to explore, reflect on, and perhaps even discover issues about ethnicity, class, age, gender, and sexual diversity.

Where to Use This Book

As editors, our first instinct would be to say this book should be used everywhere. Or at least everywhere there are people who ought to be paying attention to college, to university culture, to what an education is and how you get one, and to what all of it means. More specifically, natural venues may include transition to college/student success courses, composition courses, creative writing courses, critical thinking courses, and high school college prep courses.

How to Use This Book: A Primer for Careful Reading

Critical Thinking Points—arranged in the categories of *As You Read, After You've Read*, and *Some Possibilities for Writing*—accompany each selection, challenging students with the kinds of close and active critical reading and thinking required at the college level and providing prompts for contemplation, class discussion, and writing.

The *As You Read* questions will lend focus to a selection, help readers formulate their own questions, establish a historical and/or cultural context, or promote connections to students' lives. The *After You've Read* questions often require the kinds of debate, perspective, and points of view that make for lively and productive small-group or full-class discussion. *Some Possibilities for Writing,* at the end of each reading, are an opportunity to respond in writing in the broadest possible ways suitable for short assignments or journal entries.

The *Further Suggestions for Writing* at the end of each chapter offer a menu of varied prompts and assignments for longer, more fully developed, and perhaps more formal assignments that build the skills necessary for writing well in college. These writing prompts range from class reports to interviews, from essays to fully developed research papers that employ the traditional rhetorical strategies such as simple exposition, comparative and causal analyses, or argument and persuasion. The point, in some way or another, is to foster the attention and perspective, the self-awareness and self-assessment that are indeed *higher learning*.

These categories of questions may be necessary and helpful, but any questions from anywhere in the book might be used at any time, in any way. Although each chapter of *Higher Learning* focuses on a particular stage of college life, this book is not necessarily meant to be read sequentially from page one to the end.

Critical Reading Strategies: Questioning as You Read

Good readers question as they read, and many instinctively ask themselves "journalists' questions"—who, what, where, when, how, and why—as their eyes process each sentence. We suggest that students practice asking themselves these questions while reading and that instructors offer students more experience with this strategy by beginning each class discussion by asking students these questions as they pertain to each reading. This exercise will take just five to ten minutes at the start of the class, but it will enrich your discussion considerably.

Below is an example of this method applied to an excerpt from Mike Magnuson's memoir *Lummox: Evolution of a Man* (pages 76 to 83). Keep in mind that these prompts could elicit many possible answers and that the discussion could prompt many more questions.

Who is this piece about? Who is the author? Does that matter?

Mike Magnuson. We know from his bio that he was suspended from college for one year. He's now a college teacher.

What happens in this piece? Imagine you're writing a two-line description to go on the back of a DVD case (if this were a film) . . . what do you absolutely need to know about what goes on in the piece? What is the basic plot?

Mike gets arrested and spends Labor Day weekend in jail. He loves the food and wants to take in all the details of his experience. He reads a book that changes his life. He decides to be an intellectual like the Big Swede.

Where does this take place? Does place matter?

Eau Claire County Jail. Spending a weekend in a small town jail might be much different from being locked up in a city like New York or Chicago. Magnuson is never afraid or even intimidated.

When does it take place? Does the time period influence the piece? Does it matter if it was written recently or twenty-five years ago?

The essay takes place around 1983. If it were set in the present day, Magnuson's jail experience might be more frightening, and his sentence would likely be stricter. If this occurred today, his attempted theft would be on his record forever.

How was the piece written (poem, story, essay, etc.)? Does it matter if this is written in the first-person or third-person? Why do you think the author chose this format?

Magnuson writes his memoir about "Mike" (rather than in the first-person, "I" voice that a traditional memoir would employ). He might do this because he has evolved into "new Mike," and he's looking back at his experiences as "old Mike."

Why do you think the author wrote this? Who is the audience the author had in mind? What might have been his purpose for writing this? Who cares about the piece?

Magnuson writes about a transformative experience, something with which many readers can relate. One of the reasons that reality television is so popular in the United States is that people tend to care about stories in which characters evolve (*I was this, I had this experience, and now I'm something different*). Readers care because his story is funny and interesting: college guy gets drunk and thinks it's a great idea to steal a chair in the shape of a hand . . . when the cops come he throws his wallet in the bushes and tells them he's "Bart Starr" . . . . he spends a long weekend in the county jail, where he decides he's going to be an intellectual or at least become a good student and do what he's supposed to do.

An effective way to write a quality summary of anything—a short story from this collection, a chapter in a psychology textbook, or an article on stem-cell research—is to ask "who, what, where, when, how, and why" and answer each with concrete details. See our Web site http://www.uwec.edu/taylorb for other approaches to critical reading strategies.

A Note on the Third Edition

Significant changes have been made to the literature gathered here and to the Critical Thinking Points, Some Possibilities for Writing, Further Suggestions for Writing, and Selected Films for each chapter. We are especially pleased to add selections from Kao Kalia Yang's *The Latehomecomer: A Hmong Family Memoir,* Daniel Wolff's *How Lincoln Learned to Read: Twelve Great Americans and the Educations that Made Them,* and Alfred Lubrano's "Bricklayer's Boy," to name just a few. We have also added readings that explore alcohol abuse and other risky behavior; study-abroad experiences; Greek life; disability culture; and gay, lesbian, transgender or questioning issues. Nearly twenty of the readings are by authors who are what universities categorize as "first generation" (neither parent graduated with a bachelor's degree). Since that background often affects a person's overall experience, and since about 30 percent of entering first-year students are "first gen," we designate those authors with an asterisk in the table of contents (*).

We have a new feature in each chapter—"This Was the Assignment"—which includes a classroom-tested writing assignment and a "model" student response to that assignment. We also provide two quality student research papers on timely topics for college students—one on college students' use of Facebook and one on the difficulties of coming out—as well as "student responses to readings" for each chapter. Though the chapter titles remain the same as in our second edition, some pieces have been cut, and three to five new pieces have been added per chapter. Some questions have been deleted, and some new ones added to ask students to dig deeper and look further. The writing prompts have been rescaled so that smaller, more informal ones appear at the end of each selection, whereas longer and more formal ones are at the end of each chapter. The annotated filmographies for each chapter have been expanded and revised. Our goal in providing this book continues to be that students will not only be motivated to read, but they also will be moved to reflect and write about their own experiences, their campus, their college life in general, and the world around them.

Acknowledgments

We wish to thank the Office of Research and Sponsored Programs at the University of Wisconsin–Eau Claire and the University of Wisconsin System for their support for travel to share our research at professional conferences. We appreciate the on-going encouragement from colleagues in the Academic Skills Center and Student Support Services. Thank you to our editor, Sande Johnson, who has continued to provide us with guidance. Thank you to our reviewers who saw and commented on our book in various stages: Joseph Eng, California State University, Monterey Bay; Elisa Michals, Sacramento State University; and Jennifer Rosti, Roanoke College.

Finally, thanks to our students in the University of Wisconsin–Eau Claire's developmental education, introduction to college writing, and creative writing courses, who were our first and ongoing audience.

For additional information, activities, and resources intended to enhance the readings in this book, be sure to visit our website:

http://www.uwec.edu/taylorb.

About the Authors

Patti See teaches courses in critical thinking, learning strategies, transitions to college, third-wave feminism, and masculinities studies at the University of Wisconsin–Eau Claire. She also supervises tutoring programs for first-generation /low-income students, multicultural students, and students with disabilities.

Her stories, poems, and essays have appeared in *Salon Magazine, Women's Studies Quarterly, Journal of Development Education, The Wisconsin Academy Review,* and *HipMama,* as well as other magazines and anthologies. In addition to *Higher Learning: Reading and Writing about College,* third edition, she is the author of a poetry collection, *Love's Bluff* (Plainview Press, 2006). She speaks at universities and conferences on a variety of topics, including first-year experience, critical thinking, third-wave feminism, and the depiction of masculinities in popular film. She was the recipient of the 2004 Academic Staff Excellence in Performance Award from the University of Wisconsin–Eau Claire and the 2006 University of Wisconsin-System Regents Award for Excellence.

Bruce Taylor, Professor Emeritus of English at the University of Wisconsin–Eau Claire, has taught courses including first-year experience, introduction to college writing, creative writing, American literature, as well as in the Honors Program throughout his thirty-five years as a college teacher. He is the author of six books of poetry, including *Pity the World* (Plainview Press) and *This Day* (Juniper Press); he is the editor of seven anthologies, including the UPRIVER series of Wisconsin Poetry and Prose, and *Wisconsin Poetry,* published by the Wisconsin Academy of Sciences, Arts, and Letters. His poetry, prose, and translations have appeared in such places as *Carve Magazine, The Chicago Review, Exquisite Corpse, The Nation, Nerve, The New York Quarterly, The Northwest Review, Poetry,* and *E2ink-1: the Best of the Online Journals 2002.*

He has also served as a member of the Literature Panel of the Wisconsin Arts Board and host of The Writer's Workshop: Wisconsin ETN, and he has served as program scholar and consultant for the Wisconsin Humanities Council, the Lila Wallace Foundation, the L. E. Phillips Library, and the Annenberg/CPB Project. He has won awards and fellowships from the Wisconsin Arts Board, Fulbright-Hayes, the National Endowment for the Arts, the National Endowment for the Humanities, and the Bush Artist Foundation. He was the recipient of the 2004 Excellence in Scholarship Award from the University of Wisconsin–Eau Claire, and the 2006 Major Achievement Award from the Council of Wisconsin Writers for his lifetime of work as a poet, teacher, and community arts advocate.

We would love to hear from you. Please e-mail the authors with any feedback or suggestions at

seepk@uwec.edu   or   taylorb@uwec.edu

Credits and Permissions

Colleen Larimore. Copyright © 1997 by Cornell University. Reprinted by permission of the publisher, Cornell University Press.

"Sisterhood" by Stephanie Stillman-Spisak originally appeared in from *Out and About Campus: Personal Accounts by Lesbian, Gay, Bisexual, and Transgendered College Students*, edited by Kim Howard and Annie Stevens. Los Angeles: Alyson Books, 2000. Reprinted by permission of the author.

"Walking in America in My French Shoes" by Benedicte Bachelot used here with permission of the author.

"Lost in Italy" by Elizabeth Barney used here with permission of the author.

"First Year in College is the Riskiest" by Robert Davis and Anthony Debarros first appeared in the *USA Today* on January 25, 2006. From USA TODAY, a division of Gannett Co., Inc. Reprinted with permission.

"History as a Student" by Kayla Piper. Used by permission of the author.

Chapter Three

"Raspberries" by Jennifer Fandel. Reprinted by permission of the author.

"Ten Commandments for a College Freshman" by Joseph McCabe from *Your First Year at College: Letters to a College Freshman* by Joseph McCabe. Reprinted by permission of the author.

"Commandments for a First-Year Student (From His Mom)" by Patsy Sanchez used here with permission of the author.

"Carmen" by Jennifer Sheridan originally published in *Prairie Hearts*, Outrider Press Inc. Reprinted by permission of Outrider Press.

"Who Shall I Be? The Allure of a Fresh Start" by Jennifer Crichton. Reprinted by permission of the author.

"Welcome to Facebook" by Cody Meyers was written for English 110: Introduction to College Writing. Used here with permission of the author.

"What It's Really Like" by Frank Smoot. Reprinted by permission of the author.

"No More Kissing—AIDS Everywhere" by Michael Blumenthal. Reprinted by permission of the author.

"Dear Concerned Mother" by Jill Wolfson first appeared in *Salon.com*. Reprinted with permission of the author.

"The Undeclared Major" by Will Weaver originally appeared in *A Gravestone Made of Wheat* (1989). Reprinted with permission by the author.

"Homeward Bond" by Daisy Nguyen. Reprinted by permission of the author.

"EveryDay Use" from *In Love and Trouble: Stories of Black Women*, copyright © 1973 by Alice Walker, reprinted by permission of Harcourt, Inc.

"The Stages, Struggles and Reliefs of Coming Out" by Alicia Merclazo was written for Women's Studies 210: Culture of Third Wave Feminism. Used here by permission from the author.

Chapter Four

From *How Lincoln Learned to Read: Twelve Great Americans and the Educations that Made Them* by Daniel Wolff. Reprinted by permission of Bloomsbury USA.

Chapter Five

Supplemental Resources

INSTRUCTOR SUPPORT – Resources to simplify your life and support your students.

Book Specific

Online Instructor's Manual This manual is intended to give professors a framework or blueprint of ideas and suggestions that may assist them in providing their students with activities, journal writing, thought-provoking situations, and group activities. The test bank organized by chapter includes: multiple choice, true/false and short-answer questions that support the key features in the book. This supplement is available for download from the Instructor's Resource Center at www.pearsonhighered.com/irc

MyStudentSuccessLab Are you teaching online, in a hybrid setting, or looking to infuse exciting technology into your classroom for the first time? Then be sure to refer to the MyStudentSuccessLab section included in the coming pages of this Preface to learn more. This online solution is designed to help students build the skills they need to succeed at www.mystudentsuccesslab.com

Other Resources

"Easy access to online, book-specific teaching support is now just a click away!"
Instructor Resource Center - Register. Redeem. Login. Three easy steps that open the door to a variety of print and media resources in downloadable, digital format, available to instructors exclusively through the Pearson/Prentice Hall 'IRC'. www.pearsonhighered.com/irc

"Choose from a wide range of video resources for the classroom!"
Prentice Hall Reference Library: Life Skills Pack (ISBN: 0-13-127079-6). Contains all 4 videos, or they may be requested individually as follows:
- *Learning Styles and Self-Awareness*, 0-13-028502-1
- *Critical and Creative Thinking*, 0-13-028504-8
- *Relating to Others*, 0-13-028511-0
- *Personal Wellness*, 0-13-028514-5

Prentice Hall Reference Library: Study Skills Pack (ISBN: 0-13-127080-X). Contains all 6 videos, or they may be requested individually as follows:
- *Reading Effectively*, 0-13-028505-6
- *Listening and Memory*, 0-13-028506-4
- *Note Taking and Research*, 0-13-028508-0
- *Writing Effectively*, 0-13-028509-9
- *Effective Test Taking*, 0-13-028500-5
- *Goal Setting and Time Management*, 0-13-028503-X

Prentice Hall Reference Library: Career Skills Pack (ISBN: 0-13-118529-2). Contains all 3 videos, or they may be requested individually as follows:
- *Skills for the 21st Century – Technology*, 0-13-028512-9
- *Skills for the 21st Century – Math and Science,* 0-13-028513-7
- *Managing Career and Money*, 0-13-028516-1
- *Complete Reference Library - Life/Study Skills/Career* Video Pack on DVD (ISBN: 0-13-501095-0).

- Our Reference Library of thirteen popular video resources has now been digitized onto one DVD so students and instructors alike can benefit from the array of video clips. Featuring Life Skills, Study Skills, and Career Skills, they help to reinforce the course content in a more interactive way.

Faculty Video Resources
- Teacher Training Video 1: *Critical Thinking*, ISBN: 0-13-099432-4
- Teacher Training Video 2: *Stress Management & Communication*, ISBN: 0-13-099578-9
- Teacher Training Video 3: *Classroom Tips*, ISBN: 0-13-917205-X
- Student Advice Video, ISBN: 0-13-233206-X
- Study Skills Video, ISBN: 0-13-096095-0

Current Issues Videos
- ABC News Video Series: *Student Success Second Edition*, ISBN: 0-13-031901-5
- ABC News Video Series: *Student Success Third Edition*, ISBN: 0-13-152865-3

MyStudentSuccessLab PH Videos on DVD (ISBN: 0-13-514249-0).
- Our six most popular video resources have been digitized onto one DVD so students and instructors alike can benefit from the array of video clips. Featuring Technology, Math and Science, Managing Money and Career, Learning Styles and Self-Awareness, Study Skills, and Peer Advice, they help to reinforce the course content in a more interactive way. They are also accessible through our MSSL and course management offerings and available on VHS.

"Through partnership opportunities, we offer a variety of assessment options!"
LASSI - The LASSI is a 10-scale, 80-item assessment of students' awareness about and use of learning and study strategies. Addressing skill, will and self-regulation, the focus is on both covert and overt thoughts, behaviors, attitudes and beliefs that relate to successful learning and that can be altered through educational interventions. Available in two formats: Paper ISBN: 0-13-172315-4 or Online ISBN: 0-13-172316-2 (access card).

Noel Levitz/RMS – This retention tool measures Academic Motivation, General Coping Ability, Receptivity to Support Services, PLUS Social Motivation. It helps identify at-risk students, the areas with which they struggle, and their receptiveness to support. Available in paper or online formats, as well as short and long versions. Paper Long Form A: ISBN: 0-13-512066-7; Paper Short Form B: ISBN: 0-13-512065-9; Online Forms A,B & C: ISBN: 0-13-098158-3.

Robbins Self Assessment Library – This compilation teaches students to create a portfolio of skills. S.A.L. is a self-contained, interactive, library of 49 behavioral questionnaires that help students discover new ideas about themselves, their attitudes, and their personal strengths and weaknesses. Available in Paper, CD-Rom, and Online (Access Card) formats.

Readiness for Education at a Distance Indicator(READI) - READI is a web-based tool that assesses the overall likelihood for online learning success. READI generates an immediate score and a diagnostic interpretation of results, including recommendations for successful participation in online courses and potential remediation sources. Please visit www.readi.info for additional information. ISBN: 0-13-188967-2.

Pathway to Student Success CD-ROM
The CD is divided into several categories, each of which focuses on a specific topic that relates to students and provides them with the context, tools and strategies to enhance their educational experience. ISBN: 0-13-239314-X.

The Golden Personality Type Profiler

The Golden Personality Type Profiler™ helps students understand how they make decisions and relate to others. By completing the Golden Personality Type Profiler™ students develop a deeper understanding of their strengths, a clearer picture of how their behavior impacts others, and a better appreciation for the interpersonal style of others and how to interact with them more effectively. Using these results as a guide, students will gain the self awareness that is key to professional development and success. ISBN: 0-13-706654-6.

"For a truly tailored solution that fosters campus connections and increases retention, talk with us about custom publishing."
Pearson Custom Publishing – We are the largest custom provider for print and media shaped to your course's needs. Please visit us at www.pearsoncustom.com to learn more.

STUDENT SUPPORT – Tools to help make the grade now, and excel in school later.

CourseSmart eTextbook Available CourseSmart is an exciting new choice for students looking to save money. As an alternative to purchasing the printed textbook, students can purchase an electronic version of the same content. With a CourseSmart eTextbook, students can search the text, make notes online, print out reading assignments that incorporate lecture notes, and bookmark important passages for later review. For more information, or to purchase access to the CourseSmart eTextbook, visit www.coursesmart.com.

"Today's students are more inclined than ever to use technology to enhance their learning."
Refer to the **MyStudentSuccessLab** section of this Preface to learn about our revolutionary resource (www.mystudentsuccesslab.com) This online solution is designed to help students build the skills they need to succeed.

"Time management is the #1 challenge students face." We can help.
Prentice Hall Planner – A basic planner that includes a monthly & daily calendar plus other materials to facilitate organization. 8.5x11.

Premier Annual Planner - This specially designed, annual 4-color collegiate planner includes an academic planning/resources section, monthly planning section (2 pages/month), weekly planning section (48 weeks; July start date), which facilitate short-term as well as long-term planning. Spiral bound, 6x9. Customization is available.

"Journaling activities promote self-discovery and self-awareness."
Student Reflection Journal - Through this vehicle, students are encouraged to track their progress and share their insights, thoughts, and concerns. 8 1/2 x 11. 90 pages.

"The Student Orientation Series includes short booklets on specialized topics that facilitate greater student understanding."
S.O.S. Guides help students understand what these opportunities are, how to take advantage of them, and how to learn from their peers while doing so. They include:
- Connolly: *Learning Communities* ISBN: 0-13-232243-9
- Hoffman: *Stop Procrastination Now! 10 Simple and SUCCESSFUL Steps for Student Success,* ISBN: 0-13-513056-5
- Jabr: *English Language Learners* ISBN: 0-13-232242-0
- Watts: *Service Learning* ISBN: 0-13-232201-0

For Students!

Why is this course important?

This course will help you transition to college, introduce you to campus resources, and prepare you for success in all aspects of college, career, and life. You will:

- Develop Skills to Excel in Other Classes
- Apply Concepts from College to Your Career and Life
- Learn to Use Media Resources

How can you get the most out of the book and online resources required in this class?

Purchase your book and online resources before the First Day of Class. Register and log in to the online resources using your access code.

Develop Skills to Excel in Other Classes

- Helps you with your homework
- Prepares you for exams

Apply Concepts from College to Your Career and Life

- Provides learning techniques
- Helps you achieve your goals

Learn to Use Media Resources

- **www.mystudentsuccesslab.com** helps you build skills you need to succeed through peer-led videos, interactive exercises and projects, journaling and goal setting activities.
- Connect with real students, practice skill development, and personalize what is learned.

Want to get involved with Pearson like other students have?

Join www.PearsonStudents.com

It is a place where our student customers can incorporate their views and ideas into their learning experience. They come to find out about our programs such as the **Pearson Student Advisory Board**, **Pearson Campus Ambassador**, and the **Pearson Prize** (student scholarship!).

Here's how you can get involved:

- Tell your instructors, friends, and family members about **PearsonStudents**.
- To get daily updates on how students can boost their resumes, study tips, get involved with Pearson, and earn rewards:

  - Become a fan of **Pearson Students on Facebook**
  - Follow **@Pearson_Student on Twitter**

- Explore **Pearson Free Agent**. It allows you get involved in the publishing process, by giving student feedback.

See you on **PearsonStudents** where our student customers live. When students succeed, we succeed!

Succeed in college and beyond!
Connect, practice, and personalize with MyStudentSuccessLab.

www.mystudentsuccesslab.com

MyStudentSuccessLab is an online solution designed to help students acquire the skills they need to succeed. They will have access to peer-led video presentations and develop core skills through interactive exercises and projects that provide academic, life, and career skills that will transfer to ANY course.

It can accompany any Student Success text, or be sold as a stand-alone course offering. To become successful learners, students must consistently apply techniques to daily activities.

How will MyStudentSuccessLab make a difference?

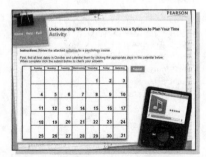

Is motivation a challenge, and if so, how do you deal with it?
Video Presentation – Experience peer led video 'by students, for students' of all ages and stages.

How would better class preparation improve the learning experience?
Practice activities – Practice skills for each topic - beginning, intermediate, and advanced - leveled by Bloom's taxonomy.

PEARSON
mystudentsuccesslab

What could you gain by building critical thinking and problem-solving skills in this class?

Apply (final project) – Complete a final project using these skills to create 'personally relevant' resources.

As an instructor, how much easier would it be to assign and use MyStudentSuccessLab if you had an Implementation guide?

Instructor Guide – Describes each activity, the skills addressed, an estimate of student time on task, and a grading rubric for the final Apply activity.

MyStudentSuccessLab Feature set:

Topic Overview: Module objectives.

Video Presentation - Connect: Real student video interviews on key issues.

Practice: Three skill-building exercises per topic provide interactive experience and practice.

Apply - Personalize: Apply what is learned by creating a personally relevant project and journal.

Resources: Plagiarism Guide, Dictionary, Calculators, and Assessments (Career, Learning Styles, and Personality Styles).

Additional Assignments: Extra suggested activities to use with each topic.

Text-Specific Study Plan (available with select books): Chapter Objectives, Practice Tests, Enrichment activities, and Flashcards.

MyStudentSuccessLab Topic List -

1. Time Management/Planning
2. Values/Goal Setting
3. Learning How You Learn
4. Listening and Taking Class Notes
5. Reading and Annotating
6. Memory and Studying
7. Critical Thinking
8. Problem-Solving
9. Information Literacy
10. Communication
11. Test Prep and Test Taking
12. Stress Management
13. Financial Literacy
14. Majors and Careers

MyStudentSuccessLab Support:

- **Demos, Registration, Log-in** - www.mystudentsuccesslab.com under "Tours and Training" and "Support."
- **Email support** - Send an inquiry to MyStudentSuccessLab@pearson.com
- **Online Training** - Join one of our weekly WebEx training sessions.
- **Peer Training** - Faculty Advocate connection for qualified adoptions.
- **Technical support** - 24 hours a day, seven days a week, at http://247pearsoned.custhelp.com

Now Available!
A 'one-stop shop' for student success.

This website offers a compilation of Pearson's training, resources, and support options all in one convenient place.

We provide variety of **Training** options to meet your needs. Events and Workshops around the country as well as Online Webinars. MyStudentSuccessLab Technology training is available too.

A wealth of **Resources** are available to address a range of interests, including assessments, online catalog, customized solutions, Instructor Resources, and Student Resources. Technology is addressed, whether you're teaching online, hybrid, or just need an engagement tool.

For **Support**, always contact your local sales professional, however, the SSCD Team is here to help anytime including Customer Service, Technical Support, Editorial, Events, Marketing, Specialists, and Faculty Advocates.

Welcome to the **Pearson SSCD Online Community** where we connect, empower, and renew with one another. Regardless of your institute origin, teaching background, or experience level, we strive to ensure there are resources available to support our mission—infusing success for EVERY student and instructor!

www.pearsonhighered.com/sscd4success

One

Where We're Coming From

LEAVING OTHER LIVES

The selections here examine how different people, places, times, and cultures affect who and what any individual becomes. This chapter explores reasons for going (or not going) to college, how formal education may or may not prepare students for adult life, the values of learning on one's own, and personal experiences of overcoming stereotypes and prejudices.

READING SELECTIONS

from *Up from Slavery*

Incurring My Mother's Displeasure

from *One Writer's Beginnings*

from *The Latehomecomer: A Hmong Family Memoir*

Saved

Miss Rinehart's Paddle

50% Chance of Lightning

Somewhere in Minnesota

LD

School's Out: One Young Man Puzzles Over His Future Without College

Eighth-Grade Final Exam: Salina, Kansas, 1895

This Was the Assignment: Disability Culture

This Was the Assignment: College Ain't Cheap

1

Up from Slavery

AN EXCERPT   Booker T. Washington

Booker T. Washington (1856–1915) was a U.S. educator who urged blacks to attempt to uplift themselves through education and economic advancement. He was born in Franklin County, Virginia, the son of a slave. From 1872 to 1875, Washington attended a newly founded school for blacks, Hampton Normal and Agricultural Institute (now Hampton University). In 1879, he became an instructor at Hampton. The school was so successful that, in 1881, Washington was appointed principal of a black school in Tuskegee, Alabama (now Tuskegee University).

The sight of it seemed to give me a new life. I felt that a new kind of existence had now begun—that life would now have a new meaning.

CRITICAL THINKING POINTS: *As you read*

1. What are some clues to the time and place?
2. The author had no idea where Hampton was or how much tuition cost. What circumstances might have led the author to have such a desire to go to college?
3. Recall a time when you felt proud of yourself for learning, simply for the sake of acquiring knowledge. What led to this?

N otwithstanding my success at Mrs. Ruffner's I did not give up the idea of going to the Hampton Institute. In the fall of 1872 I determined to make an effort to get there, although, as I have stated, I had no definite idea of the direction in which Hampton was, or of what it would cost to go there. I do not think that any one thoroughly sympathized with me in my ambition to go to Hampton unless it was my mother, and she was troubled with a grave fear that I was starting out on a 'wild-goose chase.' At any rate, I got only a half-hearted consent from her that I might start. The small amount of money that I had earned had been consumed by my stepfather and the remainder of the family, with the exception of a very few dollars, and so I had very little with which to buy clothes and pay my traveling expenses. My brother John helped me all that he could, but of course that was not a great deal, for his work was in the coal-mine, where he did not earn much, and most of what he did earn went in the direction of paying the household expenses.

Perhaps the thing that touched and pleased me most in connection with my starting for Hampton was the interest that many of the older coloured people took in the matter. They had spent the best days of their lives in slavery, and hardly expected to live to see the time when they would see a member of their race leave home to attend a boarding school. Some of these older people would give me a nickel, others a quarter, or a handkerchief.

Finally the great day came, and I started for Hampton. I had only a small, cheap satchel that contained what few articles of clothing I could get. My mother at the time was rather weak and broken in health. I hardly expected to see her again, and thus our parting was all the more sad. She, however, was very brave through it all. At that time there were no through trains connecting that part of West Virginia with eastern Virginia. Trains ran only a portion of the way, and the remainder of the distance was traveled by stage-coaches.

The distance from Malden to Hampton is about five hundred miles. I had not been away from home many hours before it began to grow painfully evident that I did not have enough money to pay my fare to Hampton. One experience I shall long remember. I had been traveling over the mountains most of the afternoon in an old-fashioned stage-coach, when, late in the evening, the coach stopped for the night at a common, unpainted house called a hotel. All the other passengers except myself were whites. In my ignorance I supposed that the little hotel existed for the purpose of accommodating the passengers who traveled on the stage-coach. The difference that the colour of one's skin would make I had not thought anything about. After all the other passengers had been shown rooms and were getting ready for supper, I shyly presented myself before the man at the desk. It is true I had practically no money in my pocket with which to pay for bed or food, but I had hoped in some way to beg my way into the good graces of the landlord, for at that season in the mountains of Virginia the weather was cold, and I wanted to get indoors for the night. Without asking as to whether I had any money, the man at the desk firmly refused to even consider the matter of providing me with food or lodging. This was my first experience in finding out what the colour of my skin meant. In some way I managed to keep warm by walking about, and so got through the night. My whole soul was so bent upon reaching Hampton that I did not have time to cherish any bitterness toward the hotelkeeper.

By walking, begging rides both in wagons and in the cars, in some way, after a number of days, I reached the city of Richmond, Virginia, about eighty-two miles from Hampton. When I reached there, tired, hungry, and dirty, it was late in the night. I had never been in a large city, and this rather added to my misery. When I reached Richmond, I was completely out of money. I had not a single acquaintance in the place, and, being unused to city ways, I did not know where to go. I applied at several places for lodging, but they all wanted money, and that was what I did not have. Knowing nothing else better to do, I walked the streets. In doing this I passed by many food-stands where fried chicken and half-moon apple pies were piled high and made to present a most tempting appearance. At that time it seemed to me that I would have promised all that I expected to possess in the future to have gotten hold of one of those chicken legs or one of those pies. But I could not get either of these, nor anything else to eat.

I must have walked the streets till after midnight. At last I became so exhausted that I could walk no longer. I was tired, I was hungry, I was everything but discouraged. Just about the time when I reached extreme physical exhaustion, I came upon a portion of a street where the board sidewalk was considerably elevated. I waited for a few minutes, till I was sure that no passers-by could see me, and then crept under the sidewalk and lay for the night upon the ground, with my satchel of clothing for a pillow. Nearly all night I could hear the tramp of feet over my head. The next morning I found myself somewhat refreshed, but I was extremely hungry, because it had been a long time since I had had sufficient food.

As soon as it became light enough for me to see my surroundings I noticed that I was near a large ship, and that this ship seemed to be unloading a cargo of pig iron. I went at once to the vessel and asked the captain to permit me to help unload the vessel in order to get money for food. The captain, a white man, who seemed to be kindhearted, consented. I worked long enough to earn money for my breakfast, and it seems to me, as I remember it now, to have been about the best breakfast that I have ever eaten. My work pleased the captain so well that he told me if I desired I could continue working for a small amount per day. This I was very glad to do. I continued working on this vessel for a number of days. After buying food with the small wages I received there was not much left to add to the amount I must get to pay my way to Hampton. In order to economize in every way possible, so as to be sure to reach Hampton in a reasonable time, I continued to sleep under the same sidewalk that gave me shelter the first night I was in Richmond. Many years after that the coloured citizens of Richmond very kindly tendered me a reception at which there must have been two thousand people present. This reception was held not far from the spot where I slept the first night I spent in that city, and I must confess that my mind was more upon the sidewalk that first gave me shelter than upon the reception, agreeable and cordial as it was.

When I had saved what I considered enough money with which to reach Hampton, I thanked the captain of the vessel for his kindness, and started again.

Without any unusual occurrence I reached Hampton, with a surplus of exactly fifty cents with which to begin my education. To me it had been a long, eventful journey; but the first sight of the large, three-story, brick school building seemed to have rewarded me for all that I had undergone in order to reach the place. If the people who gave the money to provide that building could appreciate the influence the sight of it had upon me, as well as upon thousands of other youths, they would feel all the more encouraged to make such gifts. It seemed to me to be the largest and most beautiful building I had ever seen. The sight of it seemed to give me a new life. I felt that a new kind of existence had now begun—that life would now have a new meaning. I felt that I had reached the promised land, and I resolved to let no obstacle prevent me from putting forth the highest effort to fit myself to accomplish the most good in the world.

As soon as possible after reaching the grounds of the Hampton Institute, I presented myself before the head teacher for assignment to a class. Having been so long without proper food, a bath and change of clothing, I did not, of course, make a very favourable impression upon her, and I could see at once that there were doubts in her mind about the wisdom of admitting me as a student. I felt that I could hardly blame her if she got the idea that I was a worthless loafer or tramp. For some time she did not refuse to admit me, neither did she decide in my favour, and I continued to linger about her, and to impress her in all the ways I could with my worthiness. In the meantime I saw her admitting other students, and that added greatly to my discomfort, for I felt, deep down in my heart, that I could do as well as they, if I could only get a chance to show what was in me.

After some hours had passed, the head teacher said to me: "The adjoining recitation-room needs sweeping. Take the broom and sweep it." It occurred to me at once that here was my chance. Never did I receive an order with more delight. I knew that I could sweep, for Mrs. Ruffner had thoroughly taught me how to do that when I lived with her.

I swept the recitation-room three times. Then I got a dusting-cloth and I dusted it four times. All the woodwork around the walls, every bench, table, and desk, I went over four times with my dusting-cloth. Besides, every piece of furniture had been moved and every closet and corner in the room had been thoroughly cleaned. I had the feeling that in a large measure my future depended upon the impression I made upon the teacher in the cleaning of that room. When I was through, I reported to the head teacher.

She was a 'Yankee' woman who knew just where to look for dirt. She went into the room and inspected the floor and closets; then she took her handkerchief and rubbed it on the woodwork about the walls, and over the table and benches. When she was unable to find one bit of dirt on the floor, or a particle of dust on any of the furniture, she quietly remarked, "I guess you will do to enter this institution." I was one of the happiest souls on earth. The sweeping of that room was my college examination, and never did any youth pass an examination for entrance into Harvard or Yale that gave him more genuine satisfaction. I have passed several examinations since then, but I have always felt that this was the best one I ever passed.

I have spoken of my own experience in entering the Hampton Institute. Perhaps few, if any, had anything like the same experience that I had, but about that same period there were hundreds who found their way to Hampton and other institutions after experiencing something of the same difficulties that I went through. The young men and women were determined to secure an education at any cost.

1901

CRITICAL THINKING POINTS: *After you've read*

1. Washington learns several important lessons on his journey to Hampton. What are some of them?

2. Washington says about a reception for him in Richmond, "This reception was held not far from the spot where I slept the first night I spent in that city, and I must confess that my mind was more upon the sidewalk that first gave me

shelter than upon the reception, agreeable and cordial as it was." What might such a statement say about Washington?

3. Washington says of his first assignment from the head teacher, "The sweeping of that room was my college examination, and never did any youth pass an examination for entrance into Harvard or Yale that gave him more genuine satisfaction. I have passed several examinations since then, but I have always felt that this was the best one I ever passed." What were some of the reasons this was so important to him?

SOME POSSIBILITIES FOR WRITING

1. Write a scene in which Washington, who is sleeping under the boardwalk on his way to Hampton, meets a man who attends college. Or, write a scene between Washington and another African-American man who has no aspirations for college.

2. Washington says of first seeing Hampton, "I felt that I had reached the promised land." Why was education so important to him? Do you feel it is as important for you?

3. Find *Up from Slavery* and read Chapter 8, "Teaching School in a Stable and a Hen-House." After reading the piece, compare/contrast Washington as a student and a teacher. What insights about education arise from your writing?

Incurring My Mother's Displeasure

FROM *THE SCHOOL DAYS OF AN INDIAN GIRL*   Zitkala-Sa

Zitkala-Sa (1876–1938) was a Sioux Indian. "Incurring My Mother's Displeasure" appeared in the *Atlantic Monthly* in 1900. It is a part of her larger work, *The School Days of an Indian Girl*.

Thus, homeless and heavy-hearted, I began anew my life among strangers.

CRITICAL THINKING POINTS: *As you read*

1. What are some clues to the era?
2. The language and tone of this essay are very formal. Why might that be so?
3. Speculate on what causes prejudice among ethnic groups. What are some stereotypes, past or present, of Native Americans?

In the second journey to the East I had not come without some precautions. I had a secret interview with one of our best medicine men, and when I left his wigwam I carried securely in my sleeve a tiny bunch of magic roots. This possession assured me of friends wherever I should go. So absolutely did I believe in its charms that I wore it through all the school routine for more than a year. Then, before I lost my faith in the dead roots, I lost the little buckskin bag containing all my good luck.

At the close of this second term of three years I was the proud owner of my first diploma. The following autumn I ventured upon a college career against my mother's will. I had written for her approval, but in her reply I found no encouragement. She called my notice to her neighbors' children, who had completed their education in three years. They had returned to their homes, and were then talking English with the frontier settlers. Her few words hinted that I had better give up my slow attempt to learn the white man's ways, and be content to roam over the prairies and find my living upon wild roots. I silenced her by deliberate disobedience.

Thus, homeless and heavy-hearted, I began anew my life among strangers.

As I hid myself in my little room in the college dormitory, away from the scornful and yet curious eyes of the students, I pined for sympathy. Often I wept in secret, wishing I had gone West, to be nourished by my mother's love, instead of remaining among a cold race whose hearts were frozen hard with prejudice.

During the fall and winter seasons I scarcely had a real friend, though by that time several of my classmates were courteous to me at a safe distance. My mother had not yet forgiven my rudeness to her, and I had no moment for letter-writing.

By daylight and lamplight, I spun with reeds and thistles, until my hands were tired from their weaving, the magic design which promised me the white man's respect.

At length, in the spring term, I entered an oratorical contest among the various classes. As the day of competition approached, it did not seem possible that the event was so near at hand, but it came. In the chapel the classes assembled together, with their invited guests. The high platform was carpeted, and gaily festooned with college colors. A bright white light illumined the room and outlined clearly the great polished beams that arched the domed ceiling. The assembled crowds filled the air with pulsating murmurs. When the hour for speaking arrived all were hushed. But on the wall the old clock which pointed out the trying moment ticked calmly on.

One after another I saw and heard the orators. Still, I could not realize that they longed for the favorable decision of the judges as much as I did. Each contestant received a loud burst of applause, and some were cheered heartily. Too soon my turn came, and I paused a moment behind the curtains for a deep breath. After my concluding words, I heard the same applause that the others had called out.

Upon my retreating steps, I was astounded to receive from my fellow students a large bouquet of roses tied with flowing ribbons. With the lovely flowers I fled from the stage. This friendly token was a rebuke to me for the hard feelings I had borne them.

Later, the decision of the judges awarded me the first place. Then there was a mad uproar in the hall, where my classmates sang and shouted my name at the top of their lungs; and the disappointed students howled and brayed in fearfully dissonant tin trumpets. In this excitement, happy students rushed forward to offer their congratulations. And I could not conceal a smile when they wished to escort me in a procession to the students' parlor, where all were going to calm themselves. Thanking them for the kind spirit which prompted them to make such a proposition, I walked alone with the night to my own little room.

A few weeks afterward, I appeared as the college representative in another contest. This time the competition was among orators from different colleges in our state. It was held at the state capital, in one of the largest opera houses.

Here again was a strong prejudice against my people. In the evening, as the great audience filled the house, the student bodies began warring among themselves. Fortunately, I was spared witnessing any of the noisy wrangling before the contest began. The slurs against the Indian that stained the lips of our opponents were already burning like a dry fever within my breast.

But after the orations were delivered a deeper burn awaited me. There, before that vast ocean of eyes, some college rowdies threw out a large white flag, with a drawing of a most forlorn Indian girl on it. Under this they had printed in bold black letters words that ridiculed the college which was represented by a "squaw." Such worse than barbarian rudeness embittered me. While we waited for the verdict of the judges, I gleamed fiercely upon the throngs of palefaces. My teeth were hard set, as I saw the white flag still floating insolently in the air. Then anxiously we watched the man carry toward the stage the envelope containing the final decision.

There were two prizes given, that night, and one of them was mine!

The evil spirit laughed within me when the white flag dropped out of sight, and the hands which furled it hung limp in defeat.

Leaving the crowd as quickly as possible, I was soon in my room. The rest of the night I sat in an armchair and gazed into the crackling fire. I laughed no more in triumph when thus alone. The little taste of victory did not satisfy a hunger in my heart. In my mind I saw my mother far away on the Western plains, and she was holding a charge against me.

1900

CRITICAL THINKING POINTS: *After you've read*

1. In what ways is Zitkala-Sa "homeless"?

2. Why would the narrator physically and spiritually separate herself from her people in order to go to college? What are some details from the story that support your opinion?

3. Read or reread the selection from Booker T. Washington's *Up from Slavery*. How is Zitkala-Sa's experience at college similar to Washington's? How is it different?

SOME POSSIBILITIES FOR WRITING

1. Imagine what happens when the narrator finally returns to her tribe. Write a reunion scene between Zitkala-Sa and her mother.

2. Recall a time when you purposely disobeyed your parents. What circumstances led to this? Write about the moment when you knew you would go against their wishes. What was the outcome?

3. The narrator feels isolated from her classmates because of their prejudice. Have you ever felt isolated from classmates, friends, or family? Write a scene describing your isolation or someone else's.

One Writer's Beginnings

AN EXCERPT   **Eudora Welty**

Eudora Welty (1909–2001) received her bachelor of arts degree from the University of Wisconsin–Madison in 1929. She won the Pulitzer Prize for fiction with *The Optimist's Daughter* in 1969. *One Writer's Beginnings* was nominated for the 1983 National Book Critics Circle Award.

I learned from the age of two or three that any room in our house, at any time of day, was there to read in, or to be read to.

CRITICAL THINKING POINTS: *As you read*

1. Pay attention to the things that are detailed in this essay. Why do you think the author chose the objects she did?
2. Pay attention to all the action in this essay. Why do you think she chose the actions she did?
3. Pay attention to the different ways in which the boys and girls are educated. How is this a sign of the times?

In our house on North Congress Street in Jackson, Mississippi, where I was born, the oldest of three children, in 1909, we grew up to the striking of clocks. There was a mission-style oak grandfather clock standing in the hall, which sent its gong-like strokes through the living room, dining room, kitchen, and pantry, and up the sounding board of the stairwell. Through the night, it could find its way into our ears; sometimes, even on the sleeping porch, midnight could wake us up. My parents' bedroom had a smaller striking clock that answered it. Though the kitchen clock did nothing but show the time, the dining room clock was a cuckoo clock with weights on long chains, on one of which my baby brother, after climbing on a chair to the top of the china closet, once succeeded in suspending the cat for a moment. I don't know whether or not my father's Ohio family, in having been Swiss back in the 1700s before the first three Welty brothers came to America, had anything to do with this; but we all of us have been time-minded all our lives. This was good at least for a future fiction writer, being able to learn so penetratingly, and almost first of all, about chronology. It was one of a good many things I learned almost without knowing it; it would be there when I needed it.

My father loved all instruments that would instruct and fascinate. His place to keep things was the drawer in the "library table" where lying on top of his folded maps was a telescope with brass extensions, to find the moon and the Big Dipper after supper in our front yard, and to keep appointments with eclipses. There was a folding Kodak that was brought out for Christmas, birthdays, and trips. In the back of the drawer you could find a magnifying glass, a kaleidoscope, and a gyroscope kept in a black buckram box, which he would set dancing for us on a string pulled tight. He had also supplied himself with an assortment of puzzles composed of metal rings and intersecting links and keys chained together, impossible for the rest of us, however patiently shown, to take apart; he had an almost childlike love of the ingenious.

In time, a barometer was added to our dining room wall; but we didn't really need it. My father had the country boy's accurate knowledge of the weather and its skies. He went out and stood on our front steps first thing in the morning and took a look at it and a sniff. He was a pretty good weather prophet.

"Well, I'm not," my mother would say with enormous self-satisfaction.

He told us children what to do if we were lost in a strange country. "Look for where the sky is brightest along the horizon," he said. "That reflects the nearest river. Strike out for a river and you will find habitation." Eventualities were much on his mind. In his care for us children he cautioned us to take measures against such things as being struck by lightning. He drew us all away from the windows during the severe electrical storms that are common where we live. My mother stood apart, scoffing at caution as a character failing. "Why, I always loved a storm! High winds never bothered me in West Virginia! Just listen at that! I wasn't a bit afraid of a little lightning and thunder! I'd go out on the mountain and spread my arms wide and run in a good big storm!"

So I developed a strong meteorological sensibility. In the years ahead when I wrote stories, atmosphere took its influential role from the start. Commotion in the weather and the inner feelings aroused by such a hovering disturbance emerged connected in dramatic form. (I tried a tornado first, in a story called "The Winds.")

From our earliest Christmas times, Santa Claus brought us toys that instruct boys and girls (separately) how to build things—stone blocks cut to the castle-building style, Tinker Toys, and Erector sets. Daddy made for us himself elaborate kites that needed to be taken miles out of town to a pasture long enough (and my father was not afraid of horses and cows watching) for him to run with and get up on a long cord to which my mother held the spindle, and then we children were given it to hold, tugging like something alive at our hands. They were beautiful, sound, shapely box kites, smelling delicately of office glue for their entire short lives. And of course, as soon as the boys attained anywhere near the right age, there was an electric train, the engine with its pea-sized working headlight, its line of cars, tracks equipped with switches, semaphores, its station, its bridges, and its tunnel, which blocked off all other traffic in the upstairs hall. Even from downstairs, and through the cries of excited children, the elegant rush and click of the train could be heard through the ceiling, running around and around its figure eight.

All of this, but especially the train, represents my father's fondest beliefs—in progress, in the future. With these gifts, he was preparing his children.

And so was my mother with her different gifts.

I learned from the age of two or three that any room in our house, at any time of day, was there to read in, or to be read to. My mother read to me. She'd read to me in the big bedroom in the mornings, when we were in her rocker together, which ticked in rhythm as we rocked, as though we had a cricket accompanying the story. She'd read to me in the dining room on winter afternoons in front of the coal fire, with our cuckoo clock ending the story with "Cuckoo," and at night when I'd got in my own bed. I must have given her no peace. Sometimes she read to me in the kitchen while she sat churning, and the churning sobbed along with any story. It was my ambition to have her read to me while I churned; once she granted my wish, but she read off my story before I brought her butter. She was an expressive reader. When she was reading "Puss in Boots," for instance, it was impossible not to know that she distrusted all cats.

It had been startling and disappointing to me to find out that story books had been written by people, that books were not natural wonders, coming up of themselves like grass. Yet regardless of where they came from, I cannot remember a time when I was not in love with them—with the books themselves, cover and binding and the paper they were printed on, with their smell and their weight and with their possession in my arms, captured and carried off to myself. Still illiterate, I was ready for them, committed to all the reading I could give them.

Neither of my parents had come from homes that could afford to buy many books, but though it must have been something of a strain on his salary, as the youngest officer in a young insurance company, my father was all the while carefully selecting and ordering away for what he and mother thought we children should grow up with. They bought first for the future.

Besides the bookcase in the living room, which was always called "the library," there were the encyclopedia tables and dictionary stand under windows in our dining room. Here to help us grow up arguing around the dining room table were the *Unabridged Webster*, the *Columbia Encyclopedia*, *Compton's Pictured Encyclopedia*, the *Lincoln Library of Information*, and later the *Book of Knowledge*. And the year we moved into our new house, there was room to celebrate it with the new 1925 edition of the Britannica, which my father, his face always deliberately turned toward the future, was of course disposed to think better than any previous edition.

In "the library," inside the mission-style bookcase with its three diamond-latticed glass doors, with my father's Morris chair and the glass-shaded lamp on its table beside it, were books I could soon begin on—and I did, reading them all alike and as they came, straight down their rows, top shelf to bottom. There was the set of Stoddard's Lectures, in all its late nineteenth-century vocabulary and vignettes of peasant life and quaint beliefs and customs, with matching halftone illustrations: Vesuvius erupting, Venice by moonlight, gypsies glimpsed by their campfires. I didn't know then the clue they were to my father's longing to see the rest of the world. I read straight through his other love-from-afar: the Victrola Book of the Opera, with opera after opera in synopsis, with portraits in costume of Melba, Caruso, Galli-Curci, and Geraldine Farrar, some of whose voices we could listen to on our Red Seal records.

My mother read secondarily for information; she sank as a hedonist into novels. She read Dickens in the spirit in which she would have eloped with him. The novels of her girlhood that had stayed on in her imagination, besides those of Dickens and Scott and Robert Louis Stevenson, were *Jane Eyre, Trilby, The Woman in White, Green Mansions, King Solomon's Mines.* Marie Corelli's name would crop up but I understood she had gone out of favor with my mother, who had only kept *Ardath* out of loyalty. In time she absorbed herself in Galsworthy, Edith Wharton, above all in Thomas Mann of the Joseph volumes.

St. Elmo was not in our house; I saw it often in other houses. This wildly popular Southern novel is where all the Edna Earles in our population started coming from. They're all named for the heroine, who succeeded in bringing a dissolute, sinning roué and atheist of a lover (St. Elmo) to his knees. My mother was able to forgo it. But she remembered the classic advice given to rose growers on how to water their bushes long enough: "Take a chair and St. Elmo."

To both my parents I owe my early acquaintance with a beloved Mark Twain. There was a full set of Mark Twain and a short set of Ring Lardner in our bookcase, and they were the volumes that in time united us all, parents and children.

Reading everything that stood before me was how I came upon a worn old book without a back that had belonged to my father as a child. It was called *Sanford and Merton.* Is there anyone left who recognizes it, I wonder? It is the famous moral tale written by Thomas Day in the 1780s, but of him no mention is made on the title page of this book; here it is *Sanford and Merton in Words of One Syllable* by Mary Godolphin. Here are the rich boy and the poor boy and Mr. Barlow, their teacher and interlocutor, in long discourses alternating with dramatic scenes—danger and rescue allotted to the rich and the poor respectively. It may have only words of one syllable, but one of them is "quoth." It ends with not one but two morals, both engraved on rings: "Do what you ought, come what may," and "If we would be great, we must first learn to be good."

This book was lacking its front cover, the back held on by strips of pasted paper, now turned golden, in several layers, and the pages stained, flecked, and tattered around the edges; its garish illustrations had come unattached but were preserved, laid in. I had the feeling even in my heedless childhood that this was the only book my father as a little boy had had of his own. He had held onto it, and might have gone to sleep on its coverless face: he had lost his mother when he was seven. My father had never made any mention to his own children of the book, but he had brought it along with him from Ohio to our house and shelved it in our bookcase.

My mother had brought from West Virginia that set of Dickens; those books looked sad, too—they had been through fire and water before I was born, she told me, and there they were, lined up—as I later realized, waiting for me.

I was presented, from as early as I can remember, with books of my own, which appeared on my birthday and Christmas morning. Indeed, my parents could not give me books enough. They must have sacrificed to give me on my sixth or seventh birthday—it was after I became a reader for myself—the ten-volume set of *Our Wonder World.* These were beautifully made, heavy books I would lie down with on the floor in front of the dining room hearth, and more often than the rest volume 5, *Every Child's*

Story Book, was under my eyes. There were the fairy tales—Grimm, Andersen, the English, the French, "Ali Baba and the Forty Thieves"; and there was Aesop and Reynard the Fox; there were the myths and legends, Robin Hood, King Arthur, and St. George and the Dragon, even the history of Joan of Arc; a whack of *Pilgrim's Progress* and a long piece of Gulliver. They all carried their classic illustrations. I located myself in these pages and could go straight to the stories and pictures I loved; very often "The Yellow Dwarf" was the first choice, with Walter Crane's Yellow Dwarf in full color making his terrifying appearance flanked by turkeys. Now that volume is as worn and backless and hanging apart as my father's poor *Sanford and Merton*. The precious page with Edward Lear's "Jumblies" on it has been in danger of slipping out for all these years. One measure of my love for *Our Wonder World* was that for a long time I wondered if I would go through fire and water for it as my mother had done for Charles Dickens; and the only comfort was to think I could ask my mother to do it for me.

I believe I'm the only child I know of who grew up with this treasure in the house. I used to ask others, "Did you have *Our Wonder World*?" I'd have to tell them *The Book of Knowledge* could not hold a candle to it.

I live in gratitude to my parents for initiating me—and as early as I begged for it, without keeping me waiting—into knowledge of the word, into reading and spelling, by way of the alphabet. They taught it to me at home in time for me to begin to read before starting to school. I believe the alphabet is no longer considered an essential piece of equipment for traveling through life. In my day it was the keystone to knowledge. You learned the alphabet as you learned to count to ten, as you learned "Now I lay me" and the Lord's Prayer and your father's and mother's name and address and telephone number, all in case you were lost.

1983

CRITICAL THINKING POINTS: *After you've read*

1. What kinds of people are the narrator's father and mother? How do you know that?
2. Compare and contrast what the father and the mother feel is important in an education.
3. What kinds of skills does Welty believe were important for her to learn as a writer?

SOME POSSIBILITIES FOR WRITING

1. Fill in the blank and write your own essay: "One _____ 's Beginnings."
2. Use Welty's essay as a model to write your own description of the house in which you grew up.
3. Welty says, "It had been startling and disappointing to me to find out that story books had been written by people." What in your life has held that kind of power over you? Why?

The Latehomecomer: A Hmong Family Memoir

AN EXCERPT   Kao Kalia Yang

Kao Kalia Yang earned a master of fine arts from Columbia University. Her first book, *The Latehomecomer: A Hmong Family Memoir* recounts the journey her family took, after the Vietnam War, from Laos, to a refugee camp, in Thailand, to the United States, where she and her family eventually settled in St. Paul, Minnesota. Read more about Yang at http://www.kaokaliayang.com.

In Ban Vinai Refugee Camp, I had sat on my father's shoulders, my hands secured in his hair, and I listened to him talk about how we might have a brother, how we would become educated, and how our lives would go places far beyond the horizons we saw—in America.

CRITICAL THINKING POINTS: *As you read*

1. What role does education play in Yang's life? As first-generation Americans, why is school so important for Yang and her siblings?
2. What surprises you about Yang's childhood?
3. What elements of this memoir might be categorized as an "immigrant story"?

. . .We had been in America for almost ten years. I was nearly fifteen, and Dawb had just gotten her driver's license. The children were growing up. We needed a new home—the apartment was too small. There was hardly room to breathe when the scent of jasmine rice and fish steamed with ginger mingled heavily with the scent of freshly baked pepperoni pizza—Dawb's favorite food. We had been looking for a new house for nearly six months.

It was in a poor neighborhood with houses that were ready to collapse— wooden planks falling off, color chipping away, sloping porches—and huge, old trees. There was a realty sign in the front yard, a small patch of green in front of the white house. It was one story, with a small open patio and a single wide window framed by black panels beside a black door. There was a short driveway that climbed up a little hill. No garage. It looked out of time. The house should have been on the prairie, in the early days of Minnesota. It looked liked it belonged to Laura and Mary Ingalls and a time when girls wore cotton skirts with little flowers and bonnets to keep the sun away and carried pails with their sandwiches inside. The team of two old trees in the front yard dwarfed the house. From the car, my imagination took flight. I never thought I would get a chance to live in a house that belonged to storybooks.

I asked my mom, "Are you sure this is only $36,500?"

"It was really $37,000 on the paper, but Dawb asked the man to lower the price for us and he agreed."

"It looks like at least $70,000 to me."

I couldn't wait to get out of the car. We had been looking for houses a long time—some we had liked well enough; most we couldn't afford. Now, this one that looked like a real antique was only $36,000. The deal was incredible. It felt like a miracle.

Together, we had scoured the city looking for a suitable home. My mother, father, and Dawb in the front, and the rest of us in the back, all our knees touching. We had looked all summer long, driving up and down the avenues, the corridors, the smaller streets, and the busy thoroughfares of St. Paul. On the days of fruitless hunting, my father would drive us past the mansions on Summit Avenue for inspiration. We were awed and discussed the merits of owning the structures before us, humongous and intimidating, haunting and invincible. We marveled at the bricks and the green lawns and the ivy climbing up the walls and windows.

Dawb and I posed creative arguments for why owning such a behemoth would never work for our family. These were the homes that we saw on television, the ones with the ghosts and the fun dramas, the ones with the 1980's movie stars and their loose fitting suits. These were the homes with the secret drug addicts and the eating disorders. We'd much rather live in places where men carried beverages in brown bags and walked lopsided up and down the sidewalks and a child could kick an empty beer bottle just as conveniently as a rock. We had fun with our talk, but sometimes Mom and Dad got annoyed. These houses were supposed to inspire us to work extra hard in school.

The small house before us would work. It would be our first piece of America, the first home we would buy with the money our parents earned. We were full of eagerness. Some of our cousins had purchased houses already; others were looking, just like us. It felt like we were joining the future with the past, our dreams and our lives coming together. This would be the home that the children would dream about for years to come.

Up close, we could see that the wood of the house was falling apart in places. White paint had been applied to the parts where the old paint had chipped. The floor of the porch was rotting. The black panels on either side of the window made it look bigger that it was. But that afternoon there was a feeling like the house was special, like it would be ours for a long time. I walked through the front door, into a space that was small, like an elevator. Then I made a left and entered our first home of America: 437 East York Avenue.

The house had the simplest design I have ever encountered. After the elevator-sized reception area, there were three bigger rooms all connected, each with a small bedroom to the right. There was single bathroom in between the second and third bedrooms. The first room was a designated living room. The second was an "anything-you-need-me-to-be" room (that would be used to fill capacity as a bedroom, playroom. study room, and eating room). The third was a kitchen with enough room in the center for a round dining table (a remnant of the old owners). Off the kitchen there was a door leading to an old pencil sharpener nailed in the wall. The realtor had said that the sharpener still worked. Also off the kitchen there was a small room with just enough space for a washer and drying machine and the requisite heavy-duty sink. The total area of the house was 950 square feet, and it was built in 1895. It was called a two-and-a-half bedroom house because the middle room had no closet. The entire structure smelled old, like the thrift shops we were frequenting less and less.

My mother and father were in disagreement over the house. My mother kept on hoping for better. My father's position was that we had to make do with what was before us. But they both felt that they could not afford better for us.

My father said, "We can hide from the rain and the snow in here."

"Ah-huh," we answered in various octaves.

"Someday maybe we can do better."

We all knew he was referring to education. Someday when Dawb and I became educated, and the kids grew up and did well in school too, and my mother and father no longer had to work so hard just to get enough food and pay the heating bill. That is the someday my father was waiting for. It was the someday we were all waiting for.

We moved into the house in the fall, my first year of high school. Dawb was already attending Harding High School, an inner-city school where nearly fifty percent of the student body was multicultural—many of whom were Hmong. Naturally, I would attend Harding with her. She had helped me choose my classes; I would take all the International Baccalaureate classes that I could get into, and where I couldn't, I'd take the advanced placement or college prep courses. I had gone to a small junior high school, a math and science magnet in a white neighborhood with a few Hmong kids. Then I had done well in my classes; I discovered a formula I thought quite sacred: do the homework, go to class every day, and when in class, follow the teacher with your eyes. I was still whispering in school, but the teachers took it in stride. I felt ready for the life changes that high school would bring my way.

I was feeling a strong push to reinvent myself. Without my realizing, by the time high school had begun, I had a feeling in the pit of my stomach that I had been on simmer for too long. I wanted to bubble over the top and douse the confusing fire that burned in my belly. Or else I wanted to turn the stove off. I wanted to sit cool on the burners of life, lid on, and steady. I was ready for change, but there was so little in my life that I could adjust. So life took a blurry seat.

. . . .Dawb and I had decided long before that when the time came, we would strive for the University of Minnesota. We were hearing of Hmong doctors and lawyers, both men and women, all excelling in America, building successful lives for themselves, their mothers and fathers, grandmothers and grandfathers. I had never actually met a Hmong doctor or lawyer, but they had clan names I recognized as clearly as I did my own: Vue, Thao, Vang, Xiong, Lee, Lor, Moua, Cha, Hang, Chang, Khang, Her, Chue, Pha, Kong, and Khue. Dawb and I wanted to add to the success of our clan in this growing list of Hmong people who had made lives for themselves and their families in America. We wanted to make the life journey of our family worth something. Our ambitions had grown: we contemplated changing not simply our own lives but the lives of poor children all over the world. And the key, we believed, was in school. But how far could we strive in school was unknown. We didn't tell anyone about our secret dreams.

Dawb had teachers who supported her all the way through. She had the kind of intelligence that a teacher could see (she looked every part the interested learner), could hear (her English had no accent), and could support (she soaked up information and processed it into her world for her use). I was lost, perpetually biting my lower lip: I didn't speak well or easily, and the link between what we were learning from books and living in life was harder for my mind to grasp.

In high school, this changed. I met a teacher who changed the way I saw myself in education. Her name was Mrs. Gallentin, and she opened up a possibility that I was special. She taught ninth grade English, where we read *Romeo* and *Juliet* and *Nectar in the Sieve,* as well as other literary classics. I sat near the front of the class and absorbed the books. Mrs. Gallentin had a red face and a dry sense of humor. She had little patience for kids who giggled or were fussy in their seat—students who didn't pay close enough attention to lessons and did not do their assignments on time. I had overly curvy, confident handwriting that was hard to read, and I did not have a computer, so reviewing my work was a slow process. She may have noticed me initially because of this, and her interest was compounded by both my silence and my serious approach to literature.

Mrs. Gallentin became impressed with me because I could tell the important parts of a book. I knew how to anticipate the questions on her tests. At first, I was convinced I could read her mind. But after a few thought experiments in class, I realized I was picking up understanding from the books, not from her. It was in this class that I wrote my first real essay in response to the question: Is the story of Romeo and Juliet a story of love or lust?

It took me all night long to think about the essay. I had no personal experience with love or lust. Some of my friends said that they were in love, but I was not convinced. The phone conversations they had with their boyfriends were mostly just listening to each other's breathing. After many false beginnings, I wrote about what mattered to me. I wrote about the love I felt I knew: Love is the reason my mother and father stick together in a hard life when they might each have an easier one apart; love is the reason you choose a life with someone, and you don't turn back although your heart cries sometimes and your children see you cry and you wish out loud that things were easier. Love is getting up each day and fighting the same fight only to sleep that night in the same bed beside the same person because long ago, when you were younger and you did not see so clearly, you had chosen them.

I wrote that we'll never know if Romeo and Juliet really loved because they never had the chance. I asserted that love only happened in life, not in literature because life is more complex. As soon as I wrote this essay, I started worrying about it—what if she didn't like it, what if she didn't agree, what if I had it all wrong. That was my first understanding of how writing worked, how it mattered to the writer, personally and profoundly.

I had written the essay out by hand first. I stayed up all night typing the essay on our gray typewriter at the dining table (it was the only surface in our house that was steady enough for us to really spread out our books and papers), slowly, with my index fingers (mistakes were costly). The sound of slow keys being clicked, first the right and then the left, eyes looking from keyboard to the page. Flexing careful fingers every few minutes. Trying to find a rhythm and a beat in the clicking of the keys, the mechanical whirl at the end of each line, the changing of paper. It took me a long time to think it through and follow the letters to the words, but the writing calmed something inside of me, it cooled my head: like water over a small burn in the pit of my mind. I watched eagerly as the third then fourth then fifth filled with typed letters.

My mother and father came home early in the morning. They had changed their work schedules entirely to the graveyard shift (the nominal increase in their wages was necessary to maintain the new house). They saw my eyes closing over my work and became convinced that I was their hardest working daughter. My heavy eyes followed the way they walked so tired around the kitchen, and I grew confident that I really did know love—that I had always known it. By morning, the exhausting work of writing was done. I turned it in to Mrs. Gallentin.

Mrs. Gallentin caught me in the hall later that day and said that my essay was beautiful. She said that I wrote more than an answer to the question; I was telling her the ways in which questions come from life and end in life. I had never thought of myself as a good writer. I liked stories, and in elementary school I had written gory tales about intestines coming out. I thought I was good at math and science (what my junior high school had been good at), but Mrs. Gallentin said that I had talent for literature. I didn't see it, but it pleased me to hear her say this. In the course of a semester, she opened up a real possibility that I could excel in high school and college because they were all about good reading and good writing.

I began to see a truth that my father had been asserting for a long time, long before America. In Ban Vinai Refugee Camp, I had sat on my father's shoulders, my hands secured in his hair, and I listened to him talk about how we might have a brother, how we would become educated, and how our lives would go places far beyond the horizons we saw—in America. I looked at our lives, and how could I not believe? Beyond all the spoken wishes, a dream had even come true: eight years into America and we owned a house of our own.

2008

CRITICAL THINKING POINTS: *After you've read*

1. Why does Yang say, "These houses were supposed to inspire us to work extra hard in school"?
2. How does Mrs. Gallentin change Yang's life?
3. For the World War II and baby boomer generations, the American dream included owning one's home. How do you think "the American dream" has changed for your generation?

SOME POSSIBILITIES FOR WRITING

1. Research the history of Hmong immigration to the United States and share your information with classmates.
2. Yang says that she found a formula for success that she called *sacred:* "do the homework, go to class every day, and when in class, follow the teacher with your eyes." Why might this approach work for her (and for others)? Find research to support the relevance of her approach.
3. The United States is a country made up of immigrants. Talk to your parents or grandparents about your own family's history. Write down what you find.

Saved

FROM *THE AUTOBIOGRAPHY OF MALCOLM X*   Malcolm X

While serving seven years in prison on a burglary charge, Malcolm X (born Malcolm Little; 1925–1965) experienced a life-changing conversion to Islam, honed his reading and writing skills, and emerged as a dynamic political leader of Black Muslims. He was assassinated in 1965.

. . . months passed without my even thinking about being imprisoned. In fact, up to then, I never had been so truly free in my life.

CRITICAL THINKING POINTS: *As you read*

1. What do you know about Malcolm X? How does that "back story" influence your reading of this excerpt?
2. List some of the various motivations Malcolm X has for learning.
3. Malcolm X says, "Anyone who has read a great deal can imagine the new world that opened." What are some of the elements of that world?

I became increasingly frustrated at not being able to express what I wanted to convey in letters that I wrote, especially those to Mr. Elijah Muhammad. In the street, I had been the most articulate hustler out there—I had commanded attention when I said something. But now, trying to write simple English, I not only wasn't articulate, I wasn't even functional. How would I sound writing in slang, the way I would say it, something such as "Look, daddy, let me pull your coat about a cat, Elijah Muhammad."

Many who today hear me somewhere in person, or on television, or those who read something I've said, will think I went to school far beyond the eighth grade. This impression is due entirely to my prison studies.

It had really begun back in the Charlestown Prison, when Bimbi first made me feel envy of his stock of knowledge. Bimbi had always taken charge of any conversation he was in, and I tried to emulate him. But every book I picked up had few sentences which didn't contain anywhere from one to nearly all of the words that might as well have been Chinese. When I just skipped those words, of course, I really ended up with little idea of what the book said. So I had come to the Norfolk Prison Colony still going through only book-reading motions. Pretty soon, I would have quit even these motions, unless I had received the motivation that I did.

I saw that the best thing I could do was get hold of a dictionary—to study, to learn some words. I was lucky enough to reason also that I should try to improve my penmanship. It was sad. I couldn't even write in a straight line. It was both ideas together that moved me to request a dictionary along with some tablets and pencils from the Norfolk Prison Colony school.

I spent two days just riffling uncertainly through the dictionary's pages. I'd never realized so many words existed! I didn't know *which* words I needed to learn. Finally, just to start some kind of action, I began copying.

In my slow, painstaking, ragged handwriting, I copied into my tablet everything printed on that first page, down to the punctuation marks.

I believe it took me a day. Then, aloud, I read back, to myself, everything I'd written on the tablet. Over and over, aloud, to myself, I read my own handwriting.

I woke up the next morning, thinking about those words—immensely proud to realize that not only had I written so much at one time, but I'd written words that I never knew were in the world. Moreover, with a little effort, I also could remember what many of these words meant. I reviewed the words whose meanings I didn't remember. Funny thing, from the dictionary's first page right now, that "aardvark" springs into my head. The dictionary had a picture of it, a long-tailed, long-eared, burrowing African mammal, which lives off termites caught by sticking out its tongue as an anteater does for ants.

I was so fascinated that I went on—I copied the dictionary's next page. And the same experience came when I studied that. With every succeeding page, I also learned of people and places and events from history. Actually the dictionary is like a miniature encyclopedia. Finally the dictionary's A section had filled a whole tablet—and I went on into the B's. That was the way I started copying what eventually became the entire dictionary. It went a lot faster after so much practice helped me to pick up handwriting speed. Between what I wrote in my tablet, and writing letters, during the rest of my time in prison I would guess I wrote a million words.

I suppose it was inevitable that as my word-base broadened, I could for the first time pick a book and read and now begin to understand what the book was saying. Let me tell you something: from then until I left that prison, in every free moment I had, if I was not reading in the library, I was reading on my bunk. You couldn't have gotten me out of books with a wedge. Between Mr. Muhammad's teachings, my correspondence, my visitors—usually Ella and Reginald—and my reading of books, months passed without my even thinking about being imprisoned. In fact, up to then, I never had been so truly free in my life.

The Norfolk Prison Colony's library was in the school building. A variety of classes was taught there by instructors who came from such places as Harvard and Boston universities. The weekly debates between inmate teams were also held in the school building. You would be astonished to know how worked up convict debaters and audiences would get over subjects like "Should Babies Be Fed Milk?"

Available on the prison library's shelves were books on just about every general subject. Much of the big private collection that Parkhurst had willed to the prison was still in crates and boxes in the back of the library—thousands of old books.

Some of them looked ancient: covers faded, old-time parchment-looking binding. Parkhurst, I've mentioned, seemed to have been principally interested in history and religion. He had the money and the special interest to have a lot of books that you wouldn't have in general circulation. Any college library would have been lucky to get that collection.

As you can imagine, especially in a prison where there was heavy emphasis on rehabilitation, an inmate was smiled upon if he demonstrated an unusually intense interest in books. There was a sizable number of well-read inmates, especially the popular debaters. Some were said by many to be practically walking encyclopedias. They were almost celebrities. No university would ask any student to devour literature as I did when this new world opened to me, of being able to read and *understand.*

I read more in my room than the library itself. An inmate who was known to read a lot could check out more than the permitted maximum number of books. I preferred reading in the total isolation of my own room.

When I had progressed to really serious reading, every night at about ten P.M. I would be outraged with the "lights out." It always seemed to catch me right in the middle of something engrossing.

Fortunately, right outside my door was a corridor light that cast a glow into my room. The glow was enough to read by, once my eyes adjusted to it. So when "lights out" came, I would sit on the floor where I could continue reading in that glow.

At one-hour intervals the night guards paced past every room. Each time I heard the approaching footsteps, I jumped into bed and feigned sleep. And as soon as the guard passed, I got back out of bed onto the floor area of that light-glow, where I would read for another fifty-eight minutes—until the guard approached again. That went on until three or four every morning. Three or four hours of sleep a night was enough for me. Often in the years in the streets I had slept less than that.

1965

CRITICAL THINKING POINTS: *After you've read*

1. What kind of a teacher do you think Malcolm X would have been in the class-room? What in this piece leads you to believe the way you do?

2. Malcolm X refers to skipping words he didn't know while he was reading as one of his "book-reading motions." What are some others and are they as easily remedied?

3. What might have Malcolm X learned in the streets that served him well in this experience?

SOME POSSIBILITIES FOR WRITING

1. Malcolm X says, "I didn't know *which* words I needed to learn." Pick a page at random from a dictionary and write about any words you "need" to learn.

2. Compare and contrast this piece with the selection from *Up from Slavery* presented in this book. What do you think accounts for the similarities and differences in these pieces?

3. Compare and contrast this piece with the selection from *Lummox: Evolution of a Man* later in this book. How does Magnuson's "conversion" in jail compare to that of Malcolm X? How important are some of the differences? Why?

STUDENT RESPONSE TO "SAVED"

After reading "Saved" by Malcolm X, I had a lot of different thoughts about motivation, and how either positive or negative experiences in our lives can either push us to do better or push us to do worse. I think an important thing I have learned is that it's always best to make the negative experiences of your life (like the things Malcolm X went through in the reading) work for you in a positive way. For example, Malcolm realized that his penmanship wasn't very good, and instead of letting this discourage him, he noticed room for improvement, and practiced in order to improve. Also, he used his time in prison as a positive experience to work on himself and accomplish things, rather than to feel sorry for himself and give up. I think these are very important concepts because if you let your weaknesses or bad experiences dictate your life in a negative way, you will never come back from them.

This reading made me think about my own life and what motivates me. My biggest motivators are to get my degree, not to disappoint my family, and not to fail or get suspended in the future. Instead of looking at the fact that I have failed in the past and letting it intimidate or discourage me, I will use it to my advantage by remembering it and doing things to prevent it in the future. Overall I liked the reading, and thought it proved a very good point that we can all probably relate to.

Miss Rinehart's Paddle

Jeri McCormick

Jeri McCormick teaches creative writing at senior centers and Elderhostel programs. Her poems have appeared in *Poetry Ireland Review, Cumberland Poetry Review*, and *Rosebud*. Her book of poems, *When It Came Time*, was published in 1998 by Salmon Publishing in Ireland, and she is one of the authors of *Writers Have No Age: Creative Writing For Older Adults* (2005).

the other side of power

CRITICAL THINKING POINTS: *As you read*

1. Were you the kind of student who got into trouble or the kind who did everything right?
2. The poem is saturated with violent images. What are some of them?
3. Name some of the kinds of power that teachers have over students.

The long hard rumor
had hit us years before
but there was nothing we could do
to fend sixth grade off.
One September morning
we filed into Miss Rinehart's room
to face the thick glasses,
heavy oxfords, spit curls.

The weapon occupied
her middle drawer
and was rarely used on girls,
though Betty Jo got five whacks
for her haphazard map of Brazil —
the Amazon all smeared and off-course,
Rio de Janeiro inland by inches.

I sat through six months
of imagined failures,
ended up a jittery stooge
with all *A*'s, the best parts in plays
and only now wonder
about the other side of power.

1991

CRITICAL THINKING POINTS: *After you've read*

1. What might the author mean when she calls herself "a jittery stooge / with all A's, the best parts in plays"?
2. What did you feel as you read this poem? Was it painful, funny, or sad to read? What made it so?
3. Recall elementary or middle school teachers who were especially "mean." What made them mean? What did you fear about them?

SOME POSSIBILITIES FOR WRITING

1. Many of us can recall memorable episodes from elementary, middle, or high school classrooms that changed the way we feel about teaching and/or learning. Think of such an episode. What makes it a memorable moment? What changes did the event lead to?
2. Talk to your parents and grandparents about their experiences in school. Write an essay comparing your experiences in school to those of your parents or grandparents.
3. Physical discipline is rarely practiced much anymore in this country. What other kinds of discipline do teachers and/or school systems employ? Which methods do you think are the most effective?

50% Chance of Lightning

Cristina Salat

Cristina Salat is founder of Kulana, a racially diverse artist's sanctuary in the rain forests of Hawaii. An author and filmmaker, her work has been published by Bantam Books, Children's Television Workshop, and *Popular Photography.*

Well, what's the point of being gay if I'm never going to be with anybody?

CRITICAL THINKING POINTS: *As you read*

1. Watch for the different responses Robin and Malia have toward college. What are they? Were you eager to apply to college and leave home, like Malia, or not quite ready, like Robin? Why?

2. Speculate about how Robin's mother died. What details in the story led you to that theory?

3. Are the people you know more like Malia (concrete goals, even down to the type of car she hopes to drive) or more like Robin (abstract wishes, such as simply "be happy")? Are you more like Malia or Robin? In what ways?

"I wonder if I'll ever have a girlfriend." Robin stamps her sneakers against the wet pavement, tired of waiting.

Malia laughs. "Is that all you think about?"

"Well, what's the point of being gay if I'm never going to be with anybody?" Robin shifts the big umbrella they are sharing to her other hand. Fat silver drops of rain splatter above the plastic dome. She wishes the bus would run on time for once.

"Independent women. We vowed, remember? No guy chasing," Malia says.

Robin shoots Malia a look.

"Or girl chasing," Malia adds quickly.

"You can't talk," Robin says, trying not to feel each strand of her hair as it frizzes. "You have someone."

"That's true." Malia smiles.

Robin looks at the gray, wet world through her clear umbrella. It's hat weather. Black baseball hat and hair gel. She uses both, but nothing really helps on damp days like this. "It's silly to worry how you look. Rain can make you alive if you let it!" Robin's mother used to say. She loved stormy weather almost as much as Robin didn't.

"It's Friday! How come you're so quiet?" Malia asks. "You're not obsessing about your hair, are you? It looks fine. I'd trade you in a second . . . so don't start in about my perfect Filipino hair!" She grins, reading Robin's mind.

Robin can't help smiling. They've known each other a long time.

"Guess what!" Malia changes the subject. "Tomorrow is me and Andrew's six-month anniversary. That's the longest I've ever gone out with anybody."

Robin sighs. "You guys will probably get old together." And I'll be the oldest single person on the face of the planet, she thinks gloomily.

Malia's forehead wrinkles into a slight frown. "No. I'm leaving. I can't wait to get out of here." A large electric bus lumbers to the curb and stops with a hiss. "I sent my applications out yesterday. NYU, Bryn Mawr, Hampshire, and RIT, in that order," Malia says as she boards.

They squeeze onto the heated bus between packed bodies in steaming over-coats. The bus lurches forward.

"Where did you decide?" Malia asks, grabbing onto a pole near the back.

Robin shrugs.

Malia raises one eyebrow. "It's almost Thanksgiving. You are still going to try for NYU and Hampshire with me, aren't you?"

"I guess," Robin says. "I haven't had time to decide anything yet." It's not like she hasn't been thinking about it.

College catalogs are spread across the floor of her bedroom. All she has to do is figure out where she wants to spend the next four years of her life. New York? Massachusetts? Zimbabwe? There's an endless stream of choices.

"You better make time," Malia says. "You shouldn't wait until the deadlines."

"Give me a break, okay?" Robin stares past the seated heads in front of her.

"Cranky, cranky." Malia elbows Robin's arm.

A woman wipes one hand across a steamed window for an outside view and pulls the bus cord. She vacates her seat and Malia and Robin squeeze past some-one's knees to claim it. With Malia balanced on her lap, Robin turns her head toward the window and watches the city swish by. She tries to picture herself next fall, suitcases packed, excited to be going. She's almost eighteen; she should want to leave home. A new room. New city. New friends.

I can't leave, not yet! The air in the bus is thick and warm; it's hard to breathe enough in. Outside the window, sharp edged buildings and signs fly past. Robin's head feels light and disconnected. She presses her face against the cold glass. She doesn't have to leave. She can apply to San Francisco State or USF right here in the city. Or she won't go at all. Malia's mom didn't go to college. Robin's dad didn't go either, but he wants her to. "You're smart, like your mother," he's always saying. But what if she doesn't want to go?

It's okay, Robin repeats to herself. No one can make me.

Outside the window she watches a small, mixed terrier approach the curb, sniffing the ground. Its fur is wet and matted, standing up in points. The dog steps into the stilled, waiting traffic. Robin scans the sidewalk for the dog's person. Don't they know it's dangerous to let their puppy wander into the street?

Robin stares through the window, her mind racing. Maybe it's lost. She could help. She could get off the bus and . . . A car honks loudly. Something inside her shrinks up. Malia's weight is heavy on her lap. The dog looks up and scampers back to the curb as traffic surges and the bus rumbles forward. Robin cranes her neck. She should get off, before it's too late. But she can't.

"What is it?" Malia asks, feeling Robin's shift.

Robin forces herself to lean back in the seat and breathe slowly. She's being stupid. The dog won't get run over. Its owner is probably just down the block.

They hang their jackets over the chair in Malia's small, neat room and Robin drops her baseball cap onto the desk.

"You want to see my list of goals?" Malia asks. "I read in *New Woman* if you know exactly what you want, you're more likely to get it." She hands Robin an open, spiral-bound note-book and drops next to her on the bed.

MALIA MANANSALA

Goals for Now
> Get into a good college, far away
> Major in computer science or business
> Get another part-time job for clothes, makeup, etc.
> Have fun!

Eventually
> Dressy job where I make a lot of money and get respect
> Nice apartment with classy things
> Old BMW or Jeep Cherokee (depending where I live)
> Great friends
> Marry someone loyal, sexy, and successful

"Money." Robin shakes her head. "Even if we get scholarships, we're going to be paying off college loans forever."

Malia nods. "That's why I need a big career. I'm not going to suck up to some man for money. You should make a goal list," she suggests, handing over a pen. "I need a snack."

Robin flops onto her side. Why not? At the top of a clean page, in slow, careful letters, she writes:

Goals
> Figure Out Who I Am
> Be Proud of Myself
> Fall in Love
> Do Something Good

Robin frowns at her list. How does Malia know exactly what she wants? "Hand it over." Malia comes back into the room with a tray of hot cocoa and microwaved pork buns.

"Okay, but it's not like yours."

"Do something good?" Malia makes a face. "Can you be more specific?"

"Hey, I didn't pick on your list!"

"I don't get it. When you want to do something, you just do it. This year you start telling everyone, 'I'm a lesbian, deal with it.' Why can't you be like that about college?"

"It's different," Robin says, thinking, I didn't tell everyone. My mother never got to know. Her mom drove a red Ho CRX with African pendants dangling from the rearview mirror. She took the highway a lot, to avoid city traffic. Route I South. Robin yanks her mind away.

"You are going to do more with your life than just be a lesbian, aren't you?" Malia prods.

Robin gets to her feet, shaking the damp bottoms of her baggy jeans away from her ankles. "Can I borrow something dry?"

"Come on. Seriously. What kind of job do you want?" Malia sounds like Robin's mom and dad used to—always excited about plans.

"I don't know. Something to help people," Robin says, looking through the closet.

"Peace Corps? Lawyer? Social worker?" Malia suggests.

"No," Robin says, a faded memory seeping into her mind. She used to play medicine woman when she was little, healing stuffed toy rabbits and her plastic Ujima dolls with bowls of grass-flower soup. "I always pictured myself in a fun office," she tells Malia, "where people or animals would come when they didn't feel well."

"You want to be some kind of doctor!" Malia enthuses.

Robin shakes her head. Playing medicine woman was a kid thing. "You know I can't stand blood and guts." Robin focuses her attention in the closet, taking out a black lace top and black leggings.

"How about a therapist? You could help people's minds."

"And listen to people complain all day?" Robin asks as she changes.

Malia sighs, shutting the notebook. "Well, what do you want to do tonight? I told Andrew I'd call him by four. Oh, I forgot! My mother and the jerk are going out after work. They won't be home till late. Do you want to have a party?"

"Yes!" Robin says. "Go rent some movies. I'll call for a pizza and invite everybody."

Andrew arrives first with a soggy Safeway bag tucked into his aviator jacket.

"Hey, Robbie!" he says, unpacking jumbo bottles of root beer and 7UP on the living-room table.

The doorbell rings again. Robin runs to let in Malia's friend Dan, who has brought his sister, Cybelle—a junior—and another girl. Malia has plenty of friends. Most of them are at least part Filipino.

Being a mix (African and Polish), Robin doesn't care who her friends are. She only has a few anyway, though she knows lots of people. When her mother died at the end of sophomore year, nobody knew what to say, so they acted like nothing happened. Robin still hangs out with the same people, but just because it's something to do; not because she cares.

When Malia returns from the video store, fifteen people are sprawled on the couch and floor with paper plates of mushroom and garlic pizza.

"Party woman," Andrew teases Malia, leaning down for a kiss. "You're soaked."

"It was only drizzling when I left. Sorry I took so long. I couldn't decide!" Malia takes two video cassettes out of a plastic bag. "I got a vampire movie and *The Best of Crack-Up Comedy.*"

"I love vampires!" Cybelle adjusts one of the five rhinestone studs on her left ear. "Let's get scared first."

"Go change," Andrew tells Malia. "I'll set up the movie." He nudges her toward the bedroom.

Robin watches, wondering if anyone will ever care like that about her. For some reason the wet dog she saw from the bus pops into her mind. Nobody cared enough to keep it safe.

"Hi. You're Robin Ciszek, right?" A white girl in ripped jeans and a "Save the Planet" sweatshirt sits down next to Robin on the couch. "I read your article in the school paper! I'm April, Cybelle's friend. I never thought what it feels like to be gay until I read your essay. Do you know a lot of gay people, or was the story mostly about you?" April's slate colored eyes are wide and curious.

Robin takes a big bite of pizza. It's still hard to believe she wrote an article about being gay and submitted it to the school paper. She must have been crazy.

"I hope you don't mind me asking," April says quickly. "I'm just interested."

"The story's mostly about me," she tells April. "I don't know a lot of other gay people."

"I guess you will next year," April says. "My sister goes to UC Berkeley, and she says there's like three different gay groups on campus."

Robin feels her shoulders clench up. Is college the only thing anyone can talk about? Of course, it'll be worth it to be out of high school just to get away from the stupid notes guys are taping on her locker door: ALL YOU NEED IS A REAL MAN and ROBIN C. AND MALIA M. EAT FISH.

"Personally, I'm glad I don't have to think about college for another year," April continues.

"Really? Why?" Robin asks, surprised.

April looks away, embarrassed. "It's dumb. I have this cat. I don't want to leave her."

"Guess what I brought!" Cybelle calls out as Andrew dims the living-room light. She takes a half-full bottle of brandy from her tote bag.

"I'll have a little of that," Malia says, coming back into the room in overalls and a fluffy white sweater. "To warm me up."

"Quiet—it's starting," Gary yells from the easy chair as a bold, red title flashes across the television screen.

"I want to sit on the couch," Tara giggles. "Move over, Danny."

April moves toward Robin to make room for another person. Her hip rests against Robin's. The couch armrest presses into Robin's other side.

"Oh, hold me, Andrew!" Cybelle teases Malia as eerie music fills the darkened room. Malia laughs.

April's leg relaxes against Robin's. Out of the corner of one eye, Robin looks at the girl sitting next to her. April is watching the screen. Robin's thigh sizzles.

Robin nonchalantly eases sideways until their arms and legs are touching. A faint scent of perfume tinges the air. April doesn't move away. Robin's whole left side buzzes. She sinks into the couch, holding her breath. It would be so amazing if—

If what? Just because this girl liked the article doesn't mean she's interested. Robin moves her leg away, mad at herself. On screen, a shadowy figure suddenly whirls around and grins evilly. April leans softly against Robin.

Warm drops of sweat trickle down Robin's side. The room feels dark and red. Robin could reach out, take April's hand, trace one finger over the knuckle bumps and pale, freckled skin. . . .

Halfway through the vampire movie, Robin has to go to the bathroom, bad. She is tempted, but restrains herself from squeezing April's leg as she gets up.

Away from everyone, she splashes cold water on her face, smiling. Could April really be interested? I could go back and sit away from her to see if she follows me.

Feeling hot and wild, Robin unlocks the door. It doesn't budge. She pulls harder, leaning backward, and opens it a foot.

"Hi, Robin." Cybelle grins, peeking around the corner.

"What's with you? Get away from the door," Robin says.

"Okay." Cybelle runs one hand through her porcupine patch of short, black hair. "C'mere. I want to ask you something." Cybelle pulls Robin into Malia's room. She shuts the door without flicking on the light.

"Smell my breath," she says, leaning close.

A warm rush of brandy air tickles Robin's face.

"I can't go home wasted. Do I smell like pizza or alcohol?" Cybelle asks. Her lips touch the side of Robin's mouth.

"What are you doing?" Robin asks.

Cybelle nuzzles Robin's face, tracing her lips along Robin's. "Don't you like me? Kiss me back."

Robin's heart stutters. Is this for real? Cybelle slides one hand under Robin's hair and grips the back of her neck, kissing harder.

I've wanted this for so long, Robin thinks, awkwardly moving her arms around Cybelle. It's weird not being able to see. Robin touches sharp shoulder blades through the thin cotton of Cybelle's turtleneck.

I should have helped that dog. The thought scuttles into Robin's head. Why is she thinking about that now!

Cybelle sucks on Robin's lower lip. I should have gotten off the bus and helped. I could have taken it to the pound, or home. Why didn't I do something?

Cybelle's small tongue slides into Robin's mouth. Why am I doing this? I've seen Cybelle around school and never wanted to. She's got a boyfriend. She'll probably tell everyone, "I made out with the lesbian at Malia's house," for a laugh.

Robin shifts sideways. "I have to go."

"What?"

"I'm going back to the living room." Robin feels for the wall switch and flicks on the light.

Cybelle blinks. "How come? It's okay. Nobody misses us." She smiles and tugs on Robin's arm, moving closer.

"I want to see the rest of the movie," Robin says, pulling away. It's a lame excuse, but what else can she say? "I want to kiss somebody I'm really into, and you're not it"?

Cybelle stops smiling and drops Robin's arm. "Oh sure," she laughs. "You're scared! Writing that story and you don't even know what to do! What a joke." She yanks open the door and walks out before Robin can respond.

Robin follows Cybelle to the living room and watches her take the small, open spot on the couch next to April. She glares at the back of Cybelle's spiked head. Who does she think she is? I don't have to make out if I don't want to!

Whirling around, Robin heads back to the bedroom and jams her feet into her sneakers.

"You okay?" Malia asks, coming in.

"Sure." Robin doesn't look up.

"Are you leaving? What's going on?"

"Nothing I want to talk about right now." Robin zips up her jacket. They walk to the front door. Robin flings it open. She can't wait to be outside.

"Call me tomorrow, okay? Hey." Malia grabs Robin's jacket.

Robin looks back over her shoulder. "What?"

"We're best buddies forever, right?"

If Malia moves to New York and Robin stays here . . . Nothing's forever.

"Sure," Robin says, looking away.

Malia smiles and reaches out for a hug. "I'm sorry you didn't have a good time. Let's go shopping tomorrow morning, just you and me. Okay?"

As soon as Robin steps away from Malia's house, she realizes she's forgotten her baseball cap. Angrily, she pops open her umbrella. It doesn't matter. There's a bus stop at the corner and she's just going home.

Water drops drum against the plastic shield above her head as cars zip by, their rubber tires splashing against wet asphalt. Robin glares at each car that passes. She will never own one. What if that dog got run over? She should have helped. A bolt of light illuminates the night. Robin looks helplessly down the empty street for a bus. She hates being out alone after dark, even when it's not very late.

Whenever someone worried, her dad used to say: "There's a fifty-fifty chance of something good happening." Robin's mother loved that saying. Her father hasn't said it much lately. It's hard to believe in good stuff when you're dealing with the other fifty percent. At least she ended the thing with Cybelle. That's something. Robin might want experience, but she's not desperate.

Thunder swells, filling the night. Robin cranes her neck, looking down the street. No bus. So it's fifty-fifty. Should she wait here, hoping no weirdos show up and bother her before the bus comes, or should she start walking in this lousy weather? Her parents used to take walks in the rain. They were nuts . . . but happy.

Robin starts to walk. A sharp wind whips by, threatening to turn her umbrella inside out. Okay, why not? She has nothing to lose. Robin clicks the umbrella shut. Rain falls cold against her face and settles onto her thick hair, expanding it. She walks fast, with the wooden umbrella handle held forward, staying near the street-lamps. Water trickles down her face and soaks into her clothing. She licks her lips. The rain tastes strangely good.

When she reaches the place where she saw the dog, Robin stops and studies the black road. A few torn paper bags. No blood or fur. It could be dead somewhere else. Or it could be off foraging in a garbage can or sleeping under a bush.

I'm sorry I didn't get off the bus to see if you needed help, she thinks. Next time I will. I hope you're safe. But maybe the dog didn't need help. Maybe it wasn't even scared. Maybe it was totally pleased to be out exploring and taking care of itself. Robin decides to picture the terrier that way.

From down the block a bus approaches, grumbling to a stop a few feet ahead. Robin hurries over. As the doors squeal open, she looks behind at the dark, empty street. She is afraid, but she doesn't want to be. Slowly, Robin turns away.

It is a long walk home under the wide, electric sky.

At the warm apartment on Guerrero Street, Robin finds her father asleep on their living-room couch. A paperback novel is spread open across his chest and his glasses are pushed up onto his forehead. Standing over him, dripping onto the brown shag rug, Robin feels tender and old. She removes his glasses and places the book on the glass coffee table, careful not to lose his page.

In her room, Robin drops her wet clothing to the floor and changes into an old set of flannel pajamas. Then she sits down at her drafting-table desk. Nothing's forever, and that's just the way it is. Moving college applications aside, she lifts two thick San Francisco phone books from the floor.

Robin thumbs through the thin A–L yellow pages slowly. There is something she can do. Something right.

Attorneys, Automobile . . . Bakers, Beauty . . . Carpets, Collectibles . . . Dentists, Divers . . . Environment . . . Florists . . . Health. Health clubs, health and diet, health maintenance, health service. A boxed ad catches Robin's eye.

Holistic Health Center

Dedicated to the well-being of body and mind

Licensed: nutritionists, massage therapists, acupuncturists

Courses in herbal healing, yoga, natural vision, Tai Chi

Medicine without blood and guts. Smiling to herself, Robin reaches for some loose-leaf paper and a pen. There's a new life out there, waiting for her. She just has to find it. She moves A–L aside and flips open M–Z. By ten P.M. three loose-leaf pages are filled with numbers and addresses. At the top of the first page, she writes: Call for info.

Robin stretches and climbs into bed with her new list. She rubs the soles of her bare feet against the chilled sheets. Maybe life is like rain. Alive if you let it be; lousy and depressing if you don't. She rolls onto her stomach. Under the information for the Shiatsu Institute, the College of Oriental Medicine, and the School for Therapeutic Massage, she writes: Tell Malia to get April's number from Dan. Call her?!?!?!

1994

CRITICAL THINKING POINTS: *After you've read*

1. Malia thinks that if people know exactly what they want, they're more likely to get it. Do you believe this is true? Why or why not?

2. Compare Robin's and Malia's lists of goals. Who do you think is more likely to be satisfied? Can you judge this simply from someone's goals? Why or why not?

3. Why do you think Robin doesn't get on the bus when it stops for her? What does the dog seem to represent to her? What details in the story led you to that conclusion?

SOME POSSIBILITIES FOR WRITING

1. Make two lists of your own goals: one abstract like Robin's and one concrete like Malia's. For instance, an abstract goal would be "work with people," whereas a concrete goal that is an extension of that would be "get a degree in elementary education."

2. There are advantages and disadvantages to having a life's plan like Malia does. Make a list of advantages concerning having your goals and life mapped out. Now make a list of disadvantages concerning having your goals and life mapped out.

3. Robin is harassed with notes on her locker after her article appeared in the school newspaper. Recall a time when you were teased for your ethnic background, sexual preference, or simply the way you talked or walked or something you did. Write about your experience.

Somewhere in Minnesota

Peter Klein

Peter Klein wrote this poem as an undergraduate student. His work has appeared in *The Cortland Review, The North American Review, Blackbird*, and elsewhere.

your dark eyes focused / on a brilliant future.

CRITICAL THINKING POINTS: *As you read*

1. Who do you think is the "you" in this poem?
2. Because of poetry's condensed nature, every word is important. Choose some words that you feel are "important" to this poem. Why do you think so?
3. Why might the lines end where they do? How would the poem be different if the lines were longer or shorter?

somewhere in Minnesota
there is a photograph
mailed from denver
to an uncle in duluth
who left it in a diner
on a table by the salt
it marked a woman's place
in a drugstore fiction
where it lay for years
until her freshman son
found it told his friends
the subject was his steady
then threw it in a lake
this picture was of you
your mortar board smile
gleaming softly beneath
the photographer's light
your dark eyes focused
on a brilliant future.

1979

CRITICAL THINKING POINTS: *After you've read*

1. What might the author mean by such phrases as "your mortar board smile" or "your dark eyes focused / on a brilliant future"?
2. How do the places in which the photo ends up contribute to your reading of the poem? What do these places have in common?
3. Why do you think the history of the photograph is important to the narrator?

SOME POSSIBILITIES FOR WRITING

1. Page through your own high school yearbook. Write a brief impression of the memories the pictures call to mind. Be as specific as you can in communicating these impressions.
2. Look at your parents' or grandparents' high school graduation photos and write about the people as they appeared then compared to the people as you know them now.
3. Find yearbooks in your college library from ten or twenty years ago or older. What seems to be different about the people and the university then? What seems to be still the same?

LD

Jeff Richards

Jeff Richards was born and raised in Washington, D.C. He has an MA in creative writing from Hollins College.

His twisted brain was no disability. It was a gift.

CRITICAL THINKING POINTS: *As you read*

1. What do you associate with the term "LD"?
2. How can labels, such as "LD" or "gifted," help or hinder students in school?
3. Students with "invisible" disabilities often go unnoticed by other students. What would be the benefits and disadvantages of that kind of disability?

ur minds are twisted but they are perfectly good minds. We are artistic, sensitive, impulsive, socially and emotionally immature. Spaced. We are angry, passive, withdrawn or overly extroverted. We tell stories in random order without references, and our academic skills are very slow in developing. At least that's the way we are when we are young, according to Neela Seldin, a specialist in LD who compiled the above list of our characteristics. When we grow older, we either adapt or don't adapt. Some of us drop out of high school and clerk at Kmart. Some of us graduate with Ph.Ds in nuclear physics and work for NASA. Some of us are well known: Harry Belafonte, Cher, Vince Vaughn; or leaders in their fields: Dr. Donald Coffey, a cancer researcher at Johns Hopkins; Dr. Florence Haseltine, a pioneer in women's health issues; Gaston Caperton, the educator and former governor of West Virginia; and Roger W. Wilkins, the civil rights activist. According to the company of Winston Churchill, Thomas Edison, Albert Einstein, Leonardo da Vinci, all of them either LD or afflicted by one of LD's numerous cousins, like dyslexia. Da Vinci often wrote from right to left. He had difficulty completing projects, leaving scores of complex plans and designs for posterity to try to assemble. Ms. Seldin describes the young disabled student as one who "can't make choices" and "can't stay with an activity." "Distractible, impulsive." The type to sketch out and set aside. . . .

Was I really that stupid? Was I unable to calculate fractions or percentages? Or understand what I read? I enjoyed comic books. *Fantastic Four. Archie. Spiderman.* Even the high-brow Classic Comics. One of my fondest memories was going to the drugstore to buy those comics with my dad, who seemed to enjoy them as much as I did even though he wasn't LD. I hated *Dick and Jane*. Who didn't? But comics aside,

I have to admit now, I could not read worth a damn. I was no whiz at fractions. And besides the baseball statistics I computed and recorded in a spiral notebook, I knew little of percentages. Though the terminology didn't exist at the time, I was LD.

My parents were upset at my failure to move to the next level but were undaunted, as concerned parents tend to be. They arranged for me to be tested at a diagnostic center. They enrolled me in summer school and endless tutoring sessions, and transported me to Longfellow School for Boys where I repeated sixth grade. I remember I was very depressed. I wanted to run away, join the circus or the merchant marine. I didn't want to leave my neighborhood buddies to go to this bizarre school in Bethesda full of boys who dressed up in blue blazers and ties everyday.

The summer before I went to school, they gave us a reading list—*Penrod* and *Tom Sawyer,* the usual collection of coming-of-age classics. I remember sitting in the bedroom of our rented beach house feeling the sticky, salt air, looking up occasionally from where I was bent over a book to see the yellow curtains blowing in the window. I'd hear the far-off waves against the shore, the wind in the pines, and I'd feel like I'd just woken up from a long sleep. I could read. I could *really* read. And later on, after I had finished another book, I would sit down at my desk and write exhaustive synopses and commentaries.

I hated my parents when they enrolled me at Longfellow but, when I went there and my new teacher read an excerpt from one of my book reports and said I had some good ideas, I accepted the possibility that they might be onto something. My teacher could understand my writing; I could understand him and follow his instructions; I did my tests and did my homework without copying from the encyclopedia. For the first time in my life, I didn't feel like a fraud.

However, I wasn't instantly cured of LD. It is a disability and not a disease. My mind is still twisted and always will be. What is different is that I learned how to deal with it. I'm easily distracted, so when I was in a college class I concentrated by taking elaborate notes. Many students borrowed my notes since I missed almost nothing of what the professor said. I think they benefited more than I did given my problems with memory. So I tested poorly. I made up for this in out-of-class assignments where I had time enough to think about what I was going to say. On these papers, teachers would act surprised and wonder if I was the same person who wrote the exams. My professors did not understand that I had a twisted mind, that I was as smart as anyone else, that I came to the same logical conclusions as everyone but it took me longer to get there because I was distracted by the interesting terrain I traveled on the way.

Today my daughter's teachers know what mine did not. This is both good and bad. It is good that they've found the terminology. The Internet has hundreds of Web sites that relate to Learning Disability, some of which define LD with as many as forty-eight different characteristics. Hannah has only a handful of these, many of them similar to mine: "academic skills very slow in developing, strong discrepancies in skills and knowledge, artistic, sensitive, excellent vocabulary but poor production, wants to tell but cannot retrieve words, mishears or doesn't hear, and problems with various motor development–related skills." I am amazed, on the one hand, by what a good job the nebulous "they" have done in codifying my disorder, but, on the other, I am frightened by what they plan to do with all this ammunition. They are, after all, tinkering with the human mind, my daughter's mind, in particular, and I don't find this reassuring.

I believe they are at the very beginning of understanding LD, but don't yet know how to treat it. Or if it is treatable. Or if it is a disability. Or a difference, which is closer to my view. When Hannah was in first grade she received a report card much like my own from Miss Probey. Only Miss Probey was a nice lady, even nicer when she turned into Mrs. Bernard in the middle of the year. Hannah's teacher was a prison guard. She looked like Miss Honey in *Matilda,* but acted more like Miss Trunchbull so let's call her Ms. Honeybull. Ms. Honeybull's range of normal was ludicrous. Only about three students could fit into it, two of whom were on Ritalin, the third naturally passive. She was always berating the students for one thing or another and keeping them in from recess for minor slipups such as talking out of turn in class or not keeping in line when the students walked from one classroom to another. Once, she even beat one of the students with a ruler for not identifying the location of the Nile River on a map. One of Ms. Honeybull's favorite victims was Hannah.

Hannah with her pretty, round Irish face like her mother's, thin lips, and long hair to her shoulders, flyaway hair like mine. She's been a vegetarian since she was five. She hates that we own a leather couch though she does grudgingly sit on it. When her skin touches the leather, sometimes she'd say, "This is disgusting," and eyeball us half in jest as if we are murderers.

When we received Ms. Honeybull's report card, we were upset that Hannah flunked absolutely everything. We knew she was having difficulty in her academic subjects but we had received no prior warning that it was this bad, even in art which she loves. How could she flunk art or, even more inexplicable, deportment? We were aghast with the accusation that she didn't show consideration and respect for others, that she didn't play or listen to her peers, or cooperate or share, or control herself, and on and on. This was antithetical to every experience we had ever had with our daughter. Only a kid who burned down the school deserved grades like this, said my wife. We arranged a conference with Ms. Honeybull. She defended her views. We defended ours. Nothing much was accomplished. As we left the conference room, Ms. Honeybull blurted out, "Your daughter is unteachable."

"Now I understand," I might have said but didn't. It wasn't that Hannah was unteachable. It was that Ms. Honeybull was incapable of reaching Hannah. Connie, my wife, thought it went beyond that. "They're trying to push her out of school." Which seems obvious to me now as I look back on it. We did what my parents did when we were growing up. We tested Hannah. We hired a tutor. We looked for other schools.

By the fall of the next year Hannah was enrolled in the Lab School of Washington, one of the premier schools in the world for children and adults with learning disabilities. Unlike Ms. Honeybull, the teachers are trained to deal with a wide range of students, using art, theater, dance, woodworking, hands-on experiential methods to teach academic skills. For instance, in order to build a cabinet in woodworking you must know math.

Sally Smith, the founder and director of LSW, is the recognized leader in the field of learning disabilities. In addition, she is the head of the graduate program in LD at American University, author of five books on the subject and countless articles. As tough a character as you're likely to find, she could squeeze blood out of a turnip. So the school is well endowed. But not exclusive. Most of the students are funded and come from the public schools. The waiting list to get in is endless, as is the waiting list for teachers who want to teach there. But the real judge of LSW's success is that 90 percent of the students go on to college.

Hannah is thriving in this environment. She is much further along in her reading, writing, and arithmetic than I was at her age. She is happy. The teachers never punish her. They never single her out, except for praise. They have given her the award for good behavior practically every week she has been there. If she accumulates enough of these awards over a certain period of time, she is allowed to have lunch with the handsome gym instructor that all the girls swoon over.

In the fall the Lab School gives a gala at which they honor successful people with LD. I think it was the year they invited the Fonz that a paleontologist from Johns Hopkins, Dr. Steven M. Stanley, said in his speech to the overflow audience at the Omni–Shoreham Hotel that he thought he wasn't disabled. I don't remember his words exactly but they confirmed my belief. His brain, like my own, was twisted. It took him through that same illogical Alice in Wonderland world that I go through daily, and when he came out on the other side, usually he came out with a scatter-brained idea. But sometimes when he came out, his ideas were great, the very same ideas, he thought, that made it possible for him to rise to the top of his field. His twisted brain was no disability. It was a gift. What Hannah has, what I have, what my mom had, and what our ancestors had were gifts. And yet, I'm still apprehensive for Hannah. Will she be at the Lab School forever? Or will they recommend a transfer to a more traditional school once she catches up developmentally with her peers? Either way, I wonder how well she will do in college and beyond. Will she be able to compete in the real world? My concerns are no doubt little different from other parents'. Yet other parents do not have to go to the expense, the extra time, and the heartache that Connie and I do. Somehow I feel cheated that we are forced to send Hannah to a special school with kids who are basically the same as she. I wonder why this is so, why she must be isolated from the average student population, the $1 + 1 = 2$ Crowd.

2000

CRITICAL THINKING POINTS: *After you've read*

1. Richards writes, "My professors did not understand that I had a twisted mind, that I was as smart as anyone else, that I came to the same logical conclusions as everyone but it took me longer to get there because I was distracted by the interesting terrain I traveled on the way." How does he "prove" himself in college?

2. Richards makes the point that being LD might be a disability or simply a difference. What might be the impact of each alternative point of view? What is associated with each word?

3. How is Richards better able to parent Hannah because he has a similar disability?

SOME POSSIBILITIES FOR WRITING

1. Research the effects on a generation of people—most often boys and young men—heavily medicated by drugs such as Ritalin.

2. How might public schools incorporate some of the ideologies of the Lab School?

3. Research what kinds of services are available for students with disabilities on your campus.

School's Out: One Young Man Puzzles Over His Future Without College

Laura Sessions Stepp

Laura Sessions Stepp, a Pulitzer Prize–winning journalist for *The Washington Post*, has written for fifteen years about the lives, legends, and culture of youth. She is the author of *Our Last Best Shot: Guiding Our Children Through Early Adolescence* (2001) and *Unhooked: How Young Women Pursue Sex, Delay Love and Lose at Both* (2008).

"You see these clothes I'm wearing?" he asks. "I bought them. These shoes I'm wearing? I bought them. That car out there? I'm paying for it."

CRITICAL THINKING POINTS: *As you read*

1. What are some stereotypes about high school students who choose not to go to college? Where do those stereotypes come from?
2. What kind of town does Ben Farmer live in? How does that influence him and his choices?
3. Keep a list of reasons you feel Ben did not go to college.

B en Farmer at 19, steering his silver Camaro Z28 down Main Street on a Friday night, glances at the Dairy Freeze and thinks about the buddies he graduated from high school with last year. They're off at college, probably partying tonight, the beer, the girls, at Virginia Tech, Radford, wherever.

He passes a karate studio, beauty supply store and boarded-up movie theater with a marquee begging passersby to "Shop Altavista First."

He could be at college. He had the grades, he's got the brains, but here he is, listening to the cough in his 330-horsepower engine and worrying about his spark plugs.

"There was a lot of unknowns about college," he says after he thinks about it. "It was going to be this big, tough, hard, hard time in which all you'd do is write papers, which I don't like to do." So for now he assembles air conditioning ducts in a factory, for $7 an hour, which is as much as his mother makes in her new job at the bank, her first sit-down job in all the years she's been raising him.

Nobody in his family ever went to any kind of college. His mom wanted him to go. She helped him with the application and the financial aid forms. But he didn't go, he took a $7 job in a town with a lot of $7 jobs, a little river town in central Virginia, where the Southern railroad met the Norfolk and Western, spawning a furniture factory, textile mill and other small manufacturers.

Ten to 12 hours a day, he hammers sheet metal, then goes home to shower off the dirt and fibers. Some nights he heads out to the driving range to hit golf balls. Weekends, he drives over to South Boston to watch guys do what he would like most to do, race stock cars. He has thought about signing on with a NASCAR pit crew, a great job except you're never home.

Altavista is home. He knows everybody, he's already got a job, and now he's met a girl, named Apryl East. He's having visions of a little house one day with a two-car garage, "going to work and going on vacation, not worrying where your next meal is coming from."

So now he's thinking of asking his boss at Moore's, an electrical and mechanical construction firm, if the company will pay him to take night classes at the local community college and then move him indoors to a better-paying job, a sit-down job. Apryl, who goes to Virginia Tech, encourages this line of thinking.

The fall after Ben and 70 others graduated from the local high school, 2.5 million American seniors enrolled in either a two-year or a four-year college.

Almost a million did not. They were overwhelmingly poor, male and white. Much to the surprise of social scientists who traditionally have looked for educational problems among minorities, low-income black and Hispanic men are more likely to go to college right out of high school than white guys like Ben. So are young women of any background. If Ben had a twin sister, she'd likely be enrolled.

There are Ben Farmers all over: in the coal towns of Pennsylvania, the suburban sprawl west of Sacramento and especially in the rural South. They've always been there, hidden in the pockets of America where they pump gas, assemble machine parts and put their pay on the family's kitchen table. They do work that needs to be done—building houses, running backhoes, riveting airplanes, surveying land and fixing the BMWs of upscale college types who occasionally might call them rednecks. America might well lose all its advanced-degree business school graduates with less pain than it would lose these young men.

They're proud of the work they do. At the same time, they've found it harder and harder to acquire full-time jobs with decent pay increases and good health insurance. Their earnings, adjusted for inflation, have fallen or stalled. Altavista, population 3,400, has several thousand people commuting there to work, so there are jobs. But fewer and fewer: Altavista has lost 1,300 jobs in a little over a year.

Other young Altavista men in Ben's position fear they're headed nowhere in a society that prefers paper-pushers to pipe fitters. They don't want to manage accounts payable for a living, or scan X-rays for cancerous tumors. They're proud of doing hard, physical work. But people around them say that white-collar jobs, available only with a college diploma, are the only way to win at life. This attitude, says Patricia Gandara, a professor of education at the University of California, Davis, can make these young white men feel invisible.

"Latinos and African Americans have horrendous problems, too, but at least they have a group identity," says Gandara, who studies low-income, primarily minority youths. "These poor white males don't know where in the culture they fit. Some are really alienated and angry."

Ken Gray, a professor of workforce education at Pennsylvania State University, worries about them, too. "No one's interested in the Bubbas," he says.

Ben is no Bubba, more an easygoing, smart kid with a goatee and a vague future. Off work, he wears American Eagle polo shirts, khakis and Nike sandals.

"You see these clothes I'm wearing?" he asks. "I bought them. These shoes I'm wearing? I bought them. That car out there? I'm paying for it." It's a matter of pride and obligation that richer people can't understand.

He has friends whose parents pay their school expenses, their apartment rent. One of his pals lives off campus in a nice two-bedroom apartment with a big leather couch and an air hockey table.

"On some days I wish I were him," Ben says. On other days? All he'll say about his buddy is this: "If you asked him how much his cell phone bill is, he wouldn't know."

Ben's a guy whose mother taught him to "always keep good credit and pay your bills on time." You get his drift.

His father, Walter, a truck driver who left Ben and Ben's mom when Ben was 3, hasn't played much of a role in his life. But Walter's parents, Marvin and Frances, sure have. Until his early teens, he'd spend the school months in Altavista with his mom, Patsy Moore, and all summer with Marvin and Frances, big NASCAR fans who followed the circuit.

"I think I disappointed Granny the most not going to college, and Mom second," he says.

His mom, eating dinner with Ben in his favorite restaurant, El Cazador, says she's still wondering why he didn't go to college. Hasn't he learned from her example?

Researchers would say that some kids never want to venture much farther along life's path than did the people they know and love best. Moore, a sweet woman of 42, doesn't understand this, as she explains to Ben over a taco salad that he helped her choose.

"You've seen me struggle from week to week," she says. "You can't want that."

No, he doesn't want that. But what does he want? More pressing still, what can he realistically expect to attain?

Ben has loved hot rods since he was a baby. He ran Matchbox cars over his grandmother's rug for hours at a time before he could walk, and as he got older he took up dirt bikes with a bunch of boys his age who lived in the country near his granny.

"We stayed outside all the time," he recalls.

As they got older, their little group carved a dirt track in woods of scrub pine and began racing cars and trucks. Ben's two best friends eventually acquired race cars and the gang started spending time at Big Daddy's South Boston Speedway, a NASCAR-sanctioned short track. Ben began to dream of becoming another Tony Stewart or a pit crew chief.

His teachers couldn't understand this fascination. He's such a good student, they'd sigh, as if you couldn't be interested in both math and Chevys, which happen to have a serious relationship through mechanical engineering. He pulled down A's and B's in high school, taking calculus and Latin. But his teachers didn't foresee a career in engineering, they just seemed to see a car-crazy kid.

One problem they didn't count on: His friends' families all had more money than his, and to dress the way they did and do the things they did, Ben had to get a job.

So at age fifteen he found one at the Amoco Food Shop south of town. He stopped playing high school basketball and started stocking shelves. Making money became something of an obsession. Not big money, though. That would have required college.

When Ben's friends started talking about four-year colleges, Ben would go silent. When they took the SAT in their junior year, Ben didn't. "I thought to myself, where would I find the money?"

His mom encouraged him to try a two-year school, and so he got an application to Danville Community College. But his heart wasn't in it. The message of his guidance counselor and some of his teachers, he says, was that four-year colleges or universities were the only goal worth aiming for.

Those who hold bachelor's degrees have a hard time understanding why anyone wouldn't want one. At Ben's high school, administrators took pride in the fact that they send proportionately more graduates to four-year colleges than other schools in the area. They talked about former students who chose Columbia, Duke or the University of Virginia. For Ben, even $8,000 to $10,000 a year for in-state tuition, room and board didn't seem in the cards.

Other young men in Ben's position report similar experiences.

"They were good at giving out papers to kids going to college, but didn't pay no attention to students going to community college," says Jason Spence, who makes bulletproof vests on the night shift at BGF Industries. Jason and Ben both remember sitting through school assemblies where the same students won award after award, scholarship after scholarship—to four-year schools.

Ben's mother recognized she needed someone to help jump-start her son, but when she sought out school authorities, she says, she received only an offhand kind of attention. "I'd never done this before. They told me I could take Ben to Danville and Lynchburg. It wasn't very helpful."

Ben says he asked at school if, on career day, organizers could bring in someone who worked in the racing industry. With several local drivers around, it would have been easy to find someone, but nothing happened.

"You feel like kind of an outsider," he says.

He might not have felt that way a decade ago, because young men and young women here could still come right out of high school and go to work for family-run industries offering decent starting wages and chances for promotion. They didn't need higher education to enjoy job security at places like Lane Furniture, famous for its cedar chests. But once the Lane family lost direct control of the company in the late 1980s, things started to change. Gradually the manufacturing of cedar chests and dining sets moved to the cheap labor market of China, and fewer and fewer workers filled the million-square-foot brick and wood complex that had dominated, indeed was, Altavista's skyline.

Last year, on Aug. 31, the last hope chest rolled off the assembly line. Other industries in the area started folding or cutting back, and by this past spring, the unemployment rate in central Virginia had hit a 10-year high. When a health supplements lab in town advertised for 40 new jobs, the cars lined up for interviews the first morning snaked for blocks through town.

Ben worried about his mother—she'd get a job, then be laid off under a last-hired, first-fired policy. "She's had a string of bad luck," he says.

Rather then head for college in the hope of improving their chances for a good job, Ben and other young men like him sought out jobs right away that offered health insurance, pension plans and savings programs.

Max Everhart, who lives around the corner from Ben, was one of them. Also a bright young man, he went to work at a machine bearings plant for $10 an hour plus benefits. "It's a good job," Max says. "I'm lucky to have it."

Ben felt the same way when he got hired four months ago at Moore's. With 300 employees, it's one of the few companies in town that is growing. In its vast, open garage he bends, shapes and glues ducts with men like Smoky Hudson and Melvin Mann, who have been doing this kind of work for 30 years. He has learned to respect them.

These guys "really work for their money," he says. "They get their hands dirty."

T.O. Rowland, a 33-year-old welder at Moore's, tells Ben he earns as much money as his wife, a schoolteacher with a master's degree. This makes Ben wonder again: Why do people make such a big deal over college?

This is a question that resonates only in some quarters of the educational establishment. Ken Gray, the Penn State professor, says: "The real opportunities for youth are grossly distorted by colleges. Seventy-one percent of jobs don't require anything beyond a high school education."

But that doesn't mean people can't or shouldn't keep learning, acquiring new skills. In Altavista, Central Virginia Community College runs a satellite center in the former Lane executive building here. The idea is to reach people in high-layoff areas. Center director Linda Rodriguez says the response from older workers, especially older female workers, has been terrific.

But young men like Ben aren't coming in.

When she approached high school authorities about coming to visit classes, she was met with some of the same lack of enthusiasm for community college that Ben's mom did. School authorities said there was no time in the calendar for her visits—the students were too busy taking tests—and offered a one-time assembly instead.

One evening last winter, as Ben arrived at the Amoco store to start his shift, the store manager pushed a paper napkin over to him across the counter. "Someone left this for you," he said.

On the napkin next to the beef jerky, the name Apryl East was scribbled along with a phone number. Ben smiled, remembering the blonde with the cornflower-blue eyes and infectious laugh who had stopped by a couple of weeks earlier. She was after him. Sweet.

Eight months later, the blonde is riding with him in his Camaro as they return from a football game between his old high school and hers in nearby Gretna, where she led cheers and played piccolo in the marching band. Now she's a senior at Virginia Tech, planning on teaching elementary school.

Apryl swears that her best friend left the napkin without her knowledge. Ben doesn't know whether to believe her but he also doesn't care.

He eventually did call her, they went out to a movie. Now a wallet photo of the two of them is propped next to the odometer in his beloved car.

Increasingly, their conversation involves the years to come, and tonight is no exception. Ben ran into a guy at the game whose girlfriend is taking courses in motorcar management at a community college.

"That kinda makes me want to try it," he tells Apryl.

He could choose to stay on at Moore's and go to school at the same time, "maybe get a job on computers" at Moore's. He also has had a couple of conversations with NASCAR driver Stacy Compton. Perhaps, while he's still young, he should just chuck everything—except Apryl—and enlist Compton's help signing on with a racing crew. The sponsors and money for his own car might follow.

"I am so not sure," he says.

Apryl has accepted his confusion, for now.

"I'd like you to go to college," she tells Ben, "but it's okay with me if you don't." Her three best friends are all at different universities. But neither her dad, a supervisor at Moore's, nor her mom, a secretary in a printing shop, attended college, and they've been happy together. From what she has observed at home, college isn't crucial to the married life she dreams of.

What is important, she has told Ben gently, is that he get his behind in gear. He can always try one avenue and move to another if he doesn't like it. He's not yet 20, she reminds him.

Where will he find the motivation?

"From me," she says. She laughs but she's serious. "I'm going to get out of college, come back home and tell him to do it. I can be his little mentor."

A few hours before Ben picks her up for the game, over lunch at a downtown diner, she admits that when she learned that Ben wasn't in college, "I was shocked. I told my mom he didn't get the right kind of guidance."

So why does she stick with him? "He's got a great personality. He's funny." Unlike her previous boyfriend, "he treats me well. Oh, and another thing I like about him? My dad and he have bonded. He says when we have kids, he wants to be the kind of dad he never had."

She takes a breath, then adds, "Ben's everything I ever wanted." She laughs again, then cups her hand over her mouth as if she has revealed just a little too much.

2002

CRITICAL THINKING POINTS: *After you've read*

1. Do you have any friends who are not in college? Is it difficult to explain to them what it is like? Why or why not?
2. If you could predict a future for Apryl and Ben, what might it be? Why?
3. If you were going to give Ben some advice, what would it be?

SOME POSSIBILITIES FOR WRITING

1. Compare and contrast your life now to the life you might have had if you had not gone to college.
2. In so many ways, Ben is a product of the environment and people around him. Imitating the "feature reporter" tone of this essay, write a similar one with you as the subject.
3. "No one's interested in the Bubbas," this essay asserts. Is that true? Why do you think the way you do?

Eighth-Grade Final Exam: Salina, Kansas, 1895

Various tests from the days of yore occasionally make the rounds of Internet information loops. This exam was taken from the original document on file at the Smoky Valley Genealogical Society and Library in Salina, Kansas.

What is the cost of a square farm at $15 per acre, the distance around which is 640 rods?

CRITICAL THINKING POINTS: *As you read*

1. How well do you think you would do on this test? Why?
2. Do you think your teachers could pass it? Why or why not?
3. Are there any questions for which your answer might be correct today but not in 1895? Why?

Grammar

(Time, one hour)

1. Give nine rules for the use of Capital Letters.
2. Name the Parts of Speech and define those that have no modifications.
3. Define Verse, Stanza and Paragraph.
4. What are the Principal Parts of a verb? Give Principal Parts of do, lie, lay and run.
5. Define Case, Illustrate each Case.
6. What is Punctuation? Give rules for principal marks of Punctuation.
7–10. Write a composition of about 150 words and show therein that you understand the practical use of the rules of grammar.

Arithmetic

(Time, 1.25 hours)

1. Name and define the Fundamental Rules of Arithmetic.
2. A wagon box is 2 ft. deep, 10 ft. long, and 3 ft. wide. How many bushels of wheat will it hold?

3. If a load of wheat weighs 3942 lbs., what is it worth at 50 cts.per bu, deducting 1050 lbs. for tare?

4. District No.33 has a valuation of $35,000. What is the necessary levy to carry on a school seven months at $50 per month, and have $104 for incidentals?

5. Find cost of 6720 lbs. coal at $6.00 per ton.

6. Find the interest of $512.60 for 8 months and 18 days at 7 percent.

7. What is the cost of 40 boards 12 inches wide and 16 ft. long at $20 per inch?

8. Find bank discount on $300 for 90 days (no grace) at 10 percent.

9. What is the cost of a square farm at $15 per acre, the distance around which is 640 rods?

10. Write a Bank Check, a Promissory Note, and a Receipt.

U.S. History

(Time, 45 minutes)

1. Give the epochs into which U.S. History is divided.

2. Give an account of the discovery of America by Columbus.

3. Relate the causes and results of the Revolutionary War.

4. Show the territorial growth of the United States.

5. Tell what you can of the history of Kansas.

6. Describe three of the most prominent battles of the Rebellion.

7. Who were the following: Morse, Whitney, Fulton, Bell, Lincoln, Penn, and Howe?

8. Name events connected with the following dates: 1607, 1620, 1800, 1849, and 1865.

Orthography

(Time, one hour)

1. What is meant by the following: Alphabet, phonetic orthography, etymology, syllabication?

2. What are elementary sounds? How are they classified?

3. What are the following, and give examples of each: Trigraph, sub-vocals, diphthong, cognate letters, linguals?

4. Give four substitutes for caret 'u'.

5. Give two rules for spelling words with final 'e'. Name two exceptions under each rule.

6. Give two uses of silent letters in spelling. Illustrate each.

7. Define the following prefixes and use in connection with a word: Bi, dis, mis, pre, semi, post, non, inter, mono, super.

8. Mark diacritically and divide into syllables the following, and name the sign that indicates the sound: Card, ball, mercy, sir, odd, cell, rise, blood, fare, last.

9. Use the following correctly in sentences: Cite, site, sight, fane, fain, feign, vane, vain, vein, raze, raise, rays.

10. Write 10 words frequently mispronounced and indicate pronunciation by use of diacritical marks and by syllabication.

Geography

(Time, one hour)

1. What is climate? Upon what does climate depend?

2. How do you account for the extremes of climate in Kansas?

3. Of what use are rivers? Of what use is the ocean?

4. Describe the mountains of N.A.

5. Name and describe the following: Monrovia, Odessa, Denver, Manitoba, Hecla, Yukon, St. Helena, Juan Fernandez, Aspinwall and Orinoco.

6. Name and locate the principal trade centers of the U.S.

7. Name all the republics of Europe and give the capital of each.

8. Why is the Atlantic Coast colder than the Pacific in the same latitude?

9. Describe the process by which the water of the ocean returns to the sources of rivers.

10. Describe the movements of the earth. Give inclination of the earth.

1895

CRITICAL THINKING POINTS: *After you've read*

1. Perhaps too easy an answer as to why much of this material is so foreign to you is that you were never "taught it." What are some of the reasons that is so?

2. Which sections of the test do you think you would do the best at? The worst? Why?

3. Which individual questions would be the hardest and the easiest for your class to answer? Why?

SOME POSSIBILITIES FOR WRITING

1. Design your own test (or section of a test) to give to eighth grade students in 1895. Try not to "trick" anyone or to concentrate on objects or areas that would be unfamiliar to them.

2. What are some of the most difficult tests you have taken in school? What made them difficult? Were they fair or unfair tests? What made them fair or unfair?

3. If you were to design a fair but difficult test for a course you are taking this semester, what kinds of questions might you ask? Why?

This Was the Assignment: Disability Culture

Peter Gimbel

This was the assignment: What cultural group do you belong to? What are the characteristics of that group? Consider who and what you are, based on race/ethnicity, ability, lifestyle, religion, and so on. (For instance, are you a part of "girl power" culture, "hip-hop" culture, "small town culture," "black culture"?). What does it mean to be a part of that culture?

Peter Gimbel holds a bachelor's degree from Brown University and a master's degree in social work from the University of Houston. He is a social worker at a nonprofit organization in New Jersey that promotes independent living for people with disabilities.

I feel more at home in disability culture than I do in mainstream, white culture.

CRITICAL THINKING POINTS: *As you read*

1. Pay attention to Gimbel's definition of "disability culture."
2. Many disabilities are "invisible." Which do you think would be more difficult: to have an "unseen" disability or to have a disability that might be more obvious, such as a physical disability?
3. Why does one's "cultural identity" matter? Why is this something a person reflect upon?

I am a white male with a disability. The culture of my birth is commonly abbreviated with the acronym W.A.S.P.: White, Anglo-Saxon, and Protestant. Over time, however, I have come to identify myself more as a person with a disability than as a white person, and I feel more at home in disability culture than I do in mainstream, white culture.

My cultural identity as a person with a disability is predicated on having a progressively worsening genetic disorder (Duchenne muscular dystrophy). Because I was able to walk until the age of 11, I was largely able to pass for able-bodied. Even after I began to use a wheelchair, I was told that a cure for muscular dystrophy would likely be discovered soon. My well-intentioned parents mistakenly collaborated with me in viewing my disability as a temporary setback that need not be integrated into my sense of identity.

Disability culture includes a range of beliefs and values as diverse as the members who make up this group. "Disability" is the only minority group that anyone can join . . . to become a part of it, all one has to do is acquire a disability. Because disability is such an open-ended cultural group, it includes a highly varied population who come from all cultures, races, ethnicities and nationalities. As a result, it is hard to define the beliefs and values of disability culture.

However, there are certain interests that unite nearly all people with disabilities. These interests comprise the reform of social policy toward people with disabilities, the reform of the medical system, the removal of institutional and architectural barriers to equality, and other concerns that affect daily life with a disability. The most unifying axiom of disability culture: the personal is the political.

Most people with disabilities are acutely aware that public policy affects their well-being in very real ways. Medicare and Medicaid services are critical, but so are other functions of government, such as protecting workers with disabilities from discrimination and making sure that buildings from courthouses to restaurants meet standards of wheelchair accessibility.

What I like most about the values of disability culture is the redefinition of the disability community as a minority with legitimate social and civil rights. This helps me to view myself as an empowered individual rather than a victim of circumstance.

Because of my identity as a person with a disability, I experience prejudice on an almost daily basis. It is so commonplace in my life that it is reduced to background static: I hardly even notice it anymore. This prejudice is subtle, but it is very present. I am always stared at in public places. Waiters, retail workers, and strangers on the street refer to me as "buddy," even when they would never address an able-bodied adult male in this way.

I also experience overt discrimination. I once had a waiter "forget" to take my order because he assumed that my (able-bodied) wife had ordered for both of us. I was even turned down for a social work internship whose tasks were well within my capabilities. I was told that having someone write case notes for me in a mental health clinic violated confidentiality, with no opportunity for discussion of how this problem might be resolved (for example, as at my current placement, by having the person helping me sign a confidentiality agreement).

Aside from my own cultural group as a person with a disability, I understand the culture of white people of the upper economic class. I was born into this class, but was partially removed from it as I became more visibly disabled. In this cultural context, males are expected to go into finance, corporate law, or other prestigious and highly lucrative jobs. Because of my disability, I have been largely "released" from these expectations.

2007

CRITICAL THINKING POINTS: *After you've read*

1. In your experience, is it common for people to be part of more than one "culture," as Gimbel describes?

2. Gimbel says he has been "released" from some expectations as a white male because of his disability. What might he mean?

3. Gimbel writes, "Disability culture includes a range of beliefs and values as diverse as the members who make up this group." Can you think of other groups (or groups that you're part of) for which this is true?

SOME POSSIBILITIES FOR WRITING

1. Write your own response to this assignment.

2. Research the history of civil-rights laws that protect people with disabilities.

3. Contact your school's services for students with disabilities office, and interview its coordinator. Report back to your class on the kinds of services provided.

This Was the Assignment: College Ain't Cheap

Alexander J. F. Thornton

This was the assignment: In 750 words or less, explain why you (as the most deserving person on the planet) should win a $10,000 prize for tuition and books. This contest was sponsored by mental_floss magazine, Borders and Merriam-Webster.

A former nursing major, Alexander J. F. Thornton is currently studying criminal justice at Winona State University and is part of his school's ROTC program.

I have excelled in both math and science my whole life, and nursing seems to be a good fit for me even if I have testicles.

CRITICAL THINKING POINTS: *As you read*

1. Pay attention to the details Thornton includes about himself and about male nurses. Why do you think he chooses what he does?
2. Do you think it's harder to write a short essay or a long essay? Why?
3. Why is it often difficult for students to write about themselves and their experiences?

I am the most deserving person on the planet to win this scholarship because I am a guy, and I want to become a nurse. That would make me a "male nurse." I'm sure in 2009, no one would ever say "female engineer" or "female astronaut" or even "male kindergarten teacher," but nearly everyone I know still puts *MALE* in front of "nurse" when they talk about my future career. When I graduate with a bachelor's degree in Nursing in the spring of 2013, I will join a fraternity of *male nurses*, like Gaylord "Greg" Focker from *Meet the Parents*, Walt Whitman—a Civil War nurse better known as America's poet, James Derham—a former slave of doctors who became a nurse and used his wages to buy his freedom, or even the sole "buff guy" transplant nurse in the movie *John Q*. I'm guessing all of them probably had to deal with the stereotypes of being a nurse. *Not smart enough to be a doctor? Are you gay? Do you just want to hang out with women, you pussy?*

The last stereotype is partly true. I've been accepted to Viterbo University, a premier nursing school in the Midwest where seventy percent of the students are female, and a great place for me to get a date. Viterbo is a private college in LaCrosse, Wisconsin, home of the largest six-pack of beer in the world (City Brewery lists each huge can at 14,691,592 fluid ounces—equal to over 1.2 million regular cans of beer)

57

and famous for its Oktoberfest celebration the last week of September. I've also been accepted to Winona State University, also known around the Midwest for its nursing program and with a male to female ratio of four to six, it's another good place to find a girlfriend. Winona, Minnesota was named after the Native American Princess "We-Noh-Nah," and it's the home of Sugar Loaf, a rocky limestone bluff that outlines the town. I will decide which school I'll attend based on the amount of scholarship money I earn.

Throughout early American history nurses were mostly male, but in 1901 the U.S. Army Nurse Corps was formed and only allowed female nurses. Military nursing went from being predominantly male to exclusively female. That means during World War I, World War II, and the Korean War, men could only serve as medics, not nurses. Even if a male soldier was already a Registered Nurse, he wouldn't be assigned as a nurse in the field.

Today nursing offers a well-paying, competitive, fast-paced career. The job hunt should be easy for me given the shortage of nurses in the U.S. Hopefully I will encounter flexibility while choosing which hospital or city I would like to work in. My ultimate goal is to become a Certified Registered Nurse Anesthetist (CRNA). I figure if I'm putting people to sleep they won't know whether I'm male or female.

In the U.S. today just under 6% of all Registered Nurses are male. Despite the stereotypes this is a great profession for guys like me. I have excelled in both math and science my whole life and nursing seems to be a good fit for me even if I have testicles. Am I the most deserving person on the planet to win this scholarship? I really think so.

2009

CRITICAL THINKING POINTS: *After you've read*

1. Which of Thornton's facts do you find most interesting? Why those?
2. What are other professions associated with one gender or the other?
3. Would you award Thornton a scholarship based on his essay? Why or why not?

SOME POSSIBILITIES FOR WRITING

1. Write your own response to this assignment.
2. Research scholarships at your school and elsewhere. Find and apply for at least three that seem to be a good fit for you.
3. Find a professor or a student on your campus who is in a field dominated by the opposite sex (a female computer science professor or a male elementary education student). Interview that person about his or her experiences in a male or female dominated field.

Further Suggestions for Writing— *"Where We're Coming From"*

1. What do you expect to miss the most and least about high school and/or home? Why?

2. What kind of high school student were you? What traits would you like to keep as a college student? What would you like to change and why? What could you do to facilitate this?

3. Recall a time when you were thrust into a situation where you did not quite fit in. Describe your experience. How does it compare to starting college?

4. Recall some recent experience that was new, different, foreign, and perhaps even frightening. Reflect on what you learned or how your preconceptions changed. What idea(s) gradually dawned on you?

5. Think of some significant accomplishment in your life. Write about how curiosity, discipline, risk taking, initiative, and/or enthusiasm contributed to that accomplishment. Did other qualities contribute as well?

6. Think of a time when you lacked the verbal skills you needed to communicate effectively. It may have been conducting a college interview, writing a letter to a friend, or expressing your ideas in class. Write about how it made you feel and how you coped with the problem.

7. If you participated in any organized programs in high school, describe what that activity did or did not teach you.

8. Identify a talent you have or information you possess that is unique, such as tap dancing, scuba diving, or how to make maple syrup. Write at least a page about why this is important to you and why others should know about it.

9. Aesop says, "Never trust the advice of a man in difficulties." No doubt you've received advice before coming to college. What makes for good advice? For bad? What kind of advice were you given? Which will be the easiest or the hardest for you to follow? Why?

10. Choose one of the pieces of advice in this chapter and try to convince someone that it is particularly good or bad advice.

11. Think of a problem with your high school, perhaps within a team, student organization, or group of friends. Propose some specific solutions for this problem.

12. Working in a group, examine how our society guides students to college. Did you feel that you received "the right kind of guidance"? Why or why not?

13. Some students seem eager to answer questions in class, to join the discussion, while others do not. How do you usually react in these situations? Why?

14. Interview two or three experienced students about their first year. What kinds of pressure and problems did they have? How did they handle them? Seek their advice on things you are concerned about.

15. Most people want to succeed at what they do, and college is no exception. Why and how much do you want to succeed at college? What does success at college mean to you?

16. What co-curricular activities do you plan to pursue in college? How do these activities relate to your academic or career plans?

17. Choose a campus organization you are thinking about joining and investigate it. Prepare a report on this organization to deliver to the class.

18. Find something interesting, odd, or unique about it and present your findings to the class.

19. Go to an on-campus event of any kind that you have never experienced before, such as a symphony, a ballet, a poetry reading, or a debate. The possibilities are endless. With an open mind, summarize, describe, and/or evaluate it. Do you think you would ever attend another event of this kind? Why or why not?

20. Prepare for a crucial situation that is likely to happen to you as a college student this semester. Imagine exactly what might happen and write a description of it. Explain why this situation is likely to be so crucial. Include all the possible outcomes, from the best to the worst, and figure out what you might do to prepare for the situation before it occurs.

21. Contrast "Saved" with "One Writer's Beginnings." What are some of the reasons these pieces display the differences they do? What support do you have for your position?

22. Find and watch Spike Lee's 1992 film *Malcolm X*. How does seeing this film affect your reading of the selection "Saved"?

23. Research and write a brief report about the Dawes Act (or General Allotment Act) of 1887. How do the philosophical and political implications of this act further your understanding of Zitkala-Sa's "Incurring My Mother's Displeasure"?

24. Read *Be True to Your School* by Bob Greene (1988) and/or *Please Don't Kill the Freshman: A Memoir* by Zoe Trope (2003) or similar high school memoirs. How does either of these high school experiences compare to yours or to each other? Why do you think that is so?

25. Read *Bullseye: Stories and Poems by Outstanding High School Writers* edited by Pawlak, Lourie, and Padgett (1995) and/or *Coming of Age in America: A Multicultural Anthology* edited by Frosch and Sotto (1995) and/or *Early Harvest: Student Writing from the Rural Readers Project* edited by Rachele Syme (2000), or similar collections. Which pieces seem to be the most honest to you? Why?

26. Read *Aquamarine Blue 5: Personal Stories of College Students with Autism* by Dawn Prince-Hughes (2002) and/or *Learning Outside the Lines: Two Ivy League Students with Learning Disabilities and ADHD Give You the Tools to Succeed* edited by Mooney and Cole (2002) and/or *Learning Disabilities and Life Stories* edited by Rodis, Garrod, and Boscardin (2002), or some similar collection.

After reading these experiences from these points of view, what insights and/or new awareness do you have?

27. Read *Don't Tell Me What to Do, Just Send Money: The Essential Parenting Guide to the College Years* by Johnson and Schelhas-Miller (2000) and/or *Empty Nest . . . Full Heart: The Journey from Home to College* by Andrea Van Steenhouse (2002) and/or *Letting Go: A Parents' Guide to Understanding the College Years* by Coburn and Treeger (2003), or a similar guide for parents of college students. After reading these experiences from these points of view, what insights and/or new awareness do you have?

28. Choose at least three films from the list at the end of this chapter. What do they seem to say about high school? What support do you have for your position?

29. Choose one of your responses to "Some Possibilities for Writing" in this chapter and do further research on some aspect of the topic. Write about how and why this new information would have improved your previous effort.

30. Find the original text from which one of the selections in this chapter was taken. What led you to choose the text you did? How does reading more from the text affect your original reading? Is there more you would like to know about the text, its subject, or its author? Where might you find this further information?

Selected Films—"Where We're Coming From"

Almost Famous (2000, USA). Cameron Crowe's semi-autobiographical tale of a high-school boy who is given the chance to write a story about an up-and-coming rock band as he accompanies it on their concert tour. Comedy/Drama. 122 min. R.

American Graffiti (1973, USA). The action takes place over one typical night for a group of high school graduates. Co-written and directed by George Lucas (the auteur behind the *Star Wars* trilogy). Comedy. 110 min. PG.

American Primitive (2008, USA). Tells the story of the havoc in a teenage girl's life when she discovers her widowed father is gay. Drama, 83 min. R.

Assassination of a High School President (2008, USA). At a Catholic high school, the popular girl teams up with a sophomore newspaper reporter to investigate a case of stolen SAT exams. Comedy, 93 min. R.

Boyz N the Hood (1991, USA). The film follows the stories of childhood friends who grow up in a Los Angeles ghetto. Drama. 107 min. R.

The Breakfast Club (1985, USA). Forced to spend a Saturday detention in school, five disparate high school kids find that they have more in common than they ever realized. John Hughes directed. Comedy/Drama. 97 min. R.

Breaking Away (1979, USA). Oscar winner (for best original screenplay) about a teen just out of high school searching for his identity through bicycle racing. Filmed on location at Indiana University. Comedy/Drama. 100 min. PG.

Can't Hardly Wait (1998, USA). It's graduation night for a group of high school seniors, and each of them must face the future while learning to let go of the past. Comedy. 100 min. PG-13.

Class (1983, USA). Two prep school roommates come up against class differences and a salacious secret neither one is fully aware of. Comedy/Drama. 98 min. R.

Crooklyn (1994, USA). The life of a 1970s Brooklyn family told through the viewpoint of a nine-year old girl. Spike Lee's semi-autobiographical tale of his childhood, coauthored with his sister, Joie. Comedy/Drama. 115 min. PG-13.

Do the Right Thing (1989, USA). Spike Lee's film of racial tensions that finally boil over in the Bed-Stuy district of Brooklyn during the hottest day of the summer. Comedy/Drama/Crime. 120 min. R.

The Education of Little Tree (1997, Canada). A heartwarming adaptation of the acclaimed best-seller about an eight-year-old Cherokee boy in Tennessee's Smoky Mountains during the 1930s. Drama, 112 min. PG.

Election (1999, USA). An obnoxious overachiever running for student body president is opposed by an unlikely candidate egged on by a vindictive teacher. Comedy. 103 min. R.

Elephant (2003, USA). A violent incident rocks the students and faculty at a high school in Portland, Oregon. Drama. 81 min. R.

Fame (1980, USA). Follows four students through their years in the New York City High School for the Performing Arts. The kids fall into four clearly defined stereotypes: brazen, gay and hypersensitive, prickly, and shy. Drama. 134 min. R.

Fast Times at Ridgemont High (1982, USA). Based on the factual book by Cameron Crowe, who returned to high school as an adult masquerading as a student for a year. Featured the film debuts of Forest Whitaker, Eric Stoltz, Anthony Edwards, and Nicolas Cage. Comedy. 90 min. R.

Ferris Bueller's Day Off (1986, USA). Days away from graduation, Ferris and his best friends, Cameron and Sloane, explore Chicago on a day of hooky. John Hughes directed. Comedy. 102 min. PG-13.

Heathers (1989, USA). In a half-hearted attempt at popularity, Veronica mixes with popular girls Heather I, II, and III, until she meets the darkly rebellious Jason Dean, who shows her that the flip side to popularity can be murder. Dark Comedy. 102 min. R.

Hoop Dreams (1994, USA). Recruited to attend an elite high school by professional basketball player Isaiah Thomas, Arthur Agee and William Gates are filmed for nearly five years as they struggle through successes and failures on their way to college. Documentary. 170 min. PG-13.

Hoosiers (1986, USA). A coach with a dark past and the town drunk pair up to train a small-town high-school basketball team in Indiana for the state championships. Drama. 115 min. PG.

Juno (2007, USA). Faced with an unplanned pregnancy, an offbeat young woman makes an unusual decision regarding her unborn child. Drama, 96 min. PG.

Kids (1995, USA). A young skater sets out to deflower as many virgins as possible, but things go badly when one gets tested for HIV. Drama. 91 min. R.

Mystic Pizza (1988, USA). Three young women of blue-collar Portuguese descent work in a pizzeria in the coastal town of Mystic, Connecticut, and one dreams of going to Yale. Romantic comedy. 104 min. R.

Napoleon Dynamite (2004, USA). A listless and alienated teenager decides to help his new friend win the class presidency in their small western high school, while he must deal with his bizarre family life back home. Comedy, 82 min. PG.

O (2001, USA). An update of *Othello* with a teen cast, taking place in a white prep boarding school in the South. The only black student, Odin, is the star basketball player. Drama. 95 min. R.

October Sky (1999, USA). Based on the memoir *Rocket Boys* by Homer H. Hickam Jr., this true story begins in 1957 with the Soviet Union's historic launch of the Sputnik satellite. Homer sees Sputnik as his cue to pursue a fascination with rocketry, but winning the science fair is his only ticket to college and out of life in a West Virginia coal-mining town. Drama. 108 min. PG.

Orange County (2002, USA). An Orange County teen and aspiring writer yearns for admission to Stanford. Comedy. 82 min. PG-13.

The Outsiders (1983, USA). Based upon S. E. Hinton's popular novel, *The Outsiders* follows the lives of a group of high-school-aged boys who sit on the margins of society. Drama. 91 min. PG.

Real Women Have Curves (2002, USA). The story of Ana, a first generation Mexican-American teenager, whose traditional, old-world parents want her to help provide for the family and give up her scholarship to Columbia. Drama. 87 min. PG-13.

Rebel Without a Cause (1955, USA). A James Dean classic. Dean stars as a troubled teen who comes to a new town hoping to start over and finds both friends and enemies. Drama. 111 min. N/R.

Risky Business (1983, USA). With his parents out of town, entrepreneurial Tom Cruise decides to spend the time waiting to hear from colleges dancing in his underwear and organizing a prostitution ring. By the time he gets to college, he's a wiser man. Comedy. 99 min. R.

Rushmore (1999, USA). The king of Rushmore prep school is put on academic probation. Comedy. 133 min. R.

Say Anything (1989, USA). A young kickboxer falls for the smart girl. She's college bound; he's maybe not. Comedy/Drama. 89 min. PG-13.

Sixteen Candles (1984, USA). Samantha Baker's angst-ridden love-life, as well as her sixteenth birthday, is lost in the uproar caused by her older sister's wedding. Comedy/Drama. 93 min. PG.

Thirteen (2003, USA). A thirteen-year-old girl's relationship with her mother is put to the test as she discovers drugs, sex, and petty crime in the company of her cool but troubled best friend. Drama. 100 min. R.

For critical thinking points on these films, see Appendix (p. 277).

Two

School Daze

LIFE IN THE FIRST YEAR

Many first-year students often walk around in a daze—sleep deprived, homesick, scared, overwhelmed, or feeling like a castaway in a strange land. The selections in this chapter focus on the sometimes humorous and sometimes very serious transitions, new interactions, balancing acts, and experiences that make up the first year of college.

A Day in the Life Of . . .

Greg Adams

Greg Adams is a father, teacher, songwriter, and poet who lives with his wife and daughter in his hometown of Chetek, Wisconsin. When not mesmerized by the stars or his laptop, Greg takes time to explore secondhand shops, study Isshin-Ryu karate, and record his original music.

. . . REWIND.

CRITICAL THINKING POINTS: *As you read*

1. From its title, what do you expect the poem to be about?
2. Why is this a poem and not a short story or a diary entry? What things specifically make this a poem?
3. What are some of the narrator's personality traits? How do you recognize them?

8:04 a.m., Kleenex, lamp
light, Irish Spring, Pert
Plus, boxers, pants, shirt,
Malt-O-Meal, milk, vitamin.
parking lot, bridge, college
algebra, Burger King, hot chocolate,
short story, bridge, parking
lot, keys, stereo, guitar.
local news, frozen chicken, instant
potatoes, salt, butter,
milk, aspirin, Rolaids, rented
video, beer, popcorn, Kleenex.
beer, more beer, salt, burnt
kernels, credits, STOP, Close
Up, mint floss, sleep sofa, allergy
pill, lights, REWIND.

1994

CRITICAL THINKING POINTS: *After you've read*

1. Which of these details seem to particularly reflect college life? How might that contribute to your reading of the poem?

2. Imagine you could ask the narrator, "So, how was your day?" What do you think he would say? Why?

3. Why do you think there are no verbs in the poem? What effect does that have?

SOME POSSIBILITIES FOR WRITING

1. Rewrite the poem so it is pertinent to your day. Include specific details in the way the author does. Try it again, but this time make it about a day in your life when you were in high school.

2. Write about some part of your daily routine—getting up, going to bed, walking the dog, driving to work (the more mundane the better)—as seen by a disinterested, objective third person. Try as hard as you can not to tell readers what you want them to know, but instead show them with concrete details.

3. Again, write about some part of your daily routine, but as observed by a person who wants readers to like or to dislike you. Or, as observed by a person who wants readers not to trust you. Or, from your own point of view, which reflects a particular state of mind such as happiness, depression, joy, or boredom. Try as hard as you can not to tell readers what you want them to know, but instead show them with concrete details.

My First Week at Mizzou

FROM *ANOTHER YEAR IN THE LIFE OF A NERD*   Andrew Hicks

Andrew Hicks graduated with a degree in journalism from the University of Missouri–Columbia. His online journal "The Nerd Diaries" continues his adventures through college and beyond and is available online.

I have only one class on Fridays, the omnipresent Spanish class, so that leaves plenty of time for leisure, studying and keeping up on letter correspondence. . . . Okay, you got me, I slept all afternoon.

CRITICAL THINKING POINTS: *As you read*

1. Among the first things writers should consider is their purpose and audience. What do you think are the purpose and audience of this piece? What elements lead you to think the way you do?
2. Recall your experience of first coming to campus. How was your experience different from Hicks's account? How was it similar?
3. What are some stereotypes you associate with people labeled as nerds? Why? Does the narrator conform to or violate any of these? Is he really a nerd?

August 22

The first day of the end of my life. Yes, the college experience has begun for your favorite nerd and so far it hasn't been that much different from the high school experience, except that I am now completely independent, miles from home and— oh yeah—stone cold drunk. No, of course I'm not. That statement was incorrect. I'm actually *fall-down* drunk. That last statement was also incorrect, as I've obviously never been drunk in my life. I've been exempt from peer pressure thus far in my life, except for the time those guys got me hooked on phonics, a habit I haven't been able to break since. Still, who knows what will happen to me now that I'm stuck on the grounds of a large state university, open and susceptible to all forms of temptation. I may even convert from the original "Star Trek" to "Star Trek: The Next Generation."

Dorm life, obviously, is my first experience of living in close quarters with another person, if you don't count the year and a half I was shacked up with "Golden Girl" Estelle Getty. I'd be remiss if I didn't take up valuable space in the book berating my roommate, but he's actually a pretty nice guy. A quiet guy, too. Keeps to himself. At least that's what the neighbors will tell the police after he kills me in my sleep. Think I'm being paranoid? Then you haven't seen the stack of *Soldier of Fortune* magazines, the poster of the Army guy carrying an automatic gun, the American flag hanging over the bed. Now are you starting to see the scenario? I own several Japanese electronic products, including the laptop computer I'm typing this on. What if this militant patriot decides to make sure I never buy foreign again? Still, he's probably just a normal American teenager, hence the Kathy Ireland poster on the wall. Of course, she's fully-clothed, so maybe he's not so normal after all.

At least my roommate passed one TV compatibility test, the one that asks "Do you like 'America's Funniest Home Videos'?" I could never voluntarily share a room with someone who found Bob Saget amusing. I still have to see about a second TV compatibility test, this one concerning late-night talk show hosts. As far as I'm concerned, there are two kinds of people in the world, the Letterman people and the Leno people. I've only met one Conan person in my life, but this was a McCluer student named Sumar who had continuing flashbacks to Woodstock '94, so that tells you something. My family and I are all staunch Letterman men, but of course my two best friends are Leno people, so what good does that test do? See, I've been here one day and already my theories on life are falling apart.

August 24

Today was the first day of classes. My first class on Mondays, Wednesdays and Fridays doesn't start until 10:40, but since I made no attempt to conceal that fact from my employers, I had to get up bright and early this morning to serve people their heart attacks.

The one good thing about getting up at 6:30 is that there aren't any other people using the showers. As you may imagine, with an ample body like mine, I'll never be president of the Public Showers Fan Club. I am grateful that there are stalls to separate the showers, but I still sometimes accidentally reveal too much, as evidenced a few days ago, when somebody said, "Hey, that pasty white shower curtain has a crack in it." Of course it wasn't a shower curtain, but I didn't tell the guy that.

The stalls are only shoulder high, so even though certain parts are strategically concealed, you still have to make small talk with the other people in the shower room. I've already found out saying "nice penis" doesn't cut it as far as small talk goes. And I've also found out, darn the luck, that coed dorms don't mean coed showers. *Animal House,* you lied to me!

At 10:40 I was off to Spanish class, which I had thought would be my first challenging Spanish class. After all, it had taken both ounces of my brain power to test into Spanish 2 during the Summer Welcome. Once I got to class, though, and heard the jocks and frat boys saying "*Como* . . . uh . . . my llama . . . uh . . . " I canceled any previous thoughts regarding the degree of difficulty.

My other class today was an Honors class regarding the study of the book of Revelation and other apocalyptic literature, a subject I've always found fascinating, to the point where I've actually watched the 1973 Christian movie *A Thief in the Night* more than once. Enduring a movie that bad more than once should automatically save anyone's soul from hell.

Even though the University policy states that instructors can't do anything but discuss the semester syllabus (syllabi, in the plural) on the first day, both classes did assign homework. For the Revelation class I have to walk up to complete strangers on the street and record their opinions on how the world would end, which isn't exactly a casual icebreaker for conversation. I might as well be asking them to imagine their sweet grannies burning in hellfire for all eternity.

August 25

I went to my remaining three classes today and, let me tell you, it ain't gonna be that hard for me this semester. Part of that stems from the fact that my English class centers strictly on autobiographical writing. See what I mean? All I ever do is write about myself. If only the class had been even more specific and focused on humorous autobiographical writing, I would have been set for life. But I'm sure the instructor has a sense of humor. You should have seen the suspenders he was wearing.

Three of my "instructors" are full-fledged professors, not bad for freshman courses at a large state school. The other two instructors are ambitious grad students, including my Spanish teacher, who insists on the annoying habit of speaking in Spanish all the time. She said yesterday that if you want to be good at playing football, you play football. And if you want to be good at speaking Spanish, you speak Spanish. Or something like that. I'm not sure about the exact explanation because she said it in Spanish. See, it's a no-win situation. Excuse me, *es un no-gana situacion.*

Psychology class should prove to be interesting for the mere fact that it consists of over 500 students. I have a sneaking suspicion I'm the only person in the class and the other 499 were just extras brought in for an experiment to see how I would react to the crowd. I was clever enough to anticipate that scenario and decided to throw off the results by jumping up and down, yelling "Mickey Mouse is in my pocket! You can't have him! None of you! Stand back, I have a light saber!" What I didn't anticipate was the appearance of the Mizzou police five minutes later to haul me away.

Last night we had a meeting of all the guys in my dorm. Seeing all the people I live with all at once made one thing perfectly clear to me—I have to keep my door locked at all times. As far as roommate relations go, there have been no significant developments. The guy just doesn't talk. And he keeps putting up more of the gun/military posters, the latest featuring a skull with criss-crossed guns, reading "Mess with the best, die like the rest." Oh yeah, one more thing—I haven't been sleeping too well either.

August 26

I have only one class on Fridays, the omnipresent Spanish class, so that leaves plenty of time for leisure, studying and keeping up on letter correspondence. . . . Okay, you got me, I slept all afternoon. I think I was entitled, though, after getting up at 6:30 this morning to work in the dining hall. I am gradually getting the hang of proper food-handling procedures, as today I only contaminated the food with two deadly bacteria instead of the usual three.

My first dining hall shift was a barbecue picnic at the football field, where—it has been constantly mentioned—the Astroturf has been replaced by real grass. What they didn't mention was that we were serving the Astroturf on buns with barbecue sauce for dinner. Apparently, all the rules about hygiene outlined at the orientation meeting don't apply to outdoor meals. The swarm of flies swimming in the cole slaw clued me in to that fact. Towards the end of the evening, the flies had actually constructed a miniature waterslide leading into the cole slaw and were taking turns sliding down the damn thing.

This is the first Friday night here on campus and I imagine there's plenty of drinking going on. I myself have had two pitchers of Brita filtered water, so watch out! You can tell I've loosened up out here. I used to drink only tap water, but the water here has so much lead in it there's a pencil sharpener attached to the sink.

It's been an exciting Friday night for me. A trip to the laundry room and the computer lab in the same evening. I thought the computer lab would be fairly empty due to it being Friday night and all but the first time I went in the computers were all in use. "Why aren't you people out getting drunk?" I demanded. "Leave the computer room to dorks like me who have nothing better to do." But no one budged. Oh well, I can always come back later to coerce preteen girls over the Internet.

August 29

Although there's not much spiritual conviction to be found in most Mizzou students (their philosophy in life centers more around "two boobs and a brewski" than the Bible), there are still quite a few Christian organizations on campus, many of which go to great lengths to attract students' attention. Today, for example, there was a street preacher yelling at the top of his lungs at one intersection about "fornication" and "hay-ell," with the traditional evangelist flair, the kind of college student who would be more at home at Oral Roberts University than a large state school.

As I was walking past this spectacle, I overheard a girl commenting. She was a Jim Morrison–worshiping vampire clone with purple hair and a nose ring. She said three words concerning the street preacher: "That guy's weird." I considered stopping and pointing out the full irony of the girl's comment but decided against it.

My week at Mizzou has proven to me that there are quite a few people out there who stretch the bounds of "normal," whatever that may be defined as. Today in my Revelation course a group of students reported back on their interviews with people about their opinions on the world's end. Although most respondents did have the traditional Rapture / Tribulation / Antichrist / Armageddon beliefs or the naturalistic science-geek perspective of the earth ending due to "cyclical forces," there were some that just couldn't be classified.

One person thought the earth would literally shrink to one-eighth its original size and people would have to push each other off into space to retain their position, until the only people left were murderers whom God would cast into hell. Of course, this guy's brain has probably shrunk to one-eighth its original size. . . . Another person, a Black power advocate, said that, due to negligence by white supremacists, the ozone hole would widen, giving all white people skin tumors. Only people of African origin would survive. I think this guy must have graduated from McCluer.

The professor then told us of a book manuscript with conclusive proof that the world would end on November 14, 1999, to which one person responded, "Do we get off class for it?" A humorous exchange I had nothing to do with but nevertheless felt compelled to transcribe so maybe I can sell it to *Reader's Digest* one day.

1995

CRITICAL THINKING POINTS: *After you've read*

1. Why might anyone keep a journal? What do you think would be some of the advantages of doing so?

2. What might be some of the differences between keeping a journal for yourself and going online with one? Pay attention not only to what you would say in your journal but also how you would say it.

3. Hicks wrote his *Another Year in the Life of a Nerd* series years before blogs became so popular. Why do you think that writing blogs is a current craze?

4. Imagine the author reading his journal some ten or twenty years in the future. What do you think he will think and/or feel about it then?

SOME POSSIBILITIES FOR WRITING

1. Create or re-create your own journal of your first few days of classes.

2. Imagine you are one of the characters who appears in this journal and rewrite one or more scenes from that character's point of view.

3. Write about the funniest incident that has happened to you since arriving on campus. Then write about the saddest or most disappointing incident.

Hunters and Gatherers

Jennifer Hale

"Hunters and Gatherers" is an excerpt from a journal that Jennifer Hale (b. 1977) wrote for an Introduction to College Learning Strategies course.

Not knowing what to expect for college, I was poorly prepared. I have not brought with me the special tools required for a successful transition to college life.

CRITICAL THINKING POINTS: *As you read*

1. What kind of student does the author seem to be? What specifically from the journal do you base your opinion on?
2. Each student brings his or her unique perspective to college. What is the author's perspective? What is yours?
3. Consider how the author "learned" her course work as she wrote in her journal. Have you ever used this technique of applying course work to your personal life?

D ue to the fact that I am currently a history major I have the extreme pleasure of learning the same thing in three classes. In Anthropology, US History and World History all my professors are talking about pre-historical societies and hunting/gathering groups as a foundation for the classes. This is highly beneficial for a person who selectively attends class such as I. I can take notes for one class and still do well in the others. However lackadaisical this approach may seem I have still learned a great deal. In studying hunting and gathering societies I have found parallels to my own life.

In a hunting and gathering society the food-getting strategies involve the collection of "naturally" occurring plants and animals. In this type of community there are little economic practices. Except for the occasional bartering there is no currency exchange. Primitive societies like this one are also extremely superstitious, having natural gods that provide for people and are also feared by the clan.

Maybe the connection is not clear to you, so I will give examples.

In hunting/gathering societies the food getting strategies involve the collection of naturally occurring plants and animals.

Not knowing what to expect for college, I was poorly prepared. I have not brought with me the special tools required for a successful transition to college life. These "tools" would be things like tape, nail-polish remover, highlighter, and, of course, sleeping pills. Fortunately I live in a very fertile and lush place where these things are easily attainable. However, like primitive societies, I must make offerings to the God that provides these needed "tools," namely my roommate Karen. I try to use naturally occurring products when Karen is out of the room so not to anger her but sometimes a complimentary can of Coke helps to keep the peace. Another item that I find I can't live without is cereal. Luckily for me Karen thinks all food goes bad a week after it is bought (an idea I introduced into her puny skull) so she often throws out perfectly good food. At this point I do "creative hunting/gathering" by removing the good trash (cereal) and throw the bad trash down the trash shoot. This way I am not stealing the food only recycling it. I also get points for taking out the garbage.

In this type of community there are little economic practices. Except for the occasional bartering there is no currency exchange.

Besides prison, maybe college life is the most cash free environment alive today. However true this may be, there is still a free exchange of goods. Since money is used for tobacco, alcohol, and weed, other ways of obtaining goods must be developed. After all, necessity is the mother of invention. The use of CDs from a neighbor might involve the use of one of your good sweaters. Term papers can be bought for carpeting, and let's not underplay the value of sexual favors.

Primitive societies also are extremely superstitious, having natural gods that both provide for the clan and are feared by it.

I can't stress the importance of abusing your roommate enough. Hey, the way I see it, this college thing is an egalitarian society, and we all should share. Or at least that's what I tell myself as I am eating out of the trash. However wonderful this might seem there are prices to pay. Like tuition.

1996

CRITICAL THINKING POINTS: *After you've read*

1. In what other ways might first-year students become "hunters and gatherers"? How else might they be described?
2. In addition to the concrete tools the author mentions, what kinds of personal skills are needed to make the transition to college life? Does this student possess any of those?
3. Read or reread Andrew Hicks's "My First Week at Mizzou." How is Hale similar to Hicks? How is she different?

SOME POSSIBILITIES FOR WRITING

1. Build on Hale's list of the tools necessary for college life. Make it your own personal list, however far-fetched.

2. Hale says, "Not knowing what to expect for college, I was poorly prepared." Write briefly about one way you have already realized you were poorly prepared for college. What steps should you take to rectify this situation?

3. Use specific course work from one of your classes and find parallels to your personal or social life, in the same way the author of "Hunters and Gatherers" does. Some possibilities might include concepts you've learned in your courses in psychology, sociology, economics, or any other social science field.

Lummox: Evolution of a Man

AN EXCERPT   **Mike Magnuson**

Mike Magnuson earned a one-year suspension for poor academic performance after his first year of college. This excerpt details the Labor Day weekend before he returned to classes. *Lummox* is Magnuson's third book. Read more about him at http://mikemagnuson.blogspot.com.

He's going to fill his mind with ideas and beauty, and even if nobody thinks Mike's capable of knowing this shit, knowing about beauty and truth and art and all that, by God Mike can know about it anyway.

CRITICAL THINKING POINTS: *As you read*

1. What is a "lummox"? Do you think Mike Magnuson is a lummox? Why or why not?
2. What are grounds for suspension at your school?
3. How does Magnuson teach himself to be a better reader while he's in jail?

 thin jailer is standing in the cell's doorway, requesting that Mike get on his feet. Mike complies, gets right up, and isn't wobbly one bit. He feels pretty good, all things considered. Says happily to the jailer, "I'm glad *that*'s over."

"What's that?" the jailer says.

"Being in jail."

The jailer grins, but not with amusement. Says, "You're not going home, buck. You're here till Tuesday morning."

Mike figures the jailer's giving him shit. "Give me a break, man." He says. "That's three days from now."

The jailer says, "You gotta wait till your arraignment."

Mike doesn't move. "Till Tuesday?"

"Monday, that's Labor Day. No court."

Block C in Eau Claire County Jail has twelve lock-down cells—one prisoner to a cell—that open to a barred-in holding area with three picnic-type tables in it. One of the tables is covered with books and magazines and board games, and the other two are set up for smoking and watching the TV, which is situated high up, just outside the bars.

Around 8:30 A.M. Mike arrives on Block C. The jailer assigns him to Cell 6. Tells Mike here's the shitter and here's the shower and lunch is at eleven, supper at five and lockdown at nine. And that's that. Mike's cooling out in the hoosegow. He's looking at three days of hard county time.

The place doesn't seem too intimidating, though. A few inmates are playing Risk at one of the tables, smoking cigarettes, and a guy there with long black hair and aviator glasses waits till the jailer leaves, gets up from his spot on the bench, comes right over to Mike and introduces himself.

Says he's Tom. He hopes Mike will enjoy his stay. "I'm the welcoming committee around here," he says.

He invites Mike to take a seat, which Mike does, then he offers Mike a cigarette, which he takes, then he gives Mike the straight skinny on Block C.

Tom's nine months into a yearlong stretch here for stealing a few car stereos and doing some other stupid shit, and he would get out during the week to work on Huber Law, but he can't seem to find himself a job, and, well, it's pretty goddam quiet here during the weekdays. Pretty relaxing. But on the weekends the block fills up with drunks, and that's cool with Tom because the food's a lot better on the weekends than it is during the week. Check out the feast for Sunday lunch, hey. We're talking turkey dinner with all the trimmings. And there's of course the Risk game here, which on occasion is very competitive, very quality. And there's this fine stack of magazines and books.

"I myself," Tom says, "have read every book in the stack."

"Cool," Mike says.

The other inmates on Block C aren't as talkative as Tom, but they're completely not dangerous-seeming in a way. A couple of them say they're in for bouncing checks. One guy's in for his second DUI. One guy's in for his third. Another guy, a really skinny fellow with sunken eyes, he won't say what he's in for, but Mike doesn't figure it's for anything but a fuckup.

After a while, Mike tells everybody his story. The getting-drunk-at-the-Brat-Kabin part, the stealing-the-hand, the giving-fake-names-to-the-cops, and everybody busts complete gut about it. They all say they wish they were in for what Mike's in for.

And there you have it: Mike's buddies with everybody.

Lunch is sliced roast beef with mashed potatoes, gravy, peas, and a tin cup full of milk. Awesome chow, that's for sure. He'd never be eating this good at home. And after lunch, everybody yawns and wanders off to their cells, and in no time the only sound in Block C is peaceful petty-criminal snoring, but Mike's still awake. He's in jail, man. This ain't something a person should sleep through! He's got to be remembering this so he can tell his grandchildren about it. Or something.

Okay, so there's a stack of books. Maybe he'll find something to read till his fellow inmates wake up. He's never actually enjoyed reading, and in fact he hasn't read a book cover to cover since he was ten. Some Hardy Boys book, he thinks it was. Or maybe a book about airplanes. But here in Block C: Hell, it's so quiet, basically a boredom situation while everybody's napping, he figures reading is the perfectly natural thing to do.

So there's piles of *Sports Afield* and *Outdoor Life,* all raggedy and with pages torn or missing. And there's some books with sociological type titles: *Rehabilitation of the Thief. The Social Animal. A Case Against Recidivism.* And so forth.

Finally, he finds a thin black paperback, a movie tie-in book for the film *Rollerball.* Mike didn't see *Rollerball* when it came out, must have been ten years ago, but he remembers that it was about a sort of futuristic roller derby to the death or whatever. The more he thinks about it, he remembers *Rollerball* because there were ads on TV for it and somebody was playing the beginning of Bach's Toccata and Fugue in D Minor on the organ. Toccata and Fugue in D Minor. One of Mike's all-time favorites. If *Rollerball* is about *that,* it's going to be kickass.

He takes the book to his cell, stretches out, opens it up. He's expecting music, sure, or at least a novel about roller derby, but this book isn't either of those things, not really. *Rollerball* is a book of short stories by some guy named William Harrison, a guy who's seen fit to write a preface to his book, a few pages in which he talks about all sorts of things Mike doesn't remotely understand.

William Harrison writes this:

> Nowadays a well-documented Cultural Decline has befallen us and the students in the universities are too depraved to listen to talk of standards and so, I insist, am I.

He also writes this:

> The author of the story knows this and derives considerable pleasure from this fact; he is a miniaturist—with all the minor and subversive enjoyments of that role—and he sets a small hieroglyph against the armor of the body politic.

Mike reads this whatever-it-is five or six times, grows bewildered, and promptly falls asleep.

When he wakes, the book's still balanced on his chest. Outside his cell a few inmates are gathered around one of the picnic tables, playing Risk with Tom, who seems to be winning. Tom's saying, "Strategy, I'm telling you. The game is about strategy." The inmates are playing Risk for cigarettes, betting one smoke for one country occupied, two smokes for a continent.

Mike reopens *Rollerball,* rereads that sentence about body politic. Like, what in the hell is *that?* And he decides to move forward in the book and maybe find something he can understand there. He sees a story listed on the contents page called "Rollerball Murder." The movie story. He finds it, begins to read. The story's fifteen pages long, mostly explaining the rules of roller derby to the death, and also talking about some other junk like corporations replacing governments and people being all miserable and ignorant and bloodthirsty as a result.

As far as Mike can tell, ain't no Toccata and Fugue in D Minor *anywhere* in this story. He reads the entire story three times, slowly and carefully, and the only thing he reads about music is a one-line reference to corporate hymns and brass bands on the last page. But the thing is, by the time he's read the story three times, he doesn't care if there's a Toccata in there. There's people fucking each other and getting fucked over and fucking other people over. There's action: motorcycles, dudes getting killed. And somewhere near the end of the story the main character, a fellow name of Jonathan E., realizes that playing roller derby to the death is a pretty horseshit thing to do. And Mike finds himself saying, aloud, "No kidding, it's horseshit."

Suppertime comes. Another nice meal: fried chicken and green beans and potato salad and apple cobbler. Exceptional.

And during the evening Mike joins his fellow offenders in a television film festival. The movie is your made-for-TV type about a grizzly bear loose somewhere in the Northwest, terrorizing folks renting cabins on their summer vacations. Great flick, everybody's thinking. They're cheering for the bear, hoping he rips every one of them vacationers to shreds. And the bear rips up a few, too. And everybody applauds and whistles. But near the end of the movie, when an enterprising young forest ranger manages finally to kill the bear and everything in the movie is happily-ever-after, the skinny inmate with the sunken eyes falls to pieces, breaks down and weeps. The skinny guy can't endure a happy ending on Block C.

In the morning, after pancakes and sausage, Mike resolves to spend his whole day reading. He's slept well. Sure, he stinks bad because he worked landscaping all yesterday and then got drunk and still hasn't changed his clothes or showered or brushed his teeth. But he's feeling fresh in the physical and spiritual way. This incarceration thing, he's thinking, and the solitude thing in Cell 6, it's exactly the kind of mental preparation he needs before commencing the fall term. He can pull his shit together in here.

Now, you've probably heard that people's lives can sometimes change in one moment, that somebody is one person for a long time, then they experience something incredible, and they are thereafter altered. Folks who go for Christ, they'll for sure tell you that. For He comes to touch you once. And you must be ready to accept Him. And for sure, hey: Damn near every rock 'n' roll musician you've ever heard about says something like: "After I saw the Beatles on *Ed Sullivan,* I knew I wanted to play." Or "When I heard Hendrix in London." All people do this shit; it's easier for them to say *Right here, at this very instant, that's when I knew,* than to say, *Well, I kinda poked along in life and eventually I knew what I wanted to do with myself.*

But on this Sunday morning in the Eau Claire County Jail, on Cell Block C, in cell number 6, Mike's moment comes to him, the instant where everything in his life has been pointing in this direction and everything in his life will be different afterwards.

He reads a story in *Rollerball* called "A Cook's Tale."

It's about a middle-aged man with a job. He's the head cook at the University of Minnesota Hospital. He's large and gruff and is known as the Swede. And unbeknownst to any of his coworkers in the hospital kitchen, he's read the entire Modern Library, four hundred books, in alphabetical order, over a period of eight years. The Swede's name is John Olaf, and the story is about him finally letting his secret slip.

A woman named Emma works in the hospital kitchen, and on the day the story begins, she's weepy as fuck-all because her husband who's a graduate student, has just failed a major examination. She can't work worth a hoot as a result, is defensive about her husband, saying that he's not dumb and that he's been studying very hard to pass that test, and it's the Swede's job, it's what he gets paid for, to convince her to pull herself together. He's got a kitchen to run here. And he treats Emma hard, jokes about her husband, but when he sees her weeping there before her industrial dishwasher, his heart gets meat-tenderized for her. He feels sorry for her. So he tries comforting her, and the only words that come to him are a few words from Proust. "Pain she was capable of causing me; joy, never; pain alone kept the tedious attachment alive."

This perks her up all right. She wants to know where the quote comes from, and the Swede, he tells Emma he's just heard it somewhere; he can't remember where.

They have an affair, of course, because in stories, Mike supposes, that's one of the things people do. That Swede's married to a woman who can't understand why he's spent all that money and all that time reading four hundred books of the Modern Library. Emma is married to a man who's more interested in his studies than in her. Therefore, it's natural that they should come together. But the Swede never lets on to Emma that he's read all those books. He's large, coarse, and oafish, hardly the educated-looking type, and he figures that even if he tells Emma he's read all those books, she won't believe him. To Emma, the Swede is a fresh breath of uneducated air. To the Swede, Emma is everything his wife is not. They picnic. They hang around together. They talk and all that stuff.

Near the end of the story, Emma invites the Swede to a party at her apartment, a party where her husband's friends and professors are chatting about intellectual things. The Swede gets horrifically drunk at the party. At one point, an intellectual accuses the Swede of being a Classicist, and the Swede punches him. The Swede— and Mike knows this is the point of the story—is just as smart as these intellectuals, but he doesn't know how to behave like them. He's a large, coarse, oafish dude, and nothing's going to change that.

At the very end of the story, the Swede makes love to Emma, quietly, in Emma's bedroom, while the party rages outside the door, and then he goes home to his wife, carrying a loaf of fresh-baked bread under his arm.

Lovely.

Here's the math of it, folks. Mike reads this story and can't help thinking that the Swede equals Mike Magnuson. "A Cook's Tale" is exactly the story of Mike's life—well, except for the lovemaking part and the book-reading part. But there's the Swede: large, ungainly, loud. And there's Mike: same. Which is, in Mike's view, cause for joy. In the story, see, the Swede triumphs in a small way over the world. He can't socialize properly with intellectuals? So what? The Swede *is* an intellectual, and that's all that matters about being an intellectual: being one. So Mike resolves right then and there that he's going to do something grand like the Swede's done. He's going to read four hundred books or something like that. He's going to fill his mind with ideas and beauty, and even if nobody thinks Mike's capable of knowing this shit, knowing about beauty and truth and art and all that, by God Mike can know about it anyway.

And Mike goes ahead and does school the right way. He gets his shit together. He goes to court on Tuesday morning, gets some laughs in the courtroom when the judge reads selected excerpts from the arresting officer's report aloud: "The suspect identified himself as Bart Starr. This court hasn't heard *that* one before." But the judge releases Mike to his own recognizance. And Mike walks home. On the way, he stops by the lilac where he pitched his wallet, and sure enough, the wallet's there. Nobody's touched it. This is a nice town. This is a place where nobody will steal your wallet.

And Mike cleans himself up and gets to his first class on time, and to his next class and to his next class and so on. And he does his homework. He gets some good grades on tests and papers and presentations. He speaks up in class, tries to say intelligent things and sometimes even does, and when he's not in class he's sitting at a study carrel in the library or hanging out in the Student Union, smoking cigarettes or drinking coffee with folks from his classes and discussing with them the meaning of the universe and so forth, and by God he starts making the best friends a person could have at college: the smart ones, the crazy ones, the ones with goofy haircuts and who wear goofy clothes, the ones with alternative worldviews and alternative ways of living, the ones who know they're brilliant and have every intention of overthrowing the world when they get the chance.

You add it all up: Looks like Mike's turning out okay after all.

2002

CRITICAL THINKING POINTS: *After you've read*

1. Magnuson recognizes the difference between being as smart as "intellectuals" and acting like them. Why is this important in his story?

2. What contributes to Magnuson's plan for an evolution? Is it realistic that he experiences the kind of transformation he does over just a few days? Why or why not?

3. Most memoirs or nonfiction books about the experiences of an author are written in the first person. Why do you think Magnuson wrote about his experiences in the third person? What might this accomplish? How might this piece be different if told from the first-person point of view?

SOME POSSIBILITIES FOR WRITING

1. Magnuson writes, "you've probably heard that peoples' lives can sometimes change in one moment, that somebody is one person for a long time, then

they experience something incredible, and they are thereafter altered." Have you ever experienced or witnessed this?

2. How does being in jail during the weekend before school begins affect Magnuson? Do you think Magnuson considers the repercussions of being in jail? Why or why not?

3. What characteristics of the Swede, John Olaf, in "A Cook's Tale" does Magnuson identify with? Are there any characters in books, films, or TV programs with whom you've felt some connection? How? Why?

STUDENT RESPONSE TO *LUMMOX: EVOLUTION OF A MAN*

Reading this piece made me think of myself—especially Magnuson's talk about a moment of change. This is something that I think about frequently if not daily. Since I can remember I have been looking for a moment of change, an epiphany, a personal revolution. Starting around middle school I would write down a date that I would get things together, or pick events that I thought should be a turning point. A turning point for what (?) always changed but usually involved doing better in school, gaining control of my finances, and some social goals. It's New Year's every morning and every night I reflect on the abandoned resolutions.

This mindset is something that I think about and examine all the time. But lately I have started to doubt that lasting meaningful changes in life come that way for most people. I am starting to believe that change in one's life only really comes from diligence. It's exciting for people who experience a moment of change like Mike, but I think what's really going on is that that sometimes people are fortunate enough to have an intense experience at a time when they are already ready for change, and it simply provides them with motivation long enough to form a better habit.

I would like something intense to happen and suddenly make everything seem clear and to make positive change the only option. But I don't think I can wait for that to happen anymore, instead I have to work gradually and diligently. Every time I have thought "this is my moment of change," I work hard to improve my life for a day or a week and then fade back to neglecting school and borrowing from one to pay another. I think for most people this might be the case. The desire to improve is sparked by something (parents, bad grades, suspension) but determination burns out quickly.

I like to hear about people in their time of change like Mike, but I don't think that is how I will be able to succeed in life. I didn't do this assignment on time because suspension changed me and my study habits. I am doing it for a lot of little reasons:

- Because I'm tired of school and the fastest way out is to quit failing.
- Because I told my girlfriend that it was due so that she would give me crap if I didn't do it.
- Because I'm sick of feeling like I'm behind.

- Because failing classes has increased my debt.
- Because I finally found some medication that makes writing papers less torturous.
- Because I know there are people who would give anything to have the opportunities that I have, including college.

Although I think the essay is fine, it reminded me that I can't wait for something to fix my life for me or to wake me up. Diligence is how I plan to make this semester a success, by accepting that it will be hard and it will temporarily take away from things that are important to me.

Outside In: The Life of a Commuter Student

Patti See

Patti See's poetry, fiction, and essays have been published in *Salon Magazine, HipMama, The Southeast Review, Women's Studies Quarterly*, and other publications. She is the author of a poetry collection, *Love's Bluff* (2006), and coauthor of *Higher Learning: Reading and Writing About College*, third edition.

I didn't know as a freshman that there are many ways to experience college and mine was just one of them. I didn't know that there were other students in my classes who weren't having the "traditional" college experience.

CRITICAL THINKING POINTS: *As you read*

1. What is a first-generation college student?
2. What is the significance of the title? In what ways is See "outside in"?
3. What are some general characteristics of "commuters"? What do you think of when you hear the word "commuter"?

I t was long ago and far away, the way many of us think of our undergraduate years. I started college in the mid-'80s, a time when women my age defined themselves with big hair and a closet-full of stone-washed denim. There were few causes for college students then, just *Just Say No,* and abortion if you were into that sort of thing. I pined for a cause, for a purpose, for a normal life as a college student. I was a commuter, living a community away from the university with roommates who spent winters in Florida.

I didn't know as a freshman that there are many ways to experience college and mine was just one of them. I didn't know that there were other students in my classes who weren't having the "traditional" college experience. I only focused on the fact that I wasn't living in a dorm with a stranger, trying out different men like shoes, joining a sorority or student organization, experimenting with lifestyles.

I was embarrassed that my parents didn't pay for me to go to college away from home. They gave me a place to live, a car with insurance, every meal, everything that allowed me to commute the twenty minutes to school. At eighteen I didn't realize that putting myself through college, managing work and books, might be an experience in self-reliance. As the youngest of eight children, most of whom had gone to the university closest to home, I accepted that commuting was just what my family did. Like other teenagers, I thought my family was abnormal.

Though I was the last of their children to go to college, my parents still had no idea what it was about. They saw college as extended high school, what people did these days, go to classes for another four years, get another diploma, get a job that pays more than factory work.

My father was a railroad man who worked his way up from switchman to yard master over forty years. My mother's career was built around children and rosary beads. She was never without either of them for almost forty years and had no way nor need to retire from either. I didn't consider the humble beginnings of my peers, didn't know then that half of the university population was made up of first-generation college students like me. I only focused on my own history. I didn't see myself as progress.

At new student orientation, the summer before my first semester, I watched the other first-years wander around campus with their parents, touring buildings, reading the course catalogue over lunch. I didn't even consider telling my parents about orientation. I recognized even then I was in it alone. One morning when I was suffering from something as banal as menstrual cramps or a hangover, my mother said into my pale face at breakfast, "If you feel sick at school, just go to the office and tell them you need to come home. You can do that, can't you?"

I didn't bother to explain there was no office, no one to tell, that the campus spans for miles. I nodded an "okay."

When I walked into my first class of 250 students, more bodies than my entire high school and its faculty combined, I had no point of reference. It was straight out of *The Paper Chase,* I thought then, without the sophistication. That was the first time in my life I was truly anonymous, a number, and I liked being in a flood of strangers. I graduated from a Catholic high school where everyone knew everyone else, and I was tired of it.

I learned early on that college freshmen don't talk to one another in class, and I had no way outside of class to get to know any of them. My first semester, the closest I came to forming any sort of relationship with another person on campus was with janitors and professors. We swapped a familiar nod and hello in the hallways and nothing more. My first year of college evolved around my courses and working as a supermarket cashier and a nightclub waitress. I didn't give much thought to changing my situation, or even, in retrospect, outwardly disliking it. It was just what I did. I often felt so involved in the lecture and class discussions (though I didn't actually open my mouth in class till my sophomore year) that I felt as if I was going one on one with the professor.

Around midterm, my Psych. professor wrote in the margin of a paper he returned, "Interesting insights. I'd like to talk about this sometime." My first reaction was, "Well—hadn't we?" Sure, 249 other students were in the class, but I knew he was talking to me. I just took his comments a step further. Leaving class, walking to my car, all the time I drove down Highway 53, he was there in the passenger seat, conversing with me as I wrote my paper in my mind. Students who live in the dorms or even in off-campus housing in clusters of men and women don't have the opportunity to bring their professors home with them. Why would they? They've got clubs to join, games to attend, dorms to decorate, parties to go to. Poor things. That mentality sustained me throughout my undergraduate years. I relied solely on what went on in the classroom. I thought that was all there was to college: rigid professors who lectured to blank faces. I didn't have a blank face, and after taking my professors home with me, I no longer saw them as rigid.

Intellectually, I thrived. Socially, I didn't. I hung onto the three friends from high school who were still in the area. One was a commuter like me, engaged to a mechanic and simply looking for a piece of paper that allowed her to teach. She didn't seem to care that she had no connections, since she had already begun her real life by picking out china and flatware. Sometimes we had lunch together and talked about old friends who'd gone away to school. Once we went together to the bookstore to rent our textbooks, but it felt all wrong. Too high school for me. I had already adapted to the life of a loner on campus.

Another high school friend bounced from menial job to menial job and had enough money to celebrate with me at the end of the week. We spent weekends in honky-tonk bars, under-aged but dressed much older, and talked about the people we worked with, men and women twice our age, putting in their time at jobs they hated. We promised that wouldn't happen to us.

Another friend was a mother at nineteen, a woman who once wrote poetry like me. I loaned her my American Literature text books and visited her when her boyfriend was gone. We smoked cigarettes and watched movies when the baby was asleep, and sometimes I coaxed her into talking about what she read.

My life as a student was a balancing act between my old life as a "townie" and my new life as a "college girl," perfected by the twelve-mile difference between my child-hood home and the university. I didn't get the do-over I always imagined students were given when they went away to school. I didn't get to reinvent myself, no longer a jock, a class clown, a stoner. I was just invisible. Looking back, I know that becoming nobody was the seed of my reinvention of myself. Time and distance help me recognize that without my experience I wouldn't be writing this now. But then, I was merely an outsider in both worlds. Friends and family teased me for staying home on a Saturday night reading and becoming a Beatnik. I was anonymous to other first-year students in my courses because, I thought then, I didn't live in a dorm. The saddest part of my college career, I see now, was that there were no late night talks about Neitzsche or Anne Sexton or hot men in my gym class. Anything. Nothing. I had no one to tell what I was learning, no shared knowledge, so I made a game of sharing with myself on the way to and from school. I learned a lot in my twenty-minute commute.

I wouldn't have continued in school, would have quit to work in the plastics factory, the allure of a 401(K), if not for my passion for knowledge and desire to be somebody. I didn't know at eighteen who that somebody might be, but I had an inclination I'd find it in books, not a time card.

I started out as a journalism major because it was easy to explain to my parents. They understood what journalists do. My siblings chose "working" professions: nursing, dietetics, accounting. I was the only freak hooked on knowledge for learning's sake, not a job. Early in my sophomore year I declared English, though even months before I graduated my mother told relatives, "She's going to be a journalist." I never tried to explain what a liberal-arts degree meant. Even the phrase in my mother's mouth made me self-conscious. "English major," she said, like some people say in-surance with the emphasis on the "in." It's like the way she still says someone "knows computer," something foreign and odd, too much for her mouth in one breath. I couldn't explain that I was a writer in training, taking in the world and its details until I was ready to write it. It's something I just knew, like having blue eyes. Even in high school after I bought a pair of sea-green Incredible Hulk–eyed contacts, I was still blue underneath, still a writer. It's something inside, like serendipity that works only if you know what you're looking for or where you've been.

That meant as a freshman I discovered Walt Whitman and e.e. cummings and Kate Chopin and still talked like a townie, a walking Ole-and-Leena joke who knew proper grammar. I could diagram a sentence and write a persuasive paper to save my soul, but I was still factory-worker potential. It's what I feared as a college freshman, and even after I graduated, finding myself someday dull at the machine. That fear made me drag myself out of bed every morning at 7 A.M., eat Wheaties, and drive to school. Mornings were for classes, afternoons and evenings for work. Late nights and weekend days were for homework. It wasn't ideal, but it was productive. I was never dull but sometimes led a dull life.

Throughout my four years, I had contact with other commuters, mostly former high school classmates. Though we had similar stories, tied to the area by families and not enough money for the dorms or off-campus housing, I believed my experience was somehow different. I avoided them and their offers to car pool. These were people I'd known for thirteen years, and they were beyond interesting to me then. We knew who wet her pants in second grade and who threw up at the senior class New Year's Eve party and who made out with whom on the forty yard line after the Homecoming game. These commuters represented where I came from and wanted desperately to forget, details imbedded in my hometown DNA that I thought, at eighteen, I needed to lose in order to make room for more important details.

Though I eventually had many acquaintances, I made only one friend throughout my college career, a woman who commuted her first year when she lived with her dying grandfather. We met in a five-hour-a-week French class after she transferred from a school in her hometown. The first year I knew her, she lived in an apartment with twelve other women. I often imagined myself in her place: what all of us might talk about as we made dinner or came home from the bars. Then I met some of her roommates and discovered business majors don't have intriguing late-night discussions or even intriguing discussions in daylight. I don't recall how we got to be more than passing acquaintances or the circumstances that led me to bring her home, only twenty minutes but a lifestyle away from the college town.

"You have afghans," she said when she walked through my living room. She immediately sat in my mother's chair. What she meant was, *You live in a real home, with canned goods bursting from cupboards, no one screaming drunk upstairs at 2 A.M.*

"You have a lot of trophies," she said in my bedroom. Commuters often have no reason to pack their past lives away. I told her stories about before I was anonymous. She slept over when it was too late to drive home and we drank too much wine and ordered pizza at midnight, and I almost felt like a real college student.

Sometimes we'd get tipsy during some campus bar happy hour, and I'd tell her, "You're my only friend, man." So pathetically honest that she still teases me about it.

The first time she said, "You're so smart and nice, how can that be?" She didn't have many friends herself, and it comforted me as someone who always felt on the outside of campus life.

"Commuter," I answered, and she understood.

Later as a graduate student I continued to commute, but by then it was no longer something to be embarrassed about. It was even exotic to the other 23-year-olds too old to be slumming in student housing, while I was driving home to my rented house "in the suburbs." I was still on the outside, but I had good reason to be. I went home to see my husband and put my two-year-old to bed after class. My peers went to the bar, but some of them traveled in the front seat with me as I imagined our conversations about the literature we discussed in class.

When I was given the graduate student of the year award, my mother hinted about coming to the awards banquet. It would have been the first time either of my parents was on a college campus for something besides a commencement ceremony. Selfish or appropriate, I filled my table with professors who had influenced my life or at least my degree program.

I still commute the same route to and from school, though now I'm an instructor. When I landed my first job I considered moving nearer to campus, but—odd as it sounds—I knew I'd miss the time in the car. Even now, as I write this, the bulk of it I compose in my mind as I drive home from school, a conversation with a professor or peer or old friend, who has traveled with me a long time now.

1998

CRITICAL THINKING POINTS: *After you've read*

1. How are parental expectations or pressures addressed in this essay? How does the narrator cope with what her parents seem to expect of her? What do her friends expect?

2. Why does the narrator feel isolated on campus, especially her first semester? Does she "choose" to be isolated? If so, in what ways?

3. Do you think the narrator has a positive relationship with her parents? Why or why not? What details in the essay support your answer? Can a parent–child relationship be "healthy" without being supportive? Why or why not?

SOME POSSIBILITIES FOR WRITING

1. Recall a time when you were embarrassed by your family or something in your family history.

2. See discusses the difference between her education and her parents' education. What are some differences between your education and that of your parents? What are some similarities?

3. Why do many schools require students to live in the dorms, at least for their freshman year? Does your university have any such requirement? Argue for or against mandatory student housing in an opinion piece for your school newspaper.

STUDENT RESPONSE TO "OUTSIDE IN: THE LIFE OF A COMMUTER STUDENT"

The narrator doesn't feel like she belongs because she's a commuter, and thus not getting the experiences that others living on campus might get. Well, although that may be true for some commuters, it's not simply limited to them. I have lived on campus the whole time I've attended college, and I too felt as though I was missing out.

Freshman year I really didn't have that many friends, and none of them were "real" friends. They had different priorities than me, and basically they actually knew who they were as individuals. In high school, I was defined by my friends and what others thought of me. Although it meant what I was labeled as was way off mark, it also meant that I could get away with things simply because people expected it of me. At college, however, I was a clean slate on which I could write anything, except, like the narrator, I wrote nothing. I didn't become anything at all. I didn't know the campus or the city very well, and I was intimidated by this. I also was intimidated by having to do things on my own; I'm responsible but back home there was always someone there leading me in the "right" direction. I was used to having friends, not making them, and being told what to do, not doing what I chose to do.

I Walk in Beauty

AN EXCERPT   **Davina Ruth Begaye Two Bears**

Davina Two Bears, a proud member of the Dinè Nation (Navajo), graduated from Dartmouth University in 1990 with a degree in anthropology. She is the program manager of the Navajo Nation Archaeology Department–Northern Arizona University Branch Office.

On this day I sat next to my professor, and as usual was lost. The words, ideas, arguments, and opinions whirled around me like a tornado in which I was mercilessly tossed.

CRITICAL THINKING POINTS: *As you read*

1. Human nature says that we sometimes stake our self-esteem on one failure. How and why do you think Two Bears does that?
2. What makes an Ivy League school? What might make these universities better than any others?
3. What kind of insecurities does the author have during her first year of college?

During "Freshmen Week" incoming students get a head start on *Dorm life at Dartmouth and take placement tests.*

It was during this time that our Undergraduate Advisor (UGA) group held its first meeting. I had just finished moving into Woodward, an all-female dorm. The UGA group was designed to help freshwomen/men during their first year at college. Most of the women in my dorm belonged to my group.

We decided to meet outside, and shuffled onto the front lawn, scattered with bright red and yellow leaves. As we sat in a circle, I promptly began to freeze my ass off on the damp grass. The sun was out, but it was a chilly fall day.

Our UGA, a sophomore, smiled sweetly and began to explain a name game to us. As I looked at all the unfamiliar faces, I felt afraid, intimidated, alone, and different. I was, of course, the only Navajo or Native American person in our group. A pang of home sickness stole into my heart. Our UGA finished her instructions and we began.

The rules were to put an adjective in front of our name that described us and began with the first letter of our name. The object of the game was to introduce ourselves in a way that would help us to remember everyone's name. "Musical Melody" said a proud African American woman. A friendly voice chirped, "Amiable Amy," and everyone smiled in agreement. I couldn't think of an adjective to describe me that began with D. I racked my brain for an adjective, anything! But it was useless. "Oh, why do I have to be here? I don't belong here with all these confident women. Why can't I do this simple thing?" I remember thinking. My palms were sweating, my nose was running, and my teeth began to chatter. I looked at all their faces, so fresh, so clean and confident. It was finally my turn. I still couldn't think of an adjective. In agony, I uttered "Dumb Davina." "Nooo!" they all protested. Amiable Amy interjected, "Why not Divine Davina?" I shot her a smile of gratitude, but I was horrified and embarrassed. How could I have said that and been serious? Talk about low self-esteem.

My first term at Dartmouth went well academically. I received an A, a B, and a C. But I was lonely, even though I was friends with several women in my UGA group. It was hard for me to relate to them, because I felt they did not know who I was as a Native American, and where I was coming from. They also didn't understand my insecurities. How could they, when they believed so strongly in themselves?

I look back at my first year at Dartmouth, and realize that I made it hard on myself. I took it all too seriously, but how could I have known then what I know now? It took me years to be able to think of myself in a positive light. My mother always told me, "You are no better than anybody else. Nobody is better than you." Unfortunately, at Dartmouth her gentle words were lost in my self pity.

Going home for Christmas almost convinced me to stay home. I was so happy with my family, but I didn't want to think of myself as a quitter, nor did I want anyone else to think of me that way. I came back to an even more depressing winter term. My chemistry course overwhelmed me and I flunked it.

Chemistry was torture, and I could not keep up no matter how hard I tried. A subject that I aced in high school and actually liked did me in that term, and made me feel like a loser. What went wrong? It was just too much information too fast. I was depressed, and my heart was not really in the subject. Finally, I accepted my predicament. I'm not science material, and that's that.

Why did I do so horribly? My note taking skills were my downfall. They were poor at best. The crux of my problem was trying to distinguish the important facts that I needed to write down from the useless verbiage quickly. By the time I got to writing things down, I'd already have forgotten what the professor had just said. In this way, valuable information slipped through my fingers. Not only were my note taking skills poor, but so was my ability to participate in class discussion. At Dartmouth, one was expected to follow everything that was being said, think fast, take notes, ask questions, and finally deliver eloquent opinions, answers, and arguments. It was beyond my limited experience and self-confidence to do so. "Say something!" I screamed mentally, but it was useless. Fear paralyzed me in class.

Outside of class I'd talk, but not in class amid the stares of my peers. My freshman English professor and I would have conversations in her office lasting two or three hours, but in her class, when faced with all my peers, I became mute. Once Michael Dorris, my Native American studies professor, asked me outside of class why I did not speak up in his freshman seminar on American Indian policy. I was tongue-tied. Incredibly, I felt that if I spoke up in class, I would be perceived as stupid. It did not help matters that the discussions there utterly lost me most of the time during my first couple of years at Dartmouth.

On one occasion I did speak up in an education course, "Educational Issues in Contemporary Society." It was a tough course with tons of reading. Participating in the weekly seminar was a significant part of the grade. I never talked to anyone in the class. But the professor was always nice to me, saying "Hi" whenever we ran into each other. That day was just like all the other days of the past few weeks. Seated around the oblong table were about fifteen students, the professor and a teaching assistant. The professor did not lead the discussions; he was there as a participant just like us students, and we determined the content of the seminar. I came in, sat down, and my classmates began to express themselves, taking turns at center stage. I looked from one student to another and wondered how they made it look so easy, wishing that I could, too.

On this day I sat next to my professor, and as usual was lost. The words, ideas, arguments, and opinions whirled around me like a tornado in which I was mercilessly tossed. Too many unfamiliar words, analogies, and thoughts were being expressed for my brain to comprehend, edit, sort, pile, delete, save, etc. But this was nothing new—all of my classes at Dartmouth were confusing to me and extremely difficult.

Out of the blue, as I sat there lost in thought, my professor turned his kind face toward me and asked "Davina, why don't you ever say anything?" His question was totally unexpected, but not malicious. Rather, it was asked in a respectful tone that invited an answer. Everyone stared me down; they wanted to know, too. I was caught off guard, but thought to myself: this is my chance to explain why I am the way I am. I began hesitantly, frightened out of my wits, but determined to let these people know who I was and where I was coming from.

"Well, I have a hard time here at Dartmouth. I went to school in Arizona. That's where I am from. I went to school in Tuba City, Flagstaff, Bird Springs, and Winslow, Arizona. So I've gone to school both on and off the Navajo reservation. The schools on the reservation aren't that good. But in Flagstaff, I used to be a good student. Bird Springs, which is my home community, is where I learned about Navajo culture in sixth and seventh grade. I got behind though, because the school didn't have up-to-date books. I mean we were using books from the 1950s. I really liked it though, because I learned how to sing and dance in Navajo and they taught us how to read and write the Navajo language. I learned the correct way to introduce myself in Navajo, so even though I got behind and had to catch up in the eighth grade, it was the best time of my life, and I learned a lot about my language and traditions. Then when I went to eighth grade and high school in Winslow, I had to stay in the Bureau of Indian Affairs dorm away from my family, because the bus didn't come out that far. So the dorm was for all the Navajo and Hopi students who lived too far away on the reservation. Winslow was a good school, but I don't think I was prepared for an Ivy League school like Dartmouth. I mean it's so hard being here so far away from home. I used to be in the top ten percent of my class—now I'm at the bottom of the barrel! Do you know how that makes me feel?"

I couldn't help myself and I began to sob. My words were rushing out like they had been bottled up inside for too long.

"It's awful. I feel like I can't do anything here and that the students are so much smarter than me. It seems like everyone knows so much more than me. All of you, it's so easy for you to sit there and talk. It's hard for me to do that. I envy you. I feel like I'm always lost. I hardly ever understand what you guys are talking about. It's that bad. My note taking skills aren't that good either and it causes me a lot of problems in class, makes me get behind. I mean we never had to take notes like this at Winslow. And it's hard for me to participate in class discussion. I mean at Winslow we had to, but not like this. My teacher would put a check by our name after we asked one question. We didn't sit around a table and talk like we do in here. We didn't have to really get into a subject. We didn't even have to write essays. I only wrote one term paper in my junior and senior year. My English teacher would always tell us how much writing we'd have to do in college, but he never made us write! I'm barely hanging on, but here I sit and that's why I don't participate in class discussion."

I finished my tirade. It was quiet. Nobody said a word. Then my professor leaned over and jokingly admitted, "Don't feel too bad, Davina, I don't understand what they're talking about half the time either." We all smiled, and it was as if a great weight had been lifted off my shoulders. I'm so glad he prompted me to speak that day, and his comment helped me to put it all in perspective. Not everything a Dartmouth student says is profound. It was in this class that I received a citation, which distinguishes a student's work. My professor wrote, "Courage is a sadly lacking quality in the educational world we've created. Davina dared to take steps on behalf of her own growth (and ultimately for her fellows) in an area where she could reasonably expect to be tripped by an insensitive and dominating culture. It was a privilege to accompany her." For Education 20, I received a grade of D with an academic citation, simultaneously one of the worst and best grade reports a student can receive. "Only I would receive such an absurd grade," I said to myself in exasperation, but I was proud despite the D. After that day in class, my self-confidence went up a notch. In my junior and senior years at Dartmouth I began to participate in class little by little. By the time I hit graduate school, you couldn't shut me up.

1997

CRITICAL THINKING POINTS: *After you've read*

1. Two Bears says she was determined to let her classmates know "who I was and where I was coming from." Why do you think her "tirade" in class happened when it did?

2. Two Bears says, "Not everything a Dartmouth student says is profound." What might she mean? Why is realizing this important to her progression as a student?

3. How do you feel about talking in class and answering a teacher's question? Why is this easy for some people and harder for others?

SOME POSSIBILITIES FOR WRITING

1. What do you think are or should be the best predictors of success at college?

2. Two Bears's professor says, "Courage is a sadly lacking quality in the educational world we've created." What do you think he means?

3. How does self-esteem affect the way that students learn in elementary school? In high school? In college?

Sisterhood

AN EXCERPT   Stephanie Stillman-Spisak

Stephanie J. Stillman-Spisak graduated from Colgate University and taught for Teach for America. She earned a master's degree in theological studies from Harvard and completed her PhD at the University of California at Santa Barbara, and she currently serves as a research coordinator at the Meadows Center for Preventing Educational Risk at the University of Texas at Austin.

CRITICAL THINKING POINTS: *As you read*

1. How does Stillman-Spisak take steps toward coming out?
2. What kinds of advice might you have given to the narrator at various points of the essay? Why those?
3. What do you imagine might happen have happened after the events described in this essay ended?

Junior Year, Bid Day . . .   I had come out to myself only a year before and shortly afterward had started dating Heather. I remember the two of us walking through the student union one warm fall day.

"Are you still going to rush, Steph?" Heather asked anxiously.

"I don't know. What does that mean for us? They'd never accept me if they knew who I am. Are you still going to rush?"

"I have to, Steph. Both of my parents were Greeks, and I've always wanted to do it. I don't want to be limited by us. Besides, I'm not sure if I want this to come between us. I know I'm in love with you, but I don't want that to change the other parts of my life."

. . . . I'd decided I was going to rush my junior year, even if it meant doing it without Heather (she would be studying abroad in Ecuador). By the time rush arrived, I'd come out to a handful of campus administrators and friends from home. I was feeling nervous and confused about whether to come out to everyone.

After watching many of my friends join Rho Sigma the previous year, and being introduced to the majority of the sisters through Heather, I thought my chances of getting a bid to join were fairly high. . . . I heard a knock on the door, and Amanda, a good friend who was also hoping for a Rho Sigma bid, came in and took a seat at the end of my bed. We tried to make small talk to soothe our butterflies. We talked about how much we disliked the rush process and how we were ready for it to end. My mind kept wandering back to Heather. "You know, I'm still not even sure if this is for me," I said.

"Why not?"

"I don't know. I'm not the sorority type."

"And you think I am?" she smiled. . . .

"The reason I'm not sure about joining is because, well, I'm gay."

I felt a sigh of relief. It was out there. I was out there. I had opened up to my first straight friend at Colgate. Whether or not we became sisters, at least she knew the truth.

She hugged me and said, "I'm so glad you felt safe enough to tell me." Then, with a little smile and a laugh, she added, "Okay, that might be a valid reason not to pledge."

We had an hour before picking up the bids. Amanda asked a lot of questions about how I knew and about how hard it was to keep it a secret. It felt good to finally be open about my experience and my concerns. I explained that I wasn't sure I could be myself in Rho Sigma and how tired I was of living my life as a lie. The last thing I wanted was another group of people with whom to pretend. . . .

Back in my room I called Heather in Ecuador. Our conversation was brief. I told her I had received a bid and that we were finally going to be sisters. She was glad to hear it but said I sounded hesitant. I told her I was but would write more about my thoughts later. "I'm happy for you," she said. "Be careful tonight. And Steph, I love you." Hearing those words felt good.

All of the pledges showed up at the house promptly at 10. We found our leaders and the other eight pledges in our group and headed out for the scavenger hunt, a Rho Sigma tradition. We called ourselves Team Blue and were determined to be the best pledge group in the sorority's history. In each apartment we found a group of sisters eagerly awaiting our arrival with different tasks for our group. . . . In one apartment, six sisters in short black dresses—much like the ones I used to help Heather into before formals—sat across from the eight of us in my group. We got on our knees in two lines in front of the sister in traditional pledge style.

Tammy looked at us. "Your tasks are as follows: First, name all of the sisters in front of you; second, give the name of your last hook-up at Colgate". . . .

"My name, Stephanie Stillman. My last hook-up, Mike Borderland." My palms were cold with sweat. Some guy named Mike did pursue me freshman year, but the last name was a combination of names from friends of the past. As I knelt on the floor, the fun of the night ended for me in one fell swoop. My mood had gone from joyful celebration to bitterness. I had known this would happen eventually. I also knew it wouldn't be the last time I would be asked whom I'd been dating and feel I had to hide the truth. . . .

Retreat Weekend . . .   It was a Friday evening, and the *Maroon News*, our student paper, was about to land on the doorstep with the latest on a decision to suspend a Colgate fraternity for hazing. When the papers hit the porch steps, a half-dozen sisters ran out to pick them up and bring them to the others eagerly waiting inside. But I wasn't quite as eager. In addition to articles about the decision to suspend the fraternity, the commentary section also featured an article titled "Issues of Diversity Still Need Addressing." The article commented on the need for everyone to take a stand against homophobia because it affects everyone. "Our professors, neighbors, and even our closest friends are increasingly feeling comfortable coming out of the closet," the article read. The article was mine.

With adrenaline pumping through every capillary, I watched my sisters turn to the commentary section and begin reading. I didn't say I was gay in the article, but from the context you'd have been a fool not to figure it out. Not many straight people wrote articles calling for the acceptance of LGBT students. . . . No one said anything right away. The news on the suspension took first priority. We finished our dinner and talked into the late hours of the cold and snowy night.

As the house began to empty, Tammy approached. "I loved your article."

I replied with a rather dumbfounded, "Thanks."

Lauren added, "I agree with what you said."

I was shocked. Part of me had been hoping they would bypass the article. Another part wanted them to read it and discover I was gay so I wouldn't have to pretend anymore.

LGBT Awareness Week . . .   This year I was offered the opportunity to balance out the representation of the panel. But I didn't feel ready. Instead, I sat in the audience of about twenty and tried to support friends on the panel as they shared their lives with us. After the six students spoke, the meeting opened up for questions. People asked how the LGBT students came to know about their sexuality and what they thought about marriage, children, and religion. The answers were almost routine from the students who'd been asked those same questions many times before. Then one of my sorority sisters, Anne, spoke from the back of the room.

"Do you think there's a place for gays and lesbians in fraternities and sororities?"

I felt every eye in the room turn to me, but I couldn't speak. Maybe I didn't want to reveal myself (even though I'm fairly sure everyone in the room knew I was gay). Maybe I didn't want to give the wrong answer to her question. Maybe I wasn't convinced the answer was yes. I remained silent, and Dan gave words to many of my thoughts we had discussed previously. He explained that there should be a place for gays, lesbians, and bisexual students in sororities and fraternities. Just like any organization, there is no reason why they shouldn't be there. He also spoke of the quiet struggles many gay and lesbian students undergo in the Greek system. "It's the subtle heterosexual assumptions that make it the most difficult for them to survive there," he said.

It was hard to sit with my own vulnerability and fear of exposure watching my peers take up the slack for me when, unlike me, they didn't have the first-hand experience of being gay in the Greek system. After the question period ended, I nervously approached Anne. "Thanks for your question. It needed to be asked."

"I agree. No one talks about it."

"So true. I mean, well, you know, I'm gay."

"No, really?" she said with a touch of sarcasm.

We both laughed. "Yeah, and it's hard. People assume so many things."

"I know," Anne said. "A group of us were sitting around talking about it the other night and about how painful it used to be to watch you and Heather. We all knew."

"That's what a lot of people have been telling me."

"It really is a compliment to our house. I know it's hard, and because you want to stick through it says a lot about what we stand for and the strength of the friendships in the house. I mean, we encourage diversity and brag that we're the house that holds the most of it. But among us we have a whole gamut of diversity that we don't even recognize, let alone appreciate."

"That's exactly what I think."

"People really are OK with it. And for those who aren't, they need to be. Your sexuality doesn't make a difference. And people need to know that."

2000

CRITICAL THINKING POINTS: *After you've read*

1. Stillman-Spisak's friend Dan says that "subtle heterosexual assumptions" make it the most difficult for lesbian, gay, bisexual, transgender, queer or questioning (LGBTQ) students to survive in fraternities and sororities. What do you think he means?

2. Why do you think sororities and/or fraternities might be resistant to LGBTQ students becoming members?

3. How might Stillman-Spisak have dealt with her experiences differently?

SOME POSSIBILITIES FOR WRITING

1. Stillman-Spisak says that homophobia affects everyone. Write a brief narrative about an experience you or someone you know has had about being an outsider of a group you wanted to join.

2. Argue for or against the question raised in this essay: Do you think there's a place for gays and lesbians in fraternities and sororities?

3. Prepare a report about the current status and attitudes toward LGBTQ student membership in organizations on your campus. What kinds of policies, if any, exist concerning membership of LGBTQ students at the national level for some of the larger fraternities and sororities?

Walking in My French Shoes

Benedicte Bachelot

Benedicte Bachelot was born in Bordeaux, France, and completed a master's degree in forestry and ecology at Michigan State University. She plans to earn a PhD and work as a tropical ecologist.

I didn't want to belong to the "international crew," the "outsider group;" I wanted to feel that I belonged to this place—that I was like any other American student.

CRITICAL THINKING POINTS: *As you read*

1. What is so appealing to the author about studying in the United States?
2. Why do you think the author does not want to attend orientation for international students? Why does she eventually realize she needs it?
3. Pay attention to the author's internal monologue. Why might she talk to herself throughout this piece?

First, it was the little cartoon character who sang, "*Tom Sawyer, c'est lamerique, le symbol de la liberté,*" which means, "*Tom Sawyer, it's America, symbol of freedom.*" A few years later, it was my elementary school teachers explaining how the United States managed to win World Wars I and II and save the rest of the world. Then, it was the media discussing America's power, and the Hollywood movies, enamoring me like a row of glistening shop windows on Christmas. In English class, it was the language that sounded like a melody in my head. All of these were the beginnings of my American Dream.

Everybody has dreams. Most of them are not made to be realized; they simply float about your brain like smiling clouds. Sometimes you think about them, sometimes you do not. But this particular dream of mine, my American Dream, never went away for long. It was always there, like a little prickle in my finger. Finally, my obsession materialized into a real plan when the United States offered me the ideal program for my graduate education. This plan became a reality with my admission to Michigan State University. After I was accepted there, everything went very fast. Before I could even change my mind, I was there, walking in America . . . in my French shoes!

As soon as I landed at Lansing Capital Airport, I had a very strong feeling that I was walking in a dream. It was like being in a place for the first time and already knowing everything about it, as if you were there in a past life—that peculiar, "déja vu" feeling that sets you on edge. I grabbed my luggage and hailed a taxi (somewhat disappointingly, it wasn't a yellow one, though) and asked the driver to take me to my soon-to-be "home."

When I arrived at my flat, I was exhausted from my journey but so happy to be there that I had trouble falling asleep. I couldn't stop smiling, and telling to myself (in French) "this is it, Béné: welcome back to your new life . . . dreams really do come true." Of course, then I added a scolding statement in English: "Béné, stop it; you have to think in English now!" Then suddenly, I was struck by the thought (to be honest, it was already buried somewhere in my mind) that I didn't want to be a foreigner, an outsider. I didn't want to belong to the "international crew," the "outsider group;" I wanted to feel that I belonged to this place—that I was like any other American student. Before drifting off to sleep, I made a decision: there wouldn't be any International Orientation for me!

The next morning, I woke up with this idea still fresh in my mind. I got out of bed early and started to make plans: I need to go to the Office for International Students and Scholars (OISS) to get the I-9 form, open an American bank account, buy a cell phone, register for classes; rather than seeming overwhelming all these things rushing to my head brought a lively feeling of freedom and independence. Unlike in France, everything here was brand new and I was all by myself. With that, I started my day: the first one of my new American life! At first, things went well, but as the day went on, it started getting harder, as troublesome questions began to flash in my head. How would I get my paycheck deposited into my new bank account? How do I fill out a W4 form? I need a Social Security number; where could I get one? Suddenly, I began to wonder if it was a good idea to try to deal with all of this by myself. At the end of that day, I visited the OISS website and took a peek at the International Orientation schedule. Interestingly, it appeared that they were going to go over everything I was having trouble with. Yet I was still too proud to accept the help. I was determined to be a "normal" American student. That night, when I went to bed, I felt homesick for the first time. Everything was getting out of control; it was scary and frustrating, and I just wanted to be home. I had to fight against myself in English: "Béné, this is your dream; this is what you wanted, so stop being a child!" What happened the next morning made me realize how stupid I had been.

I woke up later than usual, and when I went outside to catch my bus, nobody else was waiting. I decided to call my dad to quickly give some news to my family. While I was on the phone, I didn't pay attention and got on the wrong bus. Actually, it was the right bus, but it was going in the wrong direction. As soon as I realized, I hung up quickly and decided just to sit down and wait. I wasn't in a hurry and Bus 20 makes a big loop, so it wasn't such a big deal. As my nerves calmed, I started to look at the people around me. The bus was almost empty; there was a young Indian couple and two Chinese girls talking very fast and laughing at each other. I liked looking at them; they all seemed so happy to be here. Thirty minutes later, the bus completed its loop and was heading toward my destination. My fellow passengers had gotten off a couple of stations earlier and once again, I was alone. But I didn't really care. Eventually, an American girl got on the bus, but left a few minutes later. It always surprised me how nice the people were here. Everyone always said, "Hi; how are you?" or "Thank you; have a good day." I liked this friendly atmosphere; it made me smile. I was thinking about that when I noticed my station and suddenly realized that my bus wasn't slowing down! "O merde," I said to myself, which cannot be politely translated into English. My heart started racing as I realized that I didn't know how to make the bus stop. I stood up, but it was too late; the bus passed by my station without stopping. I was so confused, so lost. I started looking around for something equivalent to the red button you must press to get off the bus in France, but there were no buttons around for me to press. Now I was getting scared; I felt like the bus was speeding and taking me away from anything I knew! I wanted to cry. "Just go and ask the driver, Béné," I urged myself, but by now I was feeling so ashamed, there was no way I was going to ask him. Then, all of the sudden I remembered a clip from the movie "Fast and Furious." I looked up and saw the wires, suspended like some sort of tropical yellow snakes along the window of the bus. I grabbed them, and heard the nice *blip* assuring me that the bus would stop at the next station. What a relief!

At the next stop, I got off of the bus, walked for a while, and then sat down on the grass somewhere on campus. I had just lost some of my precious time and gotten very scared for one little reason: I was too proud to ask for help. I realized I was so obsessed with not being an outsider that I had become even more a stranger. I was so mad at myself, and I decided there was only one thing to do next: attend the International Orientation. "Sure I am walking in America, the country of one of my dreams," I reminded myself, "but I am still wearing my French shoes." I realized that I belong to this place as much as I belong to the International group. There is no shame in being a little bit different; that does not make you an outsider. It's just not that simple to integrate into a new country; even if it was one of your biggest dreams. The thing you have to keep in mind is that you are not alone, and there are always warm people around who will be eager to help you.

2009

CRITICAL THINKING POINTS: *After you've read*

1. Bachelot does not want to be an outsider at Michigan State. What are some other approaches she could take so she could more easily integrate into her new country?
2. How does popular culture influence her understanding of the United States?
3. Bachelot spends much time talking to herself. Is this true for you in stressful situations? What is your "self-talk" like?

SOME POSSIBILITIES FOR WRITING

1. Find and interview an international student on your campus. How does your classmate's experience in the United States compare to the author's?

2. Research the benefits of study abroad opportunities for students. What are some long-term advantages of having a global experience?

3. Read more Michigan State international student essays here: http://oiss.isp. msu.edu/feature_essay_win.php. What are some common themes throughout the essays?

Lost in Italy

Elizabeth Barney

Elizabeth Barney earned a degree from Michigan State University in special education, with a minor in teaching English to speakers of other languages. She wrote this essay after studying abroad in Rome.

The tables had turned, and I was now the strange, foreign, annoying girl who didn't have a clue what was going on.

CRITICAL THINKING POINTS: *As you read*

1. How do the author's perceptions of Rome differ from the reality once she arrives?
2. What cultural differences between the United States and Italy does the author experience?
3. What helps the author adjust to a new country and culture?

Standing in line at the post office was not my plan for the afternoon, and so when I found myself still shifting from foot to foot after waiting 20 minutes I grew restless. It wasn't difficult to see the same feelings mirrored on my line-companion's faces: wrinkled brows, tapping feet, bulging eyes, and sweat-drenched brows all seemed to cry out together, "Can we just be done already?" The line had been moving along at a slow, but steady pace when suddenly it came to an abrupt halt.

"Lo siento, no hablo Inglés," the voice faltered, apologetically. I silently groaned inside, as I watched the short man with weathered hands and thick black hair try to negotiate some form of meaning with the clerk.

"If you don't speak English, *move*," muttered an older man in front of me, and several people nodded or smiled with their eyes in agreement. As much as I felt the need to be accepting, it was hard to be understanding as this man held up the whole line, and I felt annoyed at the people who found it convenient to come here, but not speak English.

It is ironic, then, that months later, as I found myself packing for my study abroad in Rome, Italy, the one thing I did not pack was a book of Italian. What for? It was Europe, after all, and I had been assured that everybody in Europe speaks English. My plane arrived late, and I was directed to a taxi driver hired by my college. It only took a few barked orders in Italian for me to realize that he did not speak a word of English. The tables had turned, and I was now the strange, foreign, annoying girl who didn't have a clue what was going on. As we hurtled down narrow streets, narrowly missing cars, people, and animals on the packed cobblestone streets, I held my breath and listened to a steady flow of Italian chatter as the driver screamed on his cell phone and swerved with every emphatic statement. My sense of adventure was quickly smothered by my steadily growing worry. I had no idea where I was going, every thirty seconds I was catching my breath at yet another close call, and I really didn't expect to even make it to my destination in one piece. What seemed like an eternity later, we arrived at the location, and I was dropped off in front of a graffiti-covered building holding three bags and a suitcase. I stared at the building while the sweaty taxi driver sped off, still hollering at somebody on his cell phone. A woman at the front desk informed me in broken English that my destination was on the second floor. I slowly struggled up the flight of steps to discover yet another cultural difference: in Italy, the first floor is 0, and the second floor is, in reality, an American third floor. Had I known this, I would have taken the elevator. Nevertheless, I was able to acquire my apartment key and directions to the building.

What followed over the course of the next few weeks was a whirlwind of confusion, adventures, and slowly, an understanding of life through the eyes of another culture. A half hour walk to the electronics store resulted in the discovery that all stores are closed from 1 P.M.–4 P.M. for the strict 3 hour lunch break observed in Italy. Here, eating was a ritual, and there was no such thing as skipping lunch or scarfing down a burger in 30 seconds to resume a task. Three solid hours are set apart in the middle of the day to relax, renew, and truly delight in the luxurious tastes Italy has to offer. As I slowly grew to overcome the culture shock and appreciate the mindset behind these differences I faced, I also began to realize how hard it would be to adjust if it weren't for the helpful people I found myself surrounded by.

Despite the fact that I was taking a beginner Italian class and practicing on a daily basis when I went out, I still found it necessary to carry an Italian-English dictionary with me everywhere I went. This was most painfully apparent when I had to face the grocery store. It took three weeks before I was courageous enough to even approach the bread counter and try to buy bread in Italian, and I ended up coming home with the wrong food item more than once because I misread the label. The first day I arrived, it took me an hour and a half to figure out where I could get cash from an ATM. This was my first realization that most people who say "I can speak English," can probably speak about 3 sentences and name our president, but I had no room to talk, since I was the one in Italy and couldn't even perform on the same level in Italian. Everywhere I went, people patiently helped me and tried to understand what I was saying, and directed me as best they could when I was lost.

This flow of good Samaritans who helped a poor non-Italian speaker through her daily life was not uninterrupted, however. There were more than a few times when the clerk at the grocery store rolled her eyes and curled her lip at me for asking for a grocery bag after buying my groceries. I found out later you have to actually include the bags in your purchase, and if you ask for one after you have already paid, they think you are trying to rip them off. The most significant of these encounters, however, occurred when I tried to mail my first set of postcards back home. I discovered that I had bought the wrong postage stamps, and needed twenty cents more postage on each of my post cards. I arrived at the post office, to find out that the "take a number" system had *three different stations*, each for a different purpose, and I had no clue which was appropriate to mine, so I took a random number and sat down. When I got to the counter, the lady raised her eyebrows. Clearly, I had picked the wrong station.

"Posso avere . . . venti mas?" I said, trying to point as the Italian words escaped me. The postal worker thought I wanted twenty more stamps.

"No, no, no. . . . differente," I frantically protested, before breaking back into my familiar English.

The whole post office was staring at me now, and I could feel my ears turning bright red. I could see the look on all their faces, *What is this silly American girl trying to do? Who does she think she is, expecting us to be able to speak to her in English?* The statement was clear to read on the rolled eyes, scornful sneers, and smirking lips.

"I can help," a voice cut in, and I found myself face to face with an English-Italian speaker. Relief washed over me as she communicated my needs to the postage worker, who rolled her eyes at me as if to say "Well why didn't you just say so?" and quickly stamped my postcards each with twenty cents. As I left the post office that day, I was struck with the realization of how similar my situation was to that of the many immigrants who come seeking refuge in the U.S. and must quickly struggle to learn English and communicate in a strictly "English-only" world.

Just like the man at the post office back home, I found myself in a country, unable to communicate my needs and ideas due to a language barrier. If it had not been for the many understanding, patient Italians who worked with me to improve my Italian and understand what I was trying to say, I would never have been able to explore the country as I did. Because of helpful Italians, like Giuseppe, who spent hours working with my friends and me to help us improve our Italian, or Margherita, the friendly baker who used hand gestures to help recommend the best breads to me, I was able to acquire conversational Italian and experience the Italian culture in a richer, deeper way than I would have ever thought possible.

Since returning to the U.S., I started volunteering at the refugee center, and I am often frustrated with my lack of ability to communicate with low-level English speakers. I recently found my frustration growing as I tried to explain a simple English word to a refugee girl. I stopped myself, and took myself back to the summer when I was surrounded by strange words and customs. Smiling, I slowed down my speech and started pointing and using a basket of pencils as a prop to explain my point and emphasizing my words with gestures. She smiled and relaxed, and I understood. Sometimes all we need to do to help English learners develop the ability to communicate is show them the same patience that people like Giuseppe or Margherita showed to a lost American girl one summer.

2009

CRITICAL THINKING POINTS: *After you've read*

1. Why does Barney begin her essay with the scene in the post office?
2. Barney writes about seeing Rome "through the eyes of another culture." Why is this so important?
3. What are the benefits of studying abroad for a semester or a year versus enrolling in a shorter program over summer or winter break?

SOME POSSIBILITIES FOR WRITING

1. Research your university's study abroad programs. Write a report to share with your class about the opportunities.
2. If you could study in any country in the world, which would it be? Why that one? Research how you might go about studying there.
3. Read more essays by Michigan State University students studying in other countries by visiting "Tales from Abroad" at http://studyabroad.msu.edu/tales/index.html. What are some common themes throughout the essays?

First Year in College Is the Riskiest

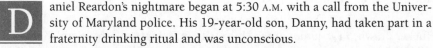

Robert Davis and Anthony Debarros

Robert Davis and Anthony Debarros are reporters for *USA Today*.

Freshmen emerge as the class most likely to make a fatal mistake.

CRITICAL THINKING POINTS: *As you read*

1. This article is filled with tragedies that happened to students their first year in college. How do the authors make you care about the students as more than mere statistics?
2. What statistics about college first-year students surprised you the most? The least?
3. What do you think can be done to prevent tragedies on college campuses?

D aniel Reardon's nightmare began at 5:30 A.M. with a call from the University of Maryland police. His 19-year-old son, Danny, had taken part in a fraternity drinking ritual and was unconscious.

When Danny began college in fall 2001, his father, a dentist in Washington, D.C., had been confident that the teenager could take care of himself. After all, Danny had spent nine months after his high school graduation traveling across Europe. But Reardon hadn't counted on anything like this.

When Danny passed out at about 11:30 P.M. on Feb. 7, 2002, fraternity members put him on a sofa, took his pulse and according to court records and police reports, took turns watching him. Early the next morning, Danny stopped breathing. Students at the fraternity house called for an ambulance about 3:30 A.M., but Danny's brain had ceased functioning when he reached the hospital. He died six days later.

In one major respect, Danny was typical of college undergraduates who die on or near campuses every year: He was a freshman who had been on campus only a few months.

A USA TODAY analysis of 620 deaths of four-year college and university students since Jan. 1, 2000, finds that freshmen are uniquely vulnerable. They account for more than one-third of undergraduate deaths in the study, although they are only 24% of the undergraduates at those institutions, according to data from the National Center for Education Statistics analyzed by the American Council on Education for USA TODAY.

College administrators, public health officials and parents increasingly have become concerned about the safety of college students after highly publicized deaths on campus from alcohol abuse and other causes.

USA TODAY set out to take a close look at the problem, to study where and how students died over a six-year period and to determine whether their deaths could have been prevented.

Overall, the analysis of hundreds of reports from media, watchdog groups, schools and police found that illnesses, homicides and motor vehicle accidents are the leading causes of death, as they are for all Americans ages 15 to 24. Suicide, which is not always reported by the media, making the count in the analysis incomplete, claims as many lives as drugs and alcohol.

But the dominant finding is that freshmen emerge as the class most likely to make a fatal mistake: Freshmen die at higher rates from illness, accounting for 40% of undergraduate deaths from natural causes. They're more likely to take their own lives; they account for 40% of all undergraduate suicides. They represent half of all undergraduate deaths from falls from windows, balconies and rooftops. More of them die on school property; 47% of the undergraduates who die on campus are freshmen. This statistic has proven the most surprising, and disturbing, to analysts, experts and parents who imagine the campus to be idyllic. And safe.

"Parents want the university to be protective," says Ann Franke, president of Wise Results, a Washington-based education law and risk management firm. But because some students arrive on campus without the skills to deal with new risks, and because they have privacy and other adult rights, "no college can guarantee 100% safety for students," she says.

Tucker Brown, 21, a junior at the University of Georgia in Athens and vice president of the student government association, says the sudden freedom college brings has an effect. "I think naturally you come to college, you don't have your parents there anymore, you know you can go crazy," he said during a USA TODAY roundtable discussion in December on college drinking. "Not that you've been waiting to go crazy, but now it is an option, especially for those people who were on a tight leash."

Helen Johnson, a Chapel Hill, N.C.-based consultant in parent relations for universities, says students face different types of risks than those facing young adults who go directly into the workforce.

These students "have the rubric of being legal adults, and yet they are not completely independent or completely capable of making adult decisions," says Johnson, author of *Don't Tell Me What to Do, Just Send the Money: The Essential Parenting Guide to the College Years*. "Kids today have been more supervised and controlled than any other generation. It means they are ill-equipped to handle the responsibility and consequences of independent life."

Though relatively few drink themselves to death as Danny Reardon did, the analysis found that about one in five of the students who died had been drinking, which impaired judgment and contributed to their deaths. "Unfortunately, we are bringing our children into an environment that is extremely dangerous," Reardon says.

According to court documents, fraternity members put Danny in a room, closed the door and told others that they would care for him and to stay out. In a lawsuit, Danny's parents said that by preventing others "who might have been more responsible" from seeing their son, the fraternity members denied Danny "the help he obviously needed under the circumstances."

"Over a period of hours until he became cyanotic," (a bluish discoloration tied to a lack of oxygen), "during which time Daniel lay unconscious, unresponsive, and with vomit running from his nose," fraternity members and others "did homework and passed about the duty to watch Daniel," the civil suit said. The other students, the suit said, "provided absolutely no reasonable assistance to Daniel, despite his obvious need for such attention and help."

Reardon sued the fraternity and reached an undisclosed settlement with some of the students and Phi Sigma Kappa, which denied liability.

Many deadly decisions are made by underdeveloped brains, experts say. Research has shown that "the brain continues to develop after 18," says Denis McCarthy, a University of Missouri-Columbia researcher. "We used to think it was done. But a lot of the areas that are still developing have to do with making judgment calls."

USA TODAY's analysis shows that Danny Reardon's death fit a pattern of fatal mistakes in judgment. Other examples:

- Boston University freshman Molly Shattuck, 19, of Ipswich, Mass., and Andrew Voluck, 20, a sophomore from Blue Bell, Pa., died together on Feb. 9, 2005, while walking on train tracks. Transportation investigators say the pair might not have known that a fast-moving train is nearly silent to those walking in its path.

- Seth Korona, 19, of Marlton, N.J., was hand-standing on a beer keg at Indiana University on Jan. 28, 2001, when he fell, suffering a fatal brain injury, the coroner said.

- Robert Meythaler, 19, of Owensboro, Ky., fell over a balcony railing at Furman University in Greenville, S.C., police said, during a spitting contest.

The signs of death were obvious to emergency medical technician Thomas Dunn as he examined Lynn Gordon "Gordie" Bailey's face on Sept. 17, 2004. Answering a 911 call, rescuers found that the college freshman had died the previous night from an alcohol overdose.

Dunn felt sorry for Bailey, 18, who had rude, sexual comments scribbled across his face. He says he knew the University of Colorado student's death would rock the state, which was still reeling from the similar death of Colorado State University sophomore Samantha Spady, 12 days earlier.

Spady, 19, of Beatrice, Neb., died after consuming 30 to 40 drinks over 11 hours, the coroner said.

As he went door-to-door inside the Chi Psi fraternity house in Boulder, Dunn, a psychology professor at the University of Northern Colorado and part-time EMT, woke up students to ensure that there were no more victims from the initiation party. Looking around the squalid house littered with empty bottles, it was Dunn's experience as a teacher that spoke to him. "I thought, 'Where did we let these kids down?'" Dunn says. "Very little about that house, from what I saw, had any evidence of scholarly pursuits. I was appalled."

As Dunn woke up still-drunken students and told fraternity leaders that Bailey was dead, he watched them go from crying to fearful and silent.

"I worried about their lives, too," he says. "We're taking these kids whose brains are not fully developed, particularly the judgment centers, and they are drinking large quantities of alcohol so their judgment goes completely out the window."

After Bailey's death, the Colorado Legislature enacted a law that grants immunity to anybody drinking illegally who calls 911 to get help for a drunken friend. Dunn says medics are now getting more calls.

National fraternity leaders are encouraging students to call for help without worrying about getting the fraternity in trouble.

"One of the biggest problems out there is students are afraid to call for help," says Geof Brown, director of alcohol-education initiatives for the North America Interfraternity Conference, which has 5,500 chapters at 800 campuses. "Our groups are taking a more proactive posture these days."

Young people in the outside world are likely to share their daily lives with adults, but students who live on or near campus are surrounded by peers. Thus their lives can be in the hands of other freshmen when they most need help.

On Jan. 29, 2002, a delay in summoning help contributed to the loss of two lives at the University of Wisconsin-Eau Claire. According to a university police report, nobody knew that Karen Hubbard, a 19-year-old freshman from Withee, Wis., was pregnant. Hubbard's weight gain had been attributed by her roommate to "the freshman 15"—the pounds often packed on during the first year of college.

Hubbard was grunting and moaning in pain inside a bathroom stall between 10 and 10:30 P.M., according to the report and handwritten accounts by the other students involved; the university refused to identify them. But Hubbard's dorm-mates left her alone when she insisted that she had a stomach flu.

Then they heard a loud splash of water and a baby crying. "I have babysat a lot over the past couple of years," one student wrote, "so to me, I clearly recognized this scream as an infant screaming."

The students left to get a resident assistant, who checked on Hubbard but accepted her statement that she just had an upset stomach. Then, the police report said, the students "heard the toilet flush three or four times, followed by a tiny baby whimper." But an hour passed before anyone peered over the edge of the stall. Hubbard bled to death that night. Her full-term baby girl, Julianna Marie Hubbard, was pulled from the toilet and revived, the police report said. But the baby died five days later.

None of the students was reprimanded, says Chuck Major, the university's housing director. "There were a lot of emotions going through the minds of a lot of the people, especially the resident assistant who was there," he says. He says the confusing question for students is: "How do I help a friend and yet not cross a boundary of being like Mom and Dad?"

College health experts say freshmen in trouble are often helped by their peers. "Student peers are actually the first ones who sense that there is something wrong," says Alan Glass, a physician on the board of the American College Health Association. "I've seen numerous examples over the course of my career where other students brought to our attention their friends who were in need of medical attention."

But Johnson, author of *Essential Parenting,* says freshmen are often ill-equipped to handle a real life-and-death situation. "The risk-taking part of their brain is fully developed, but the governor part that says 'stop' and 'wait' is not," she says. "One of the great tragedies is these young 18- or 19-year-olds will live with the knowledge that they could have done something, but they didn't."

Other freshmen have died when friends did not immediately call for help:

- Jonathan Thielen, 19, of Fridley, Minn., fell off a bunk bed in a University of Minnesota dorm early on Feb. 17, 2001, after a night of drinking, according to university police reports. Thielen began vomiting but told friends he was OK, the reports said. They helped him lie on the floor with his head on a pillow. "I assumed he was fine," the report quotes a student as saying, "because other friends of mine had fallen out of the bunk before." The report quotes another student as saying Thielen threw up a couple of more times, "but then he was sleeping OK." When students awoke the next morning, Thielen was dead of what the county medical examiner said were "traumatic head injuries due to fall."

- Travis Starr III, 19, of Martinez, Ga., fell out of the bed of a moving pickup carrying a group of students near the University of Georgia at about 2 A.M. on April 17, 2003, an Athens-Clarke County Police report said. His friends took him home to his apartment where he was groggy for most of the day, the report says. Friends took him to the hospital at 10 P.M.; he lapsed into a coma and died eight days later.

- Joseph Kepferle, 18, of Lexington Park, Md., died on March 5, 2000, from bacterial meningitis at Towson University near Baltimore. Though he had been sick during the day, "his roommates thought he was either really hung over or had a bad case of the stomach flu," says his mother, Deborah Kepferle. "It wasn't until they saw the purple rash on his stomach and trunk that they knew that was something not normal."

Because meningitis can become a life-threatening infection within hours—and because freshmen are six times more likely to contract the infection than others their age—the Centers for Disease Control and Prevention recommended this year that freshmen in dorms be vaccinated.

No matter how many safety classes colleges plan, some freshmen don't live long enough to take them. Jessica Horton, 18, of Suwanee, Ga., enrolled at the University of South Carolina, a college that for 35 years has taught students how to cope with freedoms through classes on safety called University 101. After her family helped her move in on Aug. 17, 2002, Horton stayed up visiting with friends. In the early-morning, police investigators say, she climbed out of her sixth-floor dorm window to sit on a ledge. Police later found 11 Xanax tablets and a cut straw with traces of the drug in her purse, the report said. Horton had "snorted" the anti-anxiety drug in the past, her friend told police, according to their report.

Sitting on the ledge, she smoked a Camel cigarette and talked on her cell-phone. Police believe she fell asleep there. At 6:20 A.M., a security guard saw Horton fall past a crape myrtle tree. She died before her family arrived home. The coroner found nearly twice the amount of Xanax in Horton's blood than is typically prescribed.

"It was a tragedy. When students engage in behavior that is unwise, often it is in the first weeks of school," says Dennis Pruitt, the university's vice president for student affairs. Safety efforts, he says, "don't take hold the first night, the first day or the first week. It takes some time."

2006

CRITICAL THINKING POINTS: *After you've read*

1. What do you think are the top three dangers facing college students today? What do you base your thoughts on?
2. What are some of the ways a college student can be safer?
3. If this were a college research paper, what material would need to be cited? Why?

SOME POSSIBILITIES FOR WRITING

1. Research the best way to handle a friend who has had too much to drink. Write a how-to list and post it in your residence hall.
2. Interview someone in your school's administration about how your school deals with the vulnerability of first-year students.
3. Davis and Debarros conducted research from 2000 to 2006. Compile statistics on deaths of college students since then. Do you believe the first year of college is still the "riskiest"? Why or why not?

This Was the Assignment: History as a Student

Kayla Piper

This was the assignment: Write a onepage (minimum) response describing yourself as a learner. Please consider the following questions before you respond.

- What significant events have occurred in your life as a learner? How have these events shaped your thinking and your behavior?
- What people have had an impact on your learning behavior and your attitudes?
- What are your strengths and weaknesses as a learner?
- What attitudes do you have that contribute to your success?
- What do you want from your education?
- How do you contribute to society (please be specific!)? What is your part?

Kayla Piper will graduate with a degree in English in 2012.

I wanted to do well, not just to please my mom, but because doing well in school would be my way out.

CRITICAL THINKING POINTS: *As you read*

1. How does Piper evolve as a "learner"?
2. How does the author's experience compare to yours?
3. How is Piper's love of learning affected by her childhood experiences? By becoming a mother in college?

My interest in learning has been shaped greatly by my childhood. I grew up very poor in a family of six kids being raised by a single mother. I learned early on that the only way out of poverty would be through my own devices. I had a drive that most children I knew didn't have. I wanted to do well, not just to please my mom, but because doing well in school would be my way out. There would never be anyone else I could count on to help me through life financially, and I knew I had to work hard to ensure I would never have to worry about this.

I was at a disadvantage compared to other kids growing up. We didn't have a computer in the house until I bought one my freshman year of college. This was incredibly frustrating in high school because everything had to be typed, but it really allowed me to learn skills that I would not have otherwise. I had to budget my time wisely in order to be able to stay at school or go to the library to type a paper. One good thing that came out of this was the ability to revise papers numerous times because I'd have to write them out longhand before I had a chance to type them. This is something that I still do to this day, and I am able to proofread more thoroughly this way. Not having a computer also allowed me to use my mind. Instead of Googling any fact I might need, I learned to think about it for awhile to try to come to the answer myself. Being able to hone my recall and critical thinking skills has continued to help me greatly throughout my academic career.

Because I knew that my future depended on my abilities to succeed, I think I had a different outlook on education and learning than other students. Of course, there were times that going to school was the last thing I wanted to do, but I saw value in education. This allowed me to take pride in my academics, which has continued to my current academic career. Having this attitude towards education has enabled me to be excited about learning, and that makes school so much more interesting and fun. If there is one trait I want to instill in my children, it would be to view learning in this way.

As much as I enjoy learning, it is easy for me to get overwhelmed sometimes. This is my biggest learning weakness. Wanting to do well can be a blessing and a curse. I have found that there are many times that I get upset for earning a B. This is something that I'm trying to work on. As a mother, I have to learn that sometimes things don't go right and grades suffer. There are more important things in life than a single grade. By not pressuring myself so intensely to do well, I find that my stress and anxiety levels go down which allows me to be a better mother and student.

Now that I am a mother and have someone who depends on me, my drive to succeed has gone up even further. It has allowed me to take a step back and reassess my life and decide what I really want. Because of this, my grades have gone up and I am more resourceful with my time. I used to waste hours and procrastinate until the last minute. Now I can't do that because something with my son may come up and then I wouldn't be able to finish my class work.

I have decided on taking 12 credits each semester so I won't be overwhelmed with school and not be able to be there completely for my son. Graduating as fast as I can is not worth being on the verge of a nervous breakdown for 4 years. Having a positive outlook on school makes me not want to rush through school as fast as I can. Because I've spent the time getting to know myself and my learning behaviors, I know that having fewer classes and less stress is worth the extra semester or two it will take to graduate.

2010

CRITICAL THINKING POINTS: *After you've read*

1. Why might it be helpful for college students to consider (or reconsider) their "history as a student"? What do you think you could learn from your past experiences as a student?

2. Piper claims that not having a computer actually helped her as a student. Are there other examples of how the absence of technology might help you as a student? What would they be and why might not having them help you?

3. What might be some other benefits to taking fewer credits per semester?

SOME POSSIBILITIES FOR WRITING

1. Write your own response to this assignment.

2. Recent studies show that students who grew up without a computer in their house actually did better in school. Do your own research and support or dispute this claim.

3. Write a paper in which you argue either 1) that students have an innate love of learning or 2) that teachers influence students to love learning.

Further Suggestions for Writing—"School Daze"

1. Create a list called "The Things I Learned in High School."

2. Create your own list of things you've learned in your first week or month or semester at college.

3. One of the most important study skills to develop as a college student is time management. How do you intend to manage studying, deadlines, test preparation, work, and social time?

4. Interview at least three first-year students about some of their fears in the classroom. Next, seek out students who have been on campus longer than you have and ask them for advice about these fears.

5. Browse through this semester's schedule of classes and make a list of courses you would love to take regardless of any requirements or restrictions. Explain why you would like to take these courses.

6. Research the characteristics of your freshman class. After finding out as much as you can about such things as race, ethnicity, financial background, high school class rank, and ACT or SAT scores, write a profile as a report for your class. Then consult the most recent online edition of the *Chronicle of Higher Education* and write a report on how your school's profile compares to that of other, similar universities.

7. Schools often have programs for commuters that help them get more involved in campus social activities. Contact your Dean of Students Office or Residence Life Office to find out what kinds of programs for commuters are available on your campus. Write a report to deliver to your class.

8. Working in a group, examine the issue of having a part-time job while also being a first-year student.

9. Write about your own personal attitude toward alcohol and/or drugs and how you came to that position.

10. What connection does goal setting have to success at college? Interview two upper-class students about their opinions on setting short- and long-term goals.

11. Write a paper on one of the following: "How to Make and Keep Friends at College," "How to Protect Yourself at College," "How to Cope with Homesickness," "How to Succeed as a Student Athlete," or another, similar topic of your choosing.

12. Contact your Admissions Office or Dean of Students Office to find out the number of students of color on your campus. Does your university have any student groups specifically for people of certain ethnic backgrounds? What type of support do they offer?

13. Contact your Admissions Office or Dean of Students Office to discover how many nontraditional students are enrolled. What obstacles do nontraditional

students face that traditional students do not? What support is offered to them on your campus? Write a report to be delivered to your class.

14. Argue for or against a new policy concerning alcohol on your campus.

15. Is binge drinking a problem on your campus? Begin by contacting your campus counseling services for any research they have conducted concerning binge drinking and its effects on your campus. Come up with some potential solutions to this problem.

16. Evaluate your school's program for alcohol awareness.

17. Choose a problem with your campus environment that you think would be relatively easy and inexpensive to solve, and propose a solution.

18. Do athletes on your campus have to meet the same admissions requirements as other students? What type of support services are available to student athletes? How do these services compare to those offered to the general student population?

19. In what way(s) is Patti See's search for identity or reinvention of herself in "Outside In: The Life of a Commuter Student" like Jennifer Crichton's in "'Who Shall I Be?': The Allure of a Fresh Start" in Chapter 3? How are their "re-makes" different? How do their experiences contribute to these similarities and differences?

20. Contrast the selection from Mike Magnuson's *Lummox* with Malcolm X's "Saved" in Chapter 1. Why do these pieces display the differences they do?

21. Locate some of the following poems by Langston Hughes: "Graduation," "Genius Child," "Daybreak in Alabama," "College Formal: Renaissance Casino," and "To Be Somebody" (found in either his selected or collected poems). Using these poems, write briefly on what you think Hughes's views on education might have been.

22. Find a recent college survival guide and compare it with similar guides from years ago. What insights arise from your investigation? Why do you think the way you do?

23. Read *Aquamarine Blue 5: Personal Stories of College Students with Autism* by Dawn Prince-Hughes (2002) and/or *Learning Outside the Lines: Two Ivy League Students with Learning Disabilities and ADHD Give You the Tools to Succeed* edited by Mooney and Cole (2002) and/or *Learning Disabilities and Life Stories* edited by Rodis, Garrod, and Boscardin (2002), or some similar collection.

24. Read *Coming of Age* by Lorri Hewett (1996); and/or *The Cheese Monkeys: A Novel in Two Semesters* by Chip Kidd (2002); and/or *I Am Charlotte Simmons* by Tom Wolfe (2004); and/or one of the series of adolescent novels, *College Life 101* by Wendy Corsi Staub; and/or some other novel about college life. How does the college experience portrayed in any or all of these books compare to your experience? Why do you think the way you do?

25. Read *Out & About Campus: Personal Accounts by Lesbian, Gay, Bisexual & Transgender College Students* edited by Howard and Stevens (2000) and/or *Out on Fraternity Row: Personal Accounts of Being Gay in a College Fraternity* edited by Windmeyer and Freeman (1998) or similar collections. What insights and/or new awareness have you come to from seeing these experiences from these points of view?

26. Read *Mi voz, mi vida/ My Voice, My Life: Latino College Students Tell their Life Stories* by Andrew Garrod (2007) or *Balancing Two Worlds: Asian American College Students Tell Their Life Stories* by Andrew Garrod. What similarity and difference do you find in the experiences narrated in these two books? Why do you think this is true?

27. Read *Chicken Soup for the College Soul: Inspiring and Humorous Stories for College Students*, edited by Jack Canfield (1999). Do any of the pieces inspire you? Why or why not? How do you account for the wide popularity of this book and books like it? In what ways is this collection different from this text, *Higher Learning?*

28. Choose at least three films from the list at the end of this chapter. What do they seem to say about going to college? What support do you have for your position?

29. Choose one of your responses to the "Some possibilities for writing" topics in this chapter and do further research on some aspect of the topic you addressed in your narrative. Write about how and why this new information would have improved your previous effort.

30. Find the original text from which one of the selections in this chapter was taken. What led you to choose this particular text? How does reading more from the text affect your original reading? Is there more you would like to know about the text, its subject, or its author? Where might you find this further information?

Selected Films—"School Daze"

For more choices, search IMDb.com using terms such as College, College Life, College Students.

Accepted (2006, USA). A high school slacker who is rejected by every school he applies to opts to create his own institution of higher learning. Comedy. 90 min. PG.

Bonzo Goes to College (1952, USA). A smart, spunky chimpanzee stars on the varsity football team. Comedy. 80 min. N/R

Circle of Friends (1995, Ireland–USA). Three friends from a strict Catholic small town face old inhibitions and new freedoms when they go to college in Dublin. Adapted from the Maeve Binchy novel. Romantic drama. 96 min. PG-13.

College (1927, USA). Brilliant silent film comedian Buster Keaton tries out for every sports team on campus. Comedy. 65 min. N/R.

Drive, He Said (1972, USA). Jack Nicholson directed this oddly told tale of coming-of-age angst and alienation. Scene stealer Bruce Dern plays the maniacal college basketball coach. Sports/Drama. 90 min. R.

An Education (2009, Britain). Everything sixteen year old Jenny does is in the sole pursuit of getting into Oxford until she meets a man twice her age and he gives her a different kind of education. Drama. 100 min. PG-13.

The Education of Charlie Banks (2007, USA). College student Charlie Banks has to face old problems when the bully he had an unpleasant encounter with back in high school shows up on his campus. Drama, 102 min. R.

Frosh (1993, USA). Filmmakers spent a year living in a multicultural, co-ed dormitory at Stanford University. The film documents students' difficult search for personal identity within an increasingly diverse student population. Documentary. 98 min. N/R.

The Great Debaters (2007, USA). A drama based on the true story of Melvin B. Tolson, a professor at Wiley College Texas. In 1935, he inspired students to form the school's first debate team, which went on to challenge Harvard in the national championship. Drama. 122 min. PG.

Good Will Hunting (1997, USA). Will Hunting, a janitor at MIT, has a gift for mathematics; a psychiatrist tries to help him with his gift and the rest of his life. Drama. 126 min. R.

Greetings (1968, USA). In this Vietnam War farce (an early effort by director Brian De Palma) Robert De Niro helps a buddy try to fail his physical and escape the military draft. Comedy. 88 min. R.

The Heart of Dixie (1989, USA). Three white southern college women find their lives and politics shifting as they confront the civil rights movement in the late 1950s. Drama. 96 min. PG.

Higher Learning (1995, USA). Political correctness and race issues haunt several students, whose lives intersect briefly and tragically on the campus mall. Drama. 127 min. R.

Kent State (1981, USA). Emmy-winning made-for-TV movie about the 1970 tragedy at Kent State University, in which National Guardsmen shot and killed four college protesters. Political drama. 120 min. N/R.

Legally Blonde (2002, USA). A sorority girl becomes the reigning brain at Harvard Law School. Comedy. 96 min. PG-13.

National Lampoon's Animal House (1978, USA). At a 1962 college, Dean Vernon Wormer is determined to expel the Delta House fraternity, but those rough-housers have other plans for him. Comedy. 109 min. R.

P.C.U. (1994, USA). A freshman falls in with dorm mates who organize offensive activities. A social satire of political correctness. Comedy. 81 min. PG-13.

Pretty in Pink (1986, USA). Directed by "master of the eighties teen flick" John Hughes, this film follows the story of Andie Walsh, a girl from the wrong side of the tracks who catches the eye of one of the most popular high-school hunks. Comedy/Drama. 96 min. PG-13.

Rudy (1993, USA). Based on the true story of Rudy Ruettiger, a five-foot, six-inch college student who must overcome the prejudices of his blue-collar family and an elitist university system in order to fulfill his dreams of playing on the Notre Dame football team. Drama. 116 min. PG.

School Daze (1988, USA). Homecoming weekend on a southern campus highlights how some blacks deny or affirm their racial identity. Directed by Spike Lee. Musical comedy. 114 min. R.

School Ties (1992, USA). A handsome young Jewish prep school athlete hides his religion to survive anti-Semitism in the 1950s. Drama. 107 min. PG-13.

Seniors: Four Years in Retrospect (1997, USA). The filmmakers of *Frosh* returned to Stanford three years later to see how college life had changed five of the students profiled in the earlier film. Combining extensive footage shot during senior year with prophetic clips and outtakes from *Frosh*, the two directors have produced a new film focusing on the different trajectories that students from diverse backgrounds take to a fulfilling and successful college experience. Documentary. 56 min. N/R.

For critical thinking points on these films, see Appendix (p. 277).

Three

Student Relations

FAMILY, FRIENDS, AND LOVERS

Much of the education at college takes place outside the classroom, as students learn to live in groups, view and treat one another as adults, and adapt to their changing family roles. This chapter explores parents adjusting to their children's growth, friendships that will last a lifetime or at least a semester, and the difficult choices involved in romantic relationships.

READING SELECTIONS

Raspberries

Jennifer Fandel

Jennifer Fandel earned an MFA from Mankato State University. She has published more than 30 nonfiction books for children and young adults, including biographies of inspirational figures, cultural histories of major inventions and icons, a how-to-write poetry series, and graphic novels on historical figures and inventions.

I hang on to the bush,

ready to fall heavy

full and red.

CRITICAL THINKING POINTS: *As you read*

1. Read through the poem as quickly as you can. What are your first impressions of it?
2. Make a list of words that you think are particularly powerful, beautiful, or important to this poem.
3. Speculate about the poet's age. What makes you think the way you do?

My love is heavy
as raspberries.
Silent as the fall
and red, turning
scarlet as an old heart
heavily thumping,
slow in beat, thinking.
My love is silent
as the waiting.
If only the sun and rain
could be enough.
I hang on to the bush,
ready to fall heavy
full and red.
Cupping his palm
he curves to me,
falling apart
at his touch.

1993

CRITICAL THINKING POINTS: *After you've read*

1. Why do you think the poet compares her love to raspberries? Do you think this is a good comparison? Why or why not?
2. How is this poem like other love poems you've read? How is it different?
3. If you didn't know the author's gender, would you guess this poem was written by a man or a woman? Why?

SOME POSSIBILITIES FOR WRITING

1. The poet writes, "My love is heavy as raspberries." What are three words other than *raspberries* that the poet could have used? The poet writes, "My love is silent as the waiting." What are three words other than *waiting* that could be used here? Choose at least two other words, and briefly record some of the insights and/or questions you come up with.
2. Love in the poem is an abstraction. Choose some other abstractions, such as growing up, injustice, or ambition, and render them in concrete, specific details and/or images of varying length.
3. Read or reread Frank Smoot's "What It's Really Like," later in this chapter. Both pieces might fall into the category of "love poems." How are they different? How are they the same?

Ten Commandments for a College Freshman

Joseph McCabe

Joseph McCabe (b. 1912) is an ordained minister in the United Presbyterian Church and trustee of the Princeton Theological Seminary and Herbert Hoover Presidential Library. His books include *Your First Year at College* (Westminster, 1967) and *Reason, Faith, and Love* (Parthenon, 1972).

College is a new beginning, a clean slate. . . . Burn your bad bridges. No one at college knows about that soiled baggage you've been carrying.

CRITICAL THINKING POINTS: *As you read*

1. What advice seems dated to you? What advice still seems pertinent to college students?
2. The father asks of his son, "Give me your ideas on what to scrap and what to keep." What is your response to this?
3. This piece was written in the form of a letter. What are some qualities of a letter that make this piece effective? How would this be different if it were not part of a personal letter from father to son?

Dear J.B.—

. . . As you know I am asked from time to time to talk to high school students about college and how to prepare for it. Do you think something like the following would be helpful? I'm thinking of calling it: Ten Commandments for a College Freshman. Give me your ideas on what to scrap and what to keep.

I. Thou Shalt Plan to Succeed.

Does this seem as obvious as the need for a quarterback on the football team? I don't mean *hope* to succeed. I mean that success in college will be much more likely if you really draw up a schedule of hours for study, work, and play. Lay out your day and your week. Get in the habit in high school. This will be the secret of getting things done in college and enjoying the whole experience.

II. Thou Shalt Handle Freedom Responsibly.

No one is going to tell you when to get up, go to eat, study, or go to bed. It's amazing that so many survive, and, of course, many don't. Freedom such as a student has at college is devastating for that freshman who has little sense of responsibility.

You've got to get set for freedom; it isn't doing what comes naturally.

III. Thou Shalt Spread the Joy of Learning.

Learning is an exciting adventure as you have already discovered in the best of your high school courses. Beware those who are "sent" to college, for they will be taking the attitude that education is the enemy of fun. Beware the cynics. They're on every campus and their refrain runs like this, "Poor food, dorm is like a jail, dull professors, slobby team, why did you come here?" You will sometimes wish they would take their budding ulcers or sour stomach elsewhere. But if it's an education you're after, you'll get it, and you will enjoy the process.

IV. Thou Shalt Scale Down Those Reports on the Sex and Liquor Bit.

Not every co-ed takes the pill as routinely as most takes aspirin, and the extracurricular is not a perpetual beer bust. Most fellows on campus are still looking for the girl they want to marry, and it isn't going to be the b**** who was quick to bed. When you read of students getting bombed on booze, remember you're getting a minority report.

V. Thou Shalt Plan to Commit Fun—and Often.

The world of academia has two extremes. There's the playboy who can't get a book open or the body to the library and there's the grind who never lives it up at all. You should expect to go on a real study binge, but the bookworm learns less than the fellow who knows how to make learning the leitmotif and still plays with abandon. American adults don't know how to play at all. Did they unlearn it in college?

VI. Thou Shalt Know at Least One Professor or One Dean Personally.

Even at the risk of seeming to make yourself a bore! But much more likely you will be welcomed as a student mature enough to relate to a mature person, and that will set both of you up. Invite him to the Union for coffee and he'll flip inwardly— but he'll go and he will be delighted by the invitation. At the small college this kind of relationship should come about readily, but often it doesn't. All the best universities are striving to make it happen more often. You can do this one yourself, and then say (but not to the prof or the dean), "This lowly freshman has solved the most pressing problem facing higher education in America today!" And you will be right.

VII. Thou Shalt Be Concerned.

But not simply with war on the other side of the world and the social causes of our day. Keep informed, and do what you think is right about these. But what about the cook, the maid in your dorm, the campus maintenance crew, and the night watchman? Just say, "We students appreciate you," and someone will go through the day as though it were Christmas.

VIII. Thou Shalt Be Selective.

Paper, yearbook, student government, fraternity and sorority, dances, ball games, bull sessions, dates, causes, movies, etc., etc., . . . the whole works! If you make them all, you're a bust; and if you miss them all, you're a dud. Don't spread yourself so thin that they would never miss you if you didn't show. But do choose a few, get involved, and get that good part of a college education which no classroom can ever provide.

IX. Thou Shalt Strive to Keep Healthy.

All that psychosomatic stuff has real substance. It isn't sin, it's lack of sleep that ruins so many college careers. Phys ed is required and that will get the body exercised, but there's no requirement that you eat sensibly and keep hours conducive to vigor. You will see many students just too jaded to play well or to study at all.

X. Thou Shalt Forget and Remember.

Take some time to sit down with yourself and recall those things of which you are ashamed and sorry—and then forget them. College is a new beginning, a clean slate, and all that. Burn your bad bridges. No one at college knows about that soiled baggage you've been carrying. Remember those relationships which have made life good. They were clean and decent, and to think of them is a lift. As a freshman, look back at those relationships which brought lasting joy and seek them again. Life is the fine art of forgetting—and remembering.

Well there they are, J.B. What's missing and what needs to be said better? If you forget them all, do remember the love of all of us here.

—Dad

1963

CRITICAL THINKING POINTS: *After you've read*

1. The author talks about the "soiled baggage" that someone might bring to college. What kinds of things do you think he is talking about? How might someone "burn" his or her "bad bridges"?

2. The author talks about "that good part of a college education which no classroom can ever provide." What kinds of things do you think he is talking about, and what might be "good" about them?

3. There are both "do's" and "don'ts" in McCabe's letter. What are some other common themes throughout these ten commandments? How might the son respond to this letter? How would you respond if you received this from one of your parents?

SOME POSSIBILITIES FOR WRITING

1. The father asks, "What's missing and what needs to be said better?" What do you think? Rewrite this letter, adding your thoughts. Since 1963, what has changed in the world and at college? Incorporate those changes into your updated, contemporary version of this letter.

2. McCabe says, "You've got to get set for freedom; it isn't doing what comes naturally." Write about your first few weeks of "freedom" at college. How did you react to your freedom? Did you "get set" for it, as the author advises? In what way?

3. How does the father mask his advice to his son? Do your parents give you outright advice or do they do it more subtly? Write some "obvious" advice from someone close to you. Now write some that is not so obvious.

Commandments for a First-Year Student (From His Mom)

Patsy Sanchez

Though Patsy Sanchez has worked with first-year students for many years, she just recently survived her son's first year of college. She sent him this list his first week of college.

CRITICAL THINKING POINTS: *As you read*

1. What advice is similar to advice your parent's gave you? What advice is much different?
2. Which advice do you think pertains most to you at college? Why that?
3. What advice for a first-year student might be missing?

Maybe you'll hate the jazz concert or bungee jumping or the art show or hiking along the Mississippi. But what if you love it?

---

1. Treat school like a job—put in 40–50 hours a week (15 class hours, 30 study hours) and use the rest of the time for fun.
2. Don't be afraid to tell people what you think. Be straight forward with your professors, classmates, friends, and family. Relationships can be confusing enough, especially without people saying what they really mean.
3. Listen more than you talk. Everyone loves a good listener, and you'll do better academically, personally, and professionally.
4. Underage drinking is illegal and expensive (in Winona County first offenders pay over a $250 fine, second offenders pay $390 AND forfeit their driver's license). If you choose to drink, be careful: never drink on an empty stomach, watch your open drinks so no one puts anything in them, and count your drinks. If someone you're with gets sick, stay with that person and watch that person. NEVER drink and drive—even if you've only had a few drinks (even if you're not legally intoxicated, you'll pay close to $400 on fines for violating Wisconsin and Minnesota's "absolute sobriety" law). NEVER ride with a driver who has been drinking.
5. Say hello to one new person every day—and really mean it. Most people will respond positively to a friendly smile and a hello.
6. Do at least 30 to 60 minutes of physical activity a day. It will reduce stress and keep you fit.
7. Watch what you put into your body. Junk in means you'll feel like junk.
8. Find ways to relax—Guitar Hero, Facebook, vegging in front of the TV or computer, hanging out with friends—anything to calm yourself down. The

only thing you absolutely have control over is yourself and how you react to situations. Don't worry about the rest.

9. If you're feeling bad, talk to someone. Develop a support system at school with your RA, your hall director, your advisor, and friends. If things are scary or difficult, call your mom or dad. They'll listen and give advice if you want it, but most of all give you someone to vent to. Talking can be a cure.

10. Don't smoke or chew tobacco. Both are obviously bad for you and quitting is more difficult than you can imagine.

11. Learning the mechanics of sex is easy. The emotional aspects are complicated. Beware.

12. Vote. School elections, local elections, national elections. If you vote, you have a say in how things are run. Exercise your rights, and then you can bitch about the way things are done.

13. Don't use drugs. Pills, meth, coke, marijuana—all make you unaware and downright stupid. A drug conviction will be on your record forever and affect everything from financial aid (you won't get any) to future jobs (may be harder to get). Marijuana will most likely be legalized in your lifetime. Wait.

14. Read at least one newspaper a day. Be informed about what's going on at school, in town, and in the world.

15. Try something new. Maybe you'll hate the jazz concert or bungee jumping or the art show or hiking along the Mississippi. But what if you love it? Trying new stuff is all part of your college experience.

2009

CRITICAL THINKING POINTS: *After you've read*

1. How does this piece compare to Joseph McCabe's "Ten Commandments for a College Freshman"?
2. What do you think are this mother's most important three pieces of advice? Why do you choose those?
3. Would this list be different if written from a friend or sibling's perspective rather than from a mom's? Why or why not?

SOME POSSIBILITIES FOR WRITING

1. Research your university's underage drinking rules (as well as the city ordinance and state laws concerning underage drinking). How do they compare to other places? Analyze what these rules and laws say about your school's drinking culture.
2. Choose one piece of advice and illustrate from your own experience and others you know why it seems to be "good" or "bad" advice.
3. Do an Internet search for "college advice." Compile your own list of advice from various websites. What kinds of advice seem to be the best? The worst? Why?

Carmen

Jennifer Sheridan

Jennifer Sheridan holds a Master of Fine Arts in fiction writing from Columbia College in Chicago.

I thought I might throw up after all the booze, and Aaron winking at me, so I dug another vanilla wafer out of the box and drank some tap water out of my cupped palm. Carmen lay face down on her bed, trying to light a cigarette.

CRITICAL THINKING POINTS: *As you read*

1. Why do you think the story is called "Carmen"?
2. Do you know people who are as disconnected from their academic lives as Carmen and Kate? Why are they disenchanted and disengaged characters?
3. Romantic ideas surrounding young people are promoted in movies, TV, and books. How are these romantic ideas reflected or countered in the story?

My best friend Carmen leaned against the sink and arched her back. She blew smoke at the ceiling and it curled back down the face of the mirror behind her. She was telling me the story of her virginity in that slow, sultry way she had. She'd just finished the orgasm part. We were cutting all our Monday afternoon classes and sharing a cigarette in her dorm bathroom.

It had happened over Thanksgiving break the previous week, in Greece with an older cousin who spoke no English. Late, nearly dawn. Parted French doors. An ocean.

I draped my arms over the still warm hand dryer. Carmen's tan was a deep berry color that rolled out of the sleeves of her T-shirt.

"Afterwards he paced around the room," she whispered. I pictured a leopard crisscrossing by the open window. Outside the sky would glow lavender. A breeze. The sound of water. The smell of salt and sky and beach.

"What did it feel like?"

"Watching him pace?"

"Yeah." I pictured myself in her place, lying on starched white sheets as my first lover, foreign and chiseled, paced like a wild animal.

"It was awesome," she said. "It was my favorite part." Passing the cigarette, she gave me a smile no one else for miles ever saw. She knew the pacing part would be my favorite too.

"God, Carmen, leave it to you to have the perfect first time," I said.

"Let's get drunk," she suggested. I nodded, dropping the half-smoked cigarette into the sink. It landed in a fierce sizzle.

By five-thirty the pint of Jack Daniel's was finished and the dinner migration began. When Aaron Klinger sauntered by Carmen's doorway he winked at me. Aaron Klinger who'd phone me late at night. What was I doing? Nothing much. I'd follow the scent of stale cigarettes into his bed. But it was a secret.

I thought I might throw up after all the booze, and Aaron winking at me, so I dug another vanilla wafer out of the box and drank some tap water out of my cupped palm. Carmen lay face down on her bed, trying to light a cigarette.

At six-fifteen her date appeared, standing at the door for God knows how long before I noticed him. Byron. He had black pubic curly hair on his face and head, and bugged-out eyes. His hands fluttered over his chest, landing at his sides.

Carmen insisted I come to an ancient Warren Beatty film that I'd seen twice to make sure I really hated, but what the hell, Carmen wanted me to go.

During the movie I watched her face flicker in the light coming off the screen. Occasionally I saw Byron glaring at me from the other side. I thought about Aaron, how we smoked in silence sometimes, afterward, staring at the ceiling, not touching.

"Kate," he once said. "You know Scott, the football player?"

"Yeah?"

"Well, every day he goes to this one girl's room and they do it." He leaned on one elbow and tapped his cigarette into the ashtray lying between us. I pulled the sheet up to my chin. "She makes him a cheese omelet, and that's it." Aaron rested his chin on my sheet covered chest. His greasy hair fell onto the back of my hand as I stroked the nape of his neck.

"That's great, Aaron," I said.

In the science auditorium a ten-foot Warren Beatty leaned into an open refrigerator against a half-naked Goldie Hawn.

"Juicy bootie," Carmen growled. I laughed, but I felt a hundred years old. I just wanted to go home. Maybe the phone in my hallway would be ringing. Maybe my brother would call from Yale.

"Hey, Sis, how's that Anthro class?" He'd never called me from Yale. He didn't know what classes I had.

Outside the air smelled of frost. Carmen sang a Christmas carol. Byron jammed his hands into his pockets, his eyes on Carmen, twirling in and out of sight on perfect ballet points.

"My mother is such a bitch," she said. "I hate her guts." I thought about flannel sheets against my naked skin.

"She's just drunk," I mumbled to Byron.

"Kiss me," Carmen screamed, grabbing him. She knew how bad he wanted her. I thought it was cruel, the way she treated guys. But maybe I was wrong to feel bad. Byron didn't give a shit about her either. He wanted what he wanted; we all did. At the time I gave everyone a million times more credit than they deserved.

Byron puckered his skinny chapped lips. I could see them quiver in the moonlight. Carmen wouldn't be happy about this in the morning, if she remembered it at all.

"Carmen . . ." I started. Carmen was in my face like a guard dog.

"Mind your own fucking business," she screamed.

"Yeah," said Byron. His hand gripped her arm. Carmen turned to him with a low laugh. I tried again. This time she whipped around and slapped me hard across the face. We all heard the sound. While I stroked the stinging place on my cheek his arm wrapped around her back, sliding down over her ass. She squeaked a little as he kissed her. Carmen pulled away, almost falling over backwards. Byron licked his lips and steadied her with his spindly hands.

"Good night to you," she slurred. She'd forgotten his name. Carmen disappeared into the darkness. When I found her she was throwing up in the bushes. I half-dragged her to her room.

Carmen pulled her limp dress over her head and fell naked onto the bed. She laughed at me, standing by the sink holding an empty vanilla wafer box. I could see her shape in the dim light from the hall.

"I do love you, Katie," she mumbled, rolling toward the wall. I hung her dress on the closet doorknob and stood very still on her carpet. She whimpered slightly, a sharp stab, then nothing.

I took the two steps to the side of the bed. She rolled onto her back, cradling her long arm behind her head.

"My mom," she said.

"I know," I whispered. I pulled the damp hair out of her eyes and smoothed it down along her pillow. She smelled terrible, of vomit and whiskey. She sobbed again. Her eyelids fluttered. I ran my hand over her forehead. She leaned into my fingers, cool against her hot skin. I kissed her cheek and pressed my face against hers.

Suddenly Carmen came to life. She wrapped her sweaty, strong arms around my neck and pulled my face to hers by my hair. I clamped my jaw shut, stifling a scream. Adrenaline shot through me so fast my fingers shot out straight. The next thing I knew her mouth was on mine, her lips grinding against me, her tongue forcing my teeth apart. Carmen, my best friend. Her mouth felt swollen and hot, but her tongue was cooler. It glided finally past my stubborn teeth, into my mouth. Only after she had fallen back onto the bed, eyes shut, breathing even and deep did I feel the sensation of our tongues together, like warm snakes in a twisting, sinewy pile.

When I stood up my legs wobbled. Carmen's naked chest rose and fell, half under the sheet. I staggered through the door and up the stuffy hall. One long, fluorescent light bulb flickered purple as I passed under it.

In the morning Carmen called me on the phone.

"God, Katie," she laughed. "I feel like hell."

I was angry, not because she'd slapped me but just because of everything. She wore me out. I'd watched her dance and flirt and held her head while she barfed. Carmen wasn't meant for quiet, Midwestern evenings. Her green-tinted skin and wild ways, her elegance made me hate myself.

She admitted sheepishly that she'd been pretty drunk the night before. No, she didn't remember the movie, or spilling her Raisinets, licking melted chocolate from her fingers.

"Do you remember kissing Byron?" I asked.

"I didn't."

"Do you remember slapping me?"

"Katie, I never did!"

"Yeah, you sure did."

I thought about Carmen putting badly typed love letters signed with Aaron's name in my mailbox, Carmen calling at two A.M. to talk about Ingmar Bergman, Carmen saying I looked like a Gypsy princess in the sweater I was sure people thought was weird.

"Katie, did I? Tell me I didn't."

"You didn't."

"I did, didn't I?"

"Yeah, you did."

"I'm sorry, Katie," she said. "Do you forgive me?"

I forgave Carmen. I met her for lunch. She looked the same. Standing at the bottom of the stairs leading up to the dining hall her hands did not shake. She reached for me, a fake worried look on her face.

"Help me up the stairs, daughter," she said in an old lady voice. "I feel like shit." She leaned against me as we climbed the stairs, mumbling how much coffee she would need, twenty-nine cups, black.

We blew off all our classes that day. We smoked and laughed and bought a bottle of gin. Coming out of the liquor store Carmen said she'd call her evil, stingy father for more money.

"If I'm lucky my mom will answer the phone. She always throws in an extra fifty," she said.

Sitting in the grass outside the library Carmen apologized again and shook her head, smiling into her lap. I watched her bring her cigarette to her lips. I watched her close her eyes. I listened to the ache behind her laugh that only I ever heard. I told her a thousand times to forget the whole thing. I promised to forget it myself. I really had no choice in the matter.

1996

CRITICAL THINKING POINTS: *After you've read*

1. Why does Kate seem to worship Carmen? What is Carmen's attitude toward Kate? What details in the story support this?

2. What do you think makes the scene in which Carmen kisses Kate a pivotal one in the plot?

3. How would the story be different if the two lead characters were male?

SOME POSSIBILITIES FOR WRITING

1. Kate and Carmen take turns being the mother and the daughter. Find examples of this role switching in the text. Why do you think they switch roles?

2. Compare and contrast Carmen's and Kate's attitudes toward sex.

3. Universities are notorious for promoting a lifestyle that accepts promiscuity and many sexual partners. What are your views of college life and its reputation for creating sexually active students? What do you think are some causes of this? What might be some of the results?

"Who Shall I Be?" The Allure of a Fresh Start

Jennifer Crichton

Jennifer Crichton is the author of *Delivery: A Nurse-Midwife's Story* (1986) and *Family Reunion* (1998). She holds an A.B. from Brown University and received a Master's degree in English from Columbia University in 2002.

Nothing seduces like the promise of a clean slate.

CRITICAL THINKING POINTS: *As you read*

1. Is a "fresh start" at college alluring to everyone? Why or why not?
2. Do you believe people, especially college freshmen, choose who they will become? Why or why not?
3. Crichton says, "We learn a lot about friends from the kinds of masks they choose to wear." In what ways do people choose to wear masks? Do you know anyone who does this? Do you sometimes wear masks? In what types of situations?

The student is a soul in transit, coming from one place en route to someplace else. Moving is the American way, after all. Our guiding principle is the fresh start, our foundation the big move, and nothing seduces like the promise of a clean slate.

"Do you realize how many people saw me throw up at Bob Stonehill's party in tenth grade? A lot of people," says my friend Anne. "How many forgot about it? Maybe two or three. Do you know how much I wanted to go someplace where nobody knew I threw up all over Bob Stonehill's living room in tenth grade? Very much. This may not seem like much of a justification for going away to college, but it was for me." Going away to college gives us a chance to rinse off part of our past, to shake off our burdensome reputations.

We've already survived the crises of being known, allowing how American high schools are as notoriously well-organized as totalitarian regimes, complete with secret police, punishment without trial, and banishment. High school society loves a label, cruelly infatuated with pinning down every species of student. Hilary is a klutz, Julie is a slut, and Michele a gossiping bitch who eats like a pig.

No wonder so many of us can't wait to be free of our old identities and climb inside a new skin in college. Even flattering reputations can be as confining as a pair of too-tight shoes. But identity is tricky stuff, constructed with mirrors. How you see yourself is a composite reflection of how you appear to friends, family, and lovers. In college, the fact that familiar mirrors aren't throwing back a familiar picture is both liberating and disorienting (maybe that's why so many colleges have freshman "orientation week").

"I guess you could call it an identity crisis," Andrea, a junior now, says of her freshman year. "It was the first time nobody knew who I was. I wasn't even anybody's daughter any more. I had always been the best and brightest—what was I going to do now, walk around the dorm with a sign around my neck saying 'Former High School Valedictorian'?"

For most of my college years, I was in hot pursuit of an identity crisis, especially after a Comparative Literature major informed me that the Chinese definition of "crisis" was "dangerous opportunity," with the emphasis on opportunity. On college applications, where there were blanks for your nickname, I carefully wrote "Rusty," although none of my friends (despite the fact that I have red hair) had ever, even for a whimsical moment, considered calling me that. I was the high-strung, sensitive, acne-blemished, antiauthoritarian, would-be writer. If I went through a day without some bizarre mood swing, people asked me what was wrong. I didn't even have the leeway to be the cheerful, smiling sort of girl I thought I might have it in me to be. My reputation seemed etched in stone, and I was pretty damn sick of it. As I pictured her, Rusty was the blithe spirit who would laugh everything off, shrug at perils as various as freshman mixers, bad grades, and cafeterias jammed with aloof strangers, and in general pass through a room with all the vitality and appeal of a cool gust of wind.

But when I arrived at college, Rusty had vaporized. She was simply not in the station wagon that drove me up to campus. Much of college had to do with filling in the blanks, but changing myself would not be so easy, so predictable, so clichéd.

My parents, acting as anxious overseers on the hot, humid day I took my new self to college, seemed bound by a demonic ESP to sabotage my scarcely budding new identity. After a summer planning how I would metamorphose into the great American ideal, the normal teenage girl, I heard my mother tell my roommate, "I think you'll like Jenny—she's quite the oddball." Luckily, my roommate was saturated with all kinds of information the first day of college had flung at her, and the last thing she was paying attention to were the off-the-cuff remarks this oddball's mother was making. My unmarked reputation kept its sheen as it waited for me to cautiously build it up according to plan. My parents left without any further blunders, except to brush my bangs from my eyes ("You'll get a headache, Sweetheart") and foist on what had been a blissfully bare dormitory room an excruciatingly ugly lamp from home. As soon as the station wagon became a distant mote of dust on the highway, I pulled my bangs back over my eyes in my New Wave fashion of choice, tossed the ugly lamp in the nearest trash can, and did what I came to college to do. Anonymous, alone, without even a name, I would start over and become the kind of person I was meant to be: like myself, but better, with all failures, rejections, and sexual indiscretions relegated to a history I hoped none of my new acquaintances would ever hear of.

Why was it, I wondered, when *any* change seemed possible that year, had it been so impossible in high school? For one thing people know us well enough to see when we're attempting a change, and change can look embarrassingly like a public admission of weakness. Our secret desires, and the fact that we're not entirely pleased with ourselves, are on display. To change in public under the scrutiny of the most hypercritical witnesses in the world—other high school students—is to risk failure ("Look how cool she's trying to be, the jerk!") or succeeding but betraying friends in the process ("I don't understand her any more," they say, hurt and angry) or feeling so much like a fraud that you're forced to back down. And while we live at home, parental expectations, from the lovingly hopeful to the intolerably ambitious, apply the pressure of an invisible but very effective mold.

Jacki dressed in nothing but baggy Levi's and flannel shirts for what seemed to be the endless duration of high school, even though she came to a sort of truce with her developing woman's body in eleventh grade and wasn't averse any longer to looking pretty. Looking good in college was a fantasy she savored because in high school, "I didn't want to make the attempt in public and then fail," she explains now, looking pulled-together and chic. "I thought everyone would think I was trying to look good but I only managed to look weird. And I didn't want a certain group of girls who were very image-conscious to think they'd won some kind of victory either, that I was changing to please them.

"So I waited for college, and wore nice, new clothes right off the bat so nobody would know me any other way. I had set my expectation too high, though—I sort of thought that I'd be transformed into a kind of *femme fatale* or something. When I wasn't measuring up to what I'd imagined, I almost ditched the whole thing until I realized that at least I wasn't sabotaging myself any more. When I ran into a friend from high school, even though I had gotten used to the nice way I looked, I was scared that she could see right through my disguise. That's how I felt for a long time: a slobby girl just pretending to be pulled together."

At first, any change can feel uncomfortably like a pretense, an affectation. Dana had been a punked-out druggy in high school, so worried about being considered a grind that she didn't use a fraction of her considerable vocabulary when she was around her anti-intellectual friends. She promised herself to get serious academically in college, but the first night she spent studying in the science library, she recalls, "I half-expected the other kids to look twice at me, as if my fish-out-of-water feeling was showing. Of course, it wasn't. But it was schizophrenic at first, as if I were an impostor only playing at being smart. But when you do something long enough, that thing becomes *you*. It's not playing anymore. It's what you are."

Wanting to change yourself finds its source in two wellsprings: self-hatred and self-affirmation. Self-affirmation takes what already exists in your personality (even if slightly stunted or twisted) and encourages its growth. Where self-affirmation is expansive, self-hatred is reductive, negating one's own personality while appropriating qualities external to it and applying them like thick pancake makeup.

Joan's thing was to hang out with rich kids with what can only be described as a vengeance. She dressed in Ralph Lauren, forayed to town for $75 haircuts, and complained about the tackiness of mutual friends. But after a late night of studying, Joan allowed her self-control to slip long enough to tell me of her upbringing. Her mother was a cocktail waitress and Joan had never even found out her father's name. She and her mother had trucked about from one Western trailer park to another, and Joan always went to school dogged by her wrong-side-of-the-tracks background. That Joan had come through her hardscrabble life with such strong intellectual achievement seemed a lot more credible—not to mention interesting— than the effortless achievements of many of our more privileged classmates. Joan didn't think so, and, I suppose in fear I'd blow her cover (I never did), she cut me dead after her moment's indulgence in self-revelation. Joan was rootless and anxious, alienated not only from her background but, by extension, from herself, and paid a heavy psychic price. This wasn't change: this was lies. She scared me. But we learn a lot about friends from the kinds of masks they choose to wear.

After all, role-playing to some degree is the prerogative of youth. A woman of romance, rigorous academic, trendy New Waver, intense politico, unsentimental jock, by turn—we have the chance to experiment as we decide the kind of person we want to become. And a stereotypical role, adopted temporarily, can offer refuge from the swirl of confusing choices available to us, by confining us to the limits of a type. Returning to my old self after playing a role, I find I'm slightly different, a little bit more than what I was. To contradict one's self is to transcend it.

As occasional fugitives from our families, we all sometimes do what Joan did. Sometimes you need a radical change in order to form an identity independent of your family, even if that change is a weird but transient reaction. My friend Lisa came from a family of feminists and academics. When she returned home from school for Thanksgiving, dressed as a "ditsy dame" straight out of a beach-blanket-bingo movie, she asked me, "How do you think I look? I've been planning this since tenth grade. Isn't it great?" Well, er, yes, it was great—not because she looked like a Barbie doll incarnate but because nobody would ever automatically connect her life with that of her parents again.

Another friend, Dan, went from a Southern military academy to a Quaker college in the North to execute his scheme of becoming a serious intellectual. The transformation went awry after a few months, partly because his own self was too likably irrepressible. It wouldn't lie down and play dead. "I kept running into myself like a serpent chasing its tail," as he puts it. But his openness to change resulted in a peculiar amalgamation of cultures whose charm lies in his realizing that, while he's of his background, he's not identical to it. Most of our personalities and bodies are just as stubbornly averse to being extinguished, even if the fantasy of a symbolic suicide and a renaissance from the ashes takes its obsessive tool on our thoughts now and again. But a blank slate isn't the same as a blank self, and the point of the blank slate that college provides is not to erase the past, but to sketch out a new history with a revisionist's perspective and an optimist's acts.

And what of my changes? Well, when I was friendly and happy in college, nobody gaped as though I had sprouted a tail. I learned to laugh things off as Rusty might have done, and there was one particular counterman at the corner luncheonette who called me Red, which was the closest I came to being known as Rusty.

What became of Rusty? Senior year, I stared at an announcement stating the dates that banks would be recruiting on campus, and Rusty materialized for the first time since freshman year. Rusty was a Yuppie now, and I pictured her dressed in a navy-blue suit, looking uneasily like Mary Cunningham, setting her sights on Citibank. I was still the high-strung, oversensitive, would-be writer (I'm happy to report my skin did clear up), but a little better, who left the corporate world to be Rusty. For myself, I have the slate of the rest of my life to write on.

1984

CRITICAL THINKING POINTS: *After you've read*

1. How can even flattering reputations become "as confining as a pair of too-tight shoes"?
2. What might Crichton mean when she says, "Wanting to change yourself finds its source in two wellsprings: self-hatred and self-affirmation"?
3. Crichton says her friend Dan realized that "while he's of his background, he's not identical to it." Do you feel as though you are "identical" to your background? Why or why not?

SOME POSSIBILITIES FOR WRITING

1. Crichton creates a new persona in "Rusty." Create a new persona for yourself and write a scene that shows, not tells, what this character is like by what the character does and/or by how he or she does it.
2. In what ways is a student a "soul in transit," as Crichton says? In what ways can college offer students the chance to "re-make" themselves? To "re-make" their lives? Do you believe it will happen to you? Why or why not?
3. How have you changed since you've been at college? Have you noticed yourself acting, eating, socializing, or dressing differently than you did in high school? If you don't see any noticeable changes yet, speculate about why you might or might not change dramatically.

Welcome to Facebook

Cody Meyers

Cody Meyers graduated in 2009 with a degree in Latin American studies and is an English teacher in Costa Rica.

College students' carelessness when adding content to their Facebook profile has led to personal safety problems, trouble with the law, and missed opportunities for employment.

CRITICAL THINKING POINTS: *As you read*

1. What did you learn about Facebook that surprised you?
2. What does Meyers' research add to his paper?
3. Pay attention to the types of sources Meyers uses.

I n the past decade, college students have been finding easier ways to communicate with one another. For many students, the widespread use of the Internet in the 1990's spawned communication by way of email. In recent years however, cell phone usage has grown dramatically and has become the dominant method of communication. It's quite common for the majority of students in a classroom to raise their hands when polled to see how many of them own cell phones. However, as far as meeting and befriending others, these methods have become substandard for today's university students. In order to get someone's e-mail address or cell phone number, the customary way was to initiate and have a face-to-face conversation with the person in hopes of getting their phone number or email address. However, it has just gotten easier for college students who may be too shy to engage in such an uncertain conversation.

All across the country, more and more college students have engaged in an online social networking program called Facebook. This program was created in February 2004 by Harvard student Mark Zuckerburg (Wikipedia Contributors). According to a study done by Techcrunch, a weblog dedicated to profiling and reviewing web products and companies, 85 percent of students who attend colleges that embrace Facebook have user accounts (Arrington). In an online article in *Business Week*, comScore Media Metrix, a global information provider and consultancy to which leading companies turn, has listed Facebook as the seventh-most trafficked website on the Internet as it had 5.5 billion page views last February (Rosenbush). Facebook has become one of the most widely used social networks and has connected college students all across the country.

Though this social networking tool has brought millions of college students together, some professionals wonder if it has brought them too close. The main issue concerns the responsibility of college students to regulate the content they provide on their profiles. Many students display so much personal information that it has begun to cause them problems. Along with private information, university students have had problems with adding inappropriate photos and posting offensive comments on their profiles. If these "social networkers" don't stop putting improper material on their profiles, problems will continue. College students' carelessness when adding content to their Facebook profile has led to personal safety problems, trouble with the law, and missed opportunities for employment.

College students have become too careless when adding content to their Facebook profile, and it has resulted in personal safety problems, such as cases dealing with stalking and harassment. One area of concern is giving out personal information like full names, addresses, phone numbers, and class schedules. By putting so much information on their profiles, students are providing ripe conditions for potential stalkers and harassers. Parry Aftab, an Internet privacy and security lawyer and executive director of Wired-Safety.org says students feel too "secure" about what they add onto their Facebook profiles (Bobkoff). There was a study based on Facebook's privacy issues, which was finished in December of 2005 by Harvey Jones and Jose Hiram Soltren, scholars from The Massachusetts Institute of Technology. According to their research, which was based on 70,311 downloaded profiles from students at the Massachusetts Institute of Technology, Harvard University, New York University and Oklahoma University, 70 percent of their participants did not mind displaying their name, gender, location, and interests (Jones). With the majority of students not concerned about the personal information they put on their profiles, stalking is more likely to occur.

In recent years, cyber-stalking has become a problem for college students as evident in a recent study by an organization called *Working to Halt Online Abuse*, which strives to educate Internet users about online stalking and harassment. In their study, they found that in 1,664 online cases between 2000 and 2005, nearly 48 percent of the victims fell into the ages between eighteen and thirty years (WHOA). Cyber-stalking, also referred to as "Techno-stalking," is where someone continuously tries to interact with another individual by using the Internet and in the process makes the individual feel endangered (Countryman). This can be accomplished through e-mails, chatrooms, instant messaging and now Facebook. Facebook users are more vulnerable than the others programs listed because Facebook allows individuals to send messages to one another even if they are not each other's "friend." Even though email operates in a similar manner, it is much easier to find someone's personal information using Facebook due to the powerful search features offered.

Not only can stalking be a problem in cyberspace, but it can lead to problems in everyday life. There is evidence that some students on Facebook who choose to allow individuals to see their class schedules have been stalked. Michael Sullivan, with the High Tech Crimes Bureau at the Illinois Attorney General's Office says, information put on Facebook can be used by "predators" for reasons other than the creator's initial purpose. He has also noticed that there has been an increase in concerns made by students due to "Facebook stalkers." He explained that not only has online contact become bothersome for students, but there were also occasions reported where strangers were showing up at their dorm room as well as specific points on their routes to classes (Mora). Though she hasn't faced such problems herself, one example of techno-stalking deals with Leigh Hoffman, a University of Toledo freshman who says that her friends, who had "posted personal information" on their Facebook profiles began receiving visits to their dorm rooms from strange men (Buckman).

These undesired visits can lead to harassment, which is another cause for concern among college students. One of the issues on Facebook concerning harassment is the "Poke" feature. This feature was initially thought of as somewhat of an online wink. However, Pablo Malavenda, Associate Dean of Students at Purdue University, says that "poking" has evolved into pure "flirting", and has also attained the connotation of being "creepy" among some students. He also mentions that if an individual were to be poked by the wrong person, it could lead to a case of harassment (Michalos). In addition to the "Poke," there have also been occasions when students have gotten into trouble with the "My Photos" feature because they provided inappropriate content. This feature allows students to put pictures on their profiles, which can be seen by anyone with access to the particular profile. According to an article in *The Daily Pennsyvanian*, a Penn student posted pictures of two other University of Pennsylvania students having sex. The university officials charged the student with sexual harassment because he posted the pictures using the University's servers (Schwartz).

Although college students' carelessness concerning the content they put on their profile has led to cases of stalking and harassment, there are suggestions for students to use in order to lessen these occasions. According to the Division of Student Affairs at Florida University, students should go through the privacy settings and learn how to control the amount of and to whom the information is revealed (Division). Another plan to help eliminate safety concerns has been launched by many universities including Virginia Commonwealth University. They have begun programs meant to educate students about "Internet Safety" in order to help the students protect themselves when using the Internet (Cole).

Not only can careless adding of content on Facebook lead to stalking and harassment, but it can also cause college students to get into trouble with the law. Although many police officers refuse to say outright whether or not they access Facebook, there are some who admit that they will use Facebook as a tool to further investigations. Officers like Major Cathy Atwell, University of Maryland Police spokeswoman, use Facebook to find out the suspect's "whole name" or simply just to "better understand" them (Skowronski). In addition, even though Karl Fischer, an Eau Claire Police Department Lieutenant can't remember any particular instances where the department used information from Facebook, he says that if a suspect posts comments or pictures on their profile depicting illegal activities such as underage drinking or drug usage, the police may use the evidence in their prosecution against the individual (Werlein).

There is strong evidence showing that police will indeed use Facebook to prosecute students who are careless in putting inappropriate content on their profile. For example, four students from Northern Kentucky University received fines and were required to attend a class about alcohol safety after they posted pictures on Facebook of themselves sitting around a keg in one of their dorm rooms. Though the police did not directly uncover the photos, they received the tip from an R.A. who saw the pictures on Facebook (Chalfant).

Another incident where police were able to use evidence on Facebook to prosecute students took place after a Penn State football game last fall. Students broke the law by charging the field after Penn State's stunning victory over their arch rival Ohio State. Tyrone Parham, Assistant Director of Police Operations at the Pennsylvania State University Police Department says they were notified of a group on Facebook called, "I Rushed the Field After the OSU Game (And Lived!)." He was also surprised to see that there were actually pictures displaying Penn State students rushing the field. The police were then able to identify a number of the students because the pictures were "tagged," meaning that many of the students chose to reveal their names in captions located just underneath the pictures (Maternowski).

There was a case in which putting inappropriate content on Facebook caused a problem for a Fisher College University student. According to an online article in *The Boston Globe*, this was the first case in which a college actually expelled a student dealing with the use of Facebook. The same article explained how the student publicly criticized a university officer by posting a message on Facebook saying the officer "loves to antagonize students . . . and needs to be eliminated." The student was expelled according to Dean Bonie Bagchi Williamson because he, "conspired to and damaged" the reputation of the public official (Schweitzer).

Although college students' carelessness concerning the content they display on their Facebook profiles has gotten them into trouble with the law, there are ways to eliminate these instances. Another suggestion from the Division of Student Affairs at Florida University is to regularly check "tagged" photos on your profile in order to make sure that there is no inappropriate material. It is also advisable to check the postings and messages sent from others onto your profile to be certain that there is no incriminating information on your account (Division).

As well as getting into trouble with the law, college students' carelessness when adding content onto their Facebook profile can have negative effects on their future employment. Just as career service professionals have suggested that students maintain formal voice-mail greetings and e-mail addresses when looking for internships, it is also advisable to keep Facebook profiles formal and appropriate as well (Atilano). Some employers have begun to use Facebook to find out if a particular candidate is right for the job. Lance Choy, director of the Career Development Center at Stanford University affirms that employers regularly use web searches to find information about applicants. He also says that employers will use the web even more now that Facebook has come into the picture (Fuller). However, this raises a serious question in the ethics of using Facebook as a reference tool because according to the 1964 Civil Rights Act (Title VII), employers are not allowed to single out candidates due to "race, color, religion, sex or national origin." Unfortunately for the employer, all of these characteristics can be listed or shown in pictures on a student's profile (Cole).

Setting aside whether or not it is ethical for employers to use Facebook to research possible candidates, one must wonder how it's even possible for an employer to log into Facebook assuming, of course that they are out of college. In fact it is quite simple because anyone with an ".edu" address can obtain access to Facebook (Skowronski). As alumni, employers would have full access to their job candidates' profiles if the applicants attend the same college in which the employer graduated. However this only works if the student hasn't already configured their privacy settings to block alumni from viewing their profile (Balakrishna). In addition, even if the employer is not an alumnus of the particular university, there have been cases where they have had co-workers or other interns who were alumni use their Facebook accounts to research potential candidates (Moore).

There was an instance at Indiana University where an employer accessed Facebook, and in doing so revealed inappropriate content on an employee's profile. According to Rachel Kearney, director of Career Services and Alumni Affairs at Indiana University, she has witnessed "first-hand," an employer using Facebook. She recalled a time when an employer she had been working with gained access to Facebook through one of the already hired interns. Upon finding inappropriate pictures of another recently hired intern, the employer demanded that the student's internship status be removed from the Facebook profile so people wouldn't associate the pictures with the integrity of the company (Maternowski). Another account comes from Matt Supple, Assistant Director of the Office of Fraternity and Sorority Life at the University of Maryland, who says that he has had contact with alumni whose businesses have used Facebook to review possible candidates, and in some of these reviews people lost the opportunity to be hired (Skowronski).

Although students have missed out on job opportunities due to their carelessness concerning the content they put on their Facebook profile, there are many professionals with valid opinions to help guide them in the right direction. Ken Vance, director of Public Safety at Georgia College & State University in Milledgeville, Ga., says that social networks are good for students, but they need to think about the "long-term" effects of the information they display online (Cole). Luther's Assistant Dean of Student Life, Bob Felde says he doesn't want students to have a false sense that Facebook profiles are private. He also says that students should be aware that employers may be able to see what they have on their profile (Countryman). In accordance, the Division of Student Affairs at Florida University say, "If you wouldn't speak that way in an interview, don't put it on Facebook" (Division).

The problem college students are having with Facebook is that they are being careless concerning the content they put on their profiles. Students must be cautious dealing with the content they put onto their profiles in order to protect themselves from stalkers and harassment, law violations and missed opportunities for future employment. Even though many college students have not used caution when adding material onto their profiles, they can become more responsible by using the tips provided to compensate for their lack of judgment. However, in the long-run college students need to learn that the Internet is not as private as they think. They need to understand that if they don't want certain people to know personal information, they should keep it to themselves. If university students are going to continue taking part in the Facebook phenomenon, it is important for them to learn to keep private information away from the sight of others because it can lead to severe consequences. Now if you'll excuse me, I have to update my profile.

Works Cited

Arrington, Michael. "85% of College Students use Facebook." [2005]. *Techcrunch.* 15 Apr. 2006. http://www.techcrunch.com/2005/09/07/85-of-college-students-use-facebook.

Atilano, Elizabeth. "The Double Life of Facebook." [2006]. *Loyola Marymount University.* 15 Apr. 2006. http://www.lmu.edu/Page18970.aspx.

Balakrishna, Kanya. "Facebook Becomes Tool For Employers." 21 Feb. 2006. *Yale Daily News.* 17 Apr. 2006. http://www.yaledailynews.com/article.asp?AID=31948.

Bobkoff, Dan. "In the Age of Facebook, Students Have Few Secrets." 15 Apr. 2006. *The Wesleyan Argus.* 17 Apr. 2006. http://www.wesleyanargus.com/article.php?article_id=1098.

Buckman, Rebecca. "Colleges: 'Facebook' Site May Pose Security Risks." 8 Dec. 2005. *Post-Gazette.com.* 14 Apr. 2006. http://www.post-gazette.com/pg/05342/619281.stm.

Chalfant, Drew. "Facebook Postings, Photos Incriminate Dorm Party-goers." 2 Nov. 2005. *Northern Kentucky University.* 16 Apr. 2006. http://www.thenortherner.com/media/paper527/news/2005/11/02/News/Facebook.Postings.Photos.Incriminate.Dorm.PartyGoers-1042037.shtml.

Cole, Eddie R. Jr. "The Other Face of Facebook." 27 Feb. 2006. The Tennessee State Meter. 14 Apr. 2006. http://www.tsumeter.com/vnews/display.v/ART/2006/02/27/4403a2ae0e5aa.

Countryman, Genny. "Stalkers, Employers find a Friend in Facebook." 1 Dec. 2005. *Luther College Chips.* 17 Apr. 2006. http://chips.luther.edu/modules/news/article.php?storyid=4319.

Division of Student Affairs. "Some Thoughts You Should Consider." n.d. *Florida University.* 14 Apr. 2006. http://www.uf-bocc.org/pdfs/FacebookSuggestions.pdf.

Fuller, Andrea. "Employers Snoop on Facebook." 20 Jan. 2006. *The Stanford Daily.* 16 Apr. 2006. http://daily.stanford.edu/tempo?page=content&id=19024&repository=0001_article.

Jones, Harvey and Jose Hiram Soltren. "Facebook: Threats to Privacy." 14 Dec. 2005. 14 Apr. 2006. http://72.14.203.104/search?q=cache:zpASXlBbm0AJ:www.swiss.ai.mit.edu/6805/student-papers/fall05-papers/facebook.pdf+facebook+%2B+%22page+1%22+%2B+%22page+2%22+%2B+statistics&hl=en&gl=us&ct=clnk&cd=39.

Maternowski, Kate. "Campus Police use Facebook." 25 Jan. 2006. *The Badger Herald*. 17 Apr. 2006. http://badgerherald.com/news/2006/01/25/campus_police_use_fa.php.

Maternowski, Kate. "Employers Scrutinize Facebook Profiles." 6 Feb. 2006. *Louisville Cardinal Online*. 14 Apr. 2006. http://www.louisvillecardinal.com/vnews/display.v/ART/2006/02/06/43e7f758e7f88.

Michalos, Sarah. "Officers Train to use Facebook as Tool." [c. 2005]. *The Exponent Online*. 17 Apr. 2006. http://www.purdueexponent.org/index.php/module/Issue/action/Article/article_id/2916.

Moore, Rick. "When Facebook Becomes Too Revealing." 7 Apr. 2006. *University of Minnesota News*. 16 Apr. 2006. http://www1.umn.edu/umnnews/Feature_Stories/When_Facebook_becomes_too_revealing.html.

Mora, Antonio. "Be Careful What's In Your Facebook." 3 Oct. 2005. *cbs2chicago.com*. 15 Apr. 2006. http://cbs2chicago.com/seenon/local_story_276213838.html.

Rosenbush, Steve. "Facebook's on the Block." 26 Mar. 2006. *BusinessWeek Online*. 13 Apr. 2006. http://www.businessweek.com/technology/content/mar2006/tc20060327_215976.htm.

Schwartz, Jason. "Racy Photo Lands Student in Trouble." 30 Nov. 2005. *The Daily Pennsylvanian*. 15 Apr. 2006. http://www.dailypennsylvanian.com/vnews/display.v/ART/438d5a725d606.

Schweitzer, Sarah. "Fisher College Expels Student Over Website Entries." 6 Oct. 2005. *Boston.com*. 16 Apr. 2006. http://www.boston.com/news/local/articles/2005/10/06/fisher_college_expels_student_over_website_entries.

Skowronski, Will. "University Police Incorporate Facebook to Crime-solve." 3 Feb. 2006. *Diamondbackonline.com*. 16 Apr. 2006. http://www.diamondbackonline.com/vnews/display.v/ART/2006/02/03/43e2edcc23b85.

Werlein, Matthew. "Police, Employers using Facebook." 27 Feb. 2006. *The Spectator*. 15 Apr. 2006. http://www.spectatornews.com/media/storage/paper218/news/2006/02/27/CampusNews/Police.Employers.Using.Facebook-1638325.shtml?norewrite200604191946&sourcedomain=www.spectatornews.com.

WHOA. "Online Harassment Statistics." [2005]. *Working to Halt Online Abuse*. 14 Apr. 2006. http://www.haltabuse.org/resources/stats/age.shtml.

Wikipedia Contributors. "Facebook." Wikipedia, The Free Encyclopedia. [2006]. 14 Apr. 2006, http://en.wikipedia.org/w/index.php?title=Facebook&oldid=49132476.

2006

CRITICAL THINKING POINTS: *After you've read*

1. Meyers says, "College students' carelessness when adding content to their Facebook profile has led to personal safety problems, trouble with the law, and missed opportunities for employment." Has Facebook caused any other types of problems?

2. A student affairs professional at Florida University says, "If you wouldn't speak that way in an interview, don't put it on Facebook." Do you believe this is a good guideline for students who use Facebook? Why or why not?

3. Meyers did a great deal of research for his paper. What other kinds of research might he have done? How would that have improved this paper?

SOME POSSIBILITIES FOR WRITING

1. Write a defense of Facebook. What are its strengths and advantages for college users?

2. What has changed about Facebook and social network sites since 2006? Update Meyers' research.

3. What do you think are some of the social implications of the increase in number of sites like Facebook? What opportunities and dangers do they provide?

What It's Really Like

Frank Smoot

In addition to poems and short stories, Frank Smoot has published some two hundred articles, including editorials, essays, features, interviews, and critiques of art, dance, film, literature, and music. He is currently Director of Publications and Marketing for the Chippewa Valley Museum.

you think it's too bad you'll never know each other

CRITICAL THINKING POINTS: *As you read*

1. What do you make of the title? Does this poem portray "what it's really like"? Why or why not?
2. What kind of people are the characters in this poem? List some adjectives that describe them.
3. Keep track of all the things that the narrator can and cannot know in this poem.

It would be comforting to know something
about her that would annoy you: she laughs
like a hyena or likes a kind of music that you hate.
But the truth is that she's nice and so are you,
and as you drive away from the small light
of the restaurant on the highway in another state
you think it's too bad you'll never know each other,
and you look at yourself in the rearview mirror,
your face lighted dimly by the dashboard,
and smile because she smiled at you.
You kick it out a little, thumbs tapping
to the sweet song on the radio, to which,
you have no way of knowing,
she's dancing as she closes up.

1995

148

CRITICAL THINKING POINTS: *After you've read*

1. Why is this brief moment significant enough to write about? Is it important to anyone but the characters? Why or why not?
2. Would the woman in the poem most likely be interested in the speaker? Why or why not?
3. Should the speaker of the poem have said something to the woman? Why or why not?

SOME POSSIBILITIES FOR WRITING

1. Write the next scene for one or both of the characters in the poem. Where do they go after this? Who do they talk to? What do they do?
2. Visit some gathering place for college students—a student lounge, a commons area, or a cafeteria—and write a "history" for some of the couples you see around you but know nothing about.
3. Write your own imitation of this poem: maybe "What It's Never Like," or "What It Could Have Been Like."

No More Kissing—AIDS Everywhere

Michael Blumenthal

Michael Blumenthal is the author of seven volumes of poems—most recently, *And* (2009). In 2007, he spent a month in South Africa working with orphaned infant baboons and wrote about the experience for *Natural History* and *The Washington Post Magazine*. He currently holds the Copenhaver Visiting Chair of Law at West Virginia University College of Law.

"You must remember," / he said, "that every time you make love / you tamper with fate."

CRITICAL THINKING POINTS: *As you read*

1. What are some sexual images in the poem? List them as you read.
2. Traditionally, in love poems, images of love are linked with images of death. What are some images of love that have been paired with death in this poem?
3. What might be the "etymological roots" Blumenthal writes about?

He says it to the young couple
passionately kissing on the street
and, when he does, the four of us just stand there,
laughing, on this cold wintry day in Cambridge,
nineteen hundred and eighty-eight,
as if there could be no such danger
to a kiss, as if the metaphors of love and dying
had not been literalized.

Pausing a block later, my cheeks kissed
by the cold, my lips cracking
in the January air, I think back
to what a man once told me, long before
risk had so clinical a name,
so precise a passage. *"You must remember,"*
he said, *"that every time you make love*
you tamper with fate."

Now, the early wisdoms grow clear:
the serpents slither into the year,

the elegies are writing themselves
on desires' sheets, passion and suffering
are fusing their etymological roots
into a single trunk. *Yet why should they not embrace,*
these beautiful two? They are, after all, part
of the oldest story in the world—before God,
before microbes, before the sea had licked
the earth and the air clean with its long tongue.

1989

CRITICAL THINKING POINTS: *After you've read*

1. How is this poem a reflection of the time in which it was written?
2. What might be some of the things suggested by the "oldest story in the world" that the poet refers to?
3. In what ways have the "metaphors of love and dying" been "literalized"?

SOME POSSIBILITIES FOR WRITING

1. Do you believe "that every time you make love you tamper with fate"? In what ways is this statement true? What aspects of fate are tampered with? Write a one-page response supporting or contradicting this statement.
2. Write a response from the point of view of the young couple who are kissing. What might they say to the man who yells out his warning to them? To the advice given in the second stanza? To the poet at the end of the poem?
3. In what ways has the existence of AIDS shaped your attitudes and behaviors concerning sex?

Dear Concerned Mother

Jill Wolfson

Jill Wolfson is a journalist and an author of novels for youth. She continues to volunteer in a writing program for incarcerated teens. Read more about her at www.jillwolfson.com.

My writing students in juvenile hall—addicts, thieves, gang bangers—have great parenting advice. All you have to do is ask.

CRITICAL THINKING POINTS: *As you read*

1. What kinds of advice do the students give to their teacher about her son? Why do you think they offer what they do?
2. What do you think is the best and the worst advice they give? Why?
3. What kinds of things do you think this teacher is trying to teach to her class?

I t was a Friday evening, and my 15-year-old son and I were at each other's throats. Most of the time these days, he is what my Yiddish-speaking grandmother used to call "farbissen"—sharp and sulky. He can find fault with the sky just by looking up. Between us, nothing is not an issue: his room, his grades, his behavior around the house, his friends. I harangued him a little more, let him get in the last word and headed out the front door, fuming.

On Friday nights, I run a writing class at the local juvenile hall. Most weeks, I am unrelentingly earnest with the incarcerated boys. I sweep in with my papers and books, and commence acting like everybody's dotty but ultimately harmless aunt. I wax poetic about the healing powers of writing. I show them intriguing words in the dictionary as if I am pointing out jewels. I gush over their work, frequently some of the most funny, sad, troubling, surprising, insightful and silly bits of writing you can imagine. But when I was buzzed into the hall that night, I felt sapped. I had not one iota of patience left for mankind—especially mankind of the 15-year-old, wispy mustache, smart mouth, smelly feet variety.

"It's been a real full-moon day here," a weary-looking staffer said. Great, I thought, just what I need to cap off the week—a room full of moody, pissed off, sullen gang members, addicts and thieves. My class would be smaller than usual since many of the young men had had their evening privileges revoked and were locked down in their cells. Participation in my writing program is considered a privilege, though you wouldn't have known it by the response I got when I greeted the half-dozen writers-in-waiting.

"Oh no! I'm not gonna write. Why should I write?" said Josh, a handsome boy who likes to dabble in White Power philosophy.

A young man who calls himself J-Money greeted me in his usual taunting manner. "I'm gonna write about being down for my gang. I'm gonna write about bitches and pussy."

"I have nothing to write about!" complained a boy nicknamed Storm. Storm and I often joke about how I—as much as anyone in his life—have watched him grow up, from a scared and scrawny 14-year-old street kid to a broad and buff 17-year-old with a huge dagger tattooed on his forearm. Storm, who always claims to have nothing on his mind to write about, is scheduled to stand trial as an adult for a well-publicized murder.

Soft-spoken, pasty-faced Gabe is another boy I often worry about. That night, I noticed fresh white bandages wrapped around his wrists. In juvenile hall parlance, Gabe is what is referred to as a cutter. No matter how frequently and thoroughly the staff searches him and his cell, he always manages to squirrel away a razor, a staple, the point of a pen, anything capable of carving into his flesh. Gabe also happens to be a remarkable and prolific poet. But even he was now determined to put me through the wringer: "I'm not writing tonight. That's final."

Without comment, I passed out paper and pencil and announced the evening's topic: Fear.

"What is your definition of fear?" I asked. "What are you afraid of? How do you handle your fears?" I tried putting some oomph into my voice—"Be honest. Get real with your words"—but even to my own ears I sounded flat and uninspired.

They didn't even give the topic a halfhearted try. J-Money, the king of posturing, wrote, "I ain't afraid of nothin'." Storm dashed out one poorly spelled sentence, "I'm afraid of Ben Laden and Anthrix," before pushing his paper aside. For almost everyone else in the country, this would be a perfectly valid answer. But for Storm, I knew it was bullshit. He knew I knew it was bullshit. When you are 17 years old and looking at the probability of spending the next 25 years in San Quentin, even terrorism is a comfortable abstraction, a way of running from the truth. Normally, I would have attempted to move the boys, word by word, into examining their past, present and future. But I just couldn't muster the energy to steamroll over any more adolescent negativity. When I threw up my hands, it was not just at them, but at all teenage boys, especially the one who lived in my house.

"So don't write," I said. "Just sit here and give me a lot of crap. Waste your time."

I couldn't believe I was saying this. I knew I sounded vaguely hysterical. They stared, trying to figure out whether this was some new kind of motivational trick that I had up my sleeve. Josh finally decided that my funk was for real. "Whooo! Mama! What's the matter with you today?"

"Nothing," I said. This time, I was the one who was petulant, slumped in my chair like I didn't have any bones.

"Something's bugging you. Come on."

"Problems with my son," I pouted. "You're not interested."

But I could tell by the sudden buzz of alertness in the room that they were, in fact, extremely interested. I have always made it a point to leave my own moods at the thick metal door when it slams behind me. I figure that these kids have enough problems of their own—heroin addiction, incompetent public defenders, raging hormones, girlfriends who don't write, homeboys who have ratted them out, staff members who are always on their case—without having to endure mine.

But now, why not? So I laid it all out, the full banquet of bad grades and self-destructive attitudes. I even mentioned that I had found a pipe in my son's room the week before and it scared me.

"That's what my fear is," I confessed. "I'm angry at him a lot, but I'm also afraid for him, the choices he's making."

A boy named Bobby smirked the entire time and I felt like smacking him. "Uh-oh," he said, "The Writing Lady's son be smoking the weed, doing the doob, getting high. He's gonna be in here before long. Don't worry, Writing Lady, we'll take good care of him."

"Thanks a million, Bobby," I said sarcastically. But then, Josh jumped to my defense. "Shut up, Bobby, what the fuck you saying? Don't you see this is serious?"

And then, in imitation of every psychologist who had ever interviewed him for court, Josh leaned in and looked at me with earnest, intelligent eyes: "Just don't go nagging him. Nag, nag, nag. That's what's drove me crazy with my mom."

"So what I am supposed to do?"

"Back off him like my mom finally did me. He'll get it on his own."

I mulled this over. "I don't mean any disrespect, Josh. But you've got a serious drug problem and your life isn't exactly doing so hot. I'd rather he doesn't wind up in here while he's figuring things out for himself."

A half-dozen voices joined in with comments. I had never seen all of them so charged up at once before. It dawned on me then how I am the one always dishing out advice to them, not just about synonyms, but about how to deal with drugs, how to do better in school, how to make productive use of the endless hours they spend alone in their cells. The pattern is the same with all the adults in their lives, from parents to probation officers.

But how often are these young men—so often scolded and lectured, so often in the wrong—asked for their advice? How often do guys with names like Storm and J-Money get asked what they think, what they know about the world? How often do they get to give their expertise? And on the subject of troubled, uncommunicative teens, they are definitely the experts.

"Let's scrap writing about fear," I suggested. "Instead, let's pretend you are all advice columnists in the newspaper and I have written to you with my problem. What would you tell me?"

With little coaxing, they got to work. A half hour later, they read their columns aloud. I sat in my chair and let their answers wash over me. Their opinions, like a lot of their writing, reflected a desperate eagerness to be heard and to help. I felt their support and their solace. I could see their pasts, so much of what was right and so much of what was wrong. In their words, I also got some meaningful and some seriously twisted parenting advice.

A quiet 15-year-old named Omar spoke for the first time ever in class: "Dear Concerned Mother. You got to do something with him. I used to think nobody should tell me nothing. But now that I'm a dad myself, I tell my girlfriend we got to draw some lines with my son. My mom never drew lines and look at me. Don't listen to what Josh says. You should take things away from him. Lock him in his room. Ground him. Slap him across the back of the head if you have to."

At that, Gabe shouted "No!" I don't know the details of Gabe's family life. He never writes directly about it, but I once asked a staff person who replied, "Anything awful you can think of has been done to that boy by his parents."

"Whatever you do," he read from his paper, "don't, don't, don't hit him. That's child abuse. Hitting will only make a kid more frustrated and scared. That's a reason kids run away."

Others continued:

Dear Concerned Mother,

I feel that your son can't talk to you because of the way you react. You must be judging him. Lecture him but don't ever hit him. At the same time, tell him that it's his life and he has to do what he wants. If he makes the right choice, let him know. If he makes the wrong choice, ask him what he has learned from it. His choices will be a learning experience. If he has to learn the hard way, so be it!

Dear Concerned Mother,

Treat your son with respect. Buy him anything he wants. Don't yell at him. Don't hit him.

Dear Concerned Mother,

It's not your fault that your teenager is like that. He's going through a state where he thinks he's this person, but he's not—if you know what I mean. You could try to help but he'll just turn it down. He probably doesn't feel comfortable talking to you because he thinks you don't understand. Get to know him. Study the way he is and then get him to trust you.

Dear Concerned Mother,

He's going to try drugs. That's just the way it is. You could put him in sports to occupy his time. When I was playing football, I didn't have time for drugs. That was before I messed up and landed here.

Dear Concerned Mother,

Don't take him to a therapist. God forbid! He'll just sit there. It'll go in one ear and out the other.

Dear Concerned Mother,

Don't lock him in his room and duck tape the door shut like my step-mother used to do.

When it was Storm's turn, he began:

Dear Concerned Mother,

Your kid probably has a lot of stress right now. In elementary school, he only had one teacher and one class, right? Now he's got six classes and six teachers who are on him all the time. That's hard on a kid. Give him some space. You need to point out when he's doing something good—not just when he's messing up or only if he gets straight A's or wins the whole damn science fair.

And don't throw him against a wall and then throw him out of the house. That's what my dad did and how I wound up on the streets.

Oh yeah, and take him places. Take him miniature golfing. Have fun with him. You don't want your kid to learn from other people because he'll learn to steal and do things like that. You want him to get as much fun from YOU as he can. Tell him to dress punk and then say, "Guess what? We're going to a concert, you and me." I would have liked my mom to do something like that.

When Storm got to the end of his advice, he looked away sheepishly, caught with his tough-guy demeanor down. "But that's just my opinion," he added.

The writing workshop was over. They handed in their papers and left me with a lot to think about. Josh stayed behind for a few minutes.

"Good luck with your son," he said. "Did it help?"

"I think so. Yes, it definitely did."

"I got one more question for you. Does your son have a dad?"

I nodded yes and recalled what Josh had told me about his own father, how he "runs a prison." I knew Josh didn't mean that his dad is the warden. A longtime con, his father is the one who calls all the shots—from drug dealing to revenge killings—among the prisoners.

"Is he like a regular dad who does stuff with him? Baseball and shit like that?"

"Yes," I say.

"Well, you don't have to worry then." He patted me lightly on the shoulder, a wise old soul reassuring someone just getting her feet wet in the teenage parenting business. "Maybe he's doing some wild shit now. But hang in. Anyone who's got you and a dad around is going to be OK."

2001

CRITICAL THINKING POINTS: *After you've read*

1. Teachers often have lots of advice for their students. What if the tables were turned? What kinds of advice would you give to teachers if you could? Why would you advise them the way you would?
2. What would be some of the challenges and/or rewards of teaching a class like this?
3. What do you think the students might have learned from this class? What about the teacher? Why?

SOME POSSIBILITIES FOR WRITING

1. What might be some of the problems and/or advantages of being a child of a teacher? Why do you think the way you do?
2. Recall a time when teachers shared something personal in class, perhaps a problem they were having or a joy. How did the class react? Why do you think this was so?
3. The "Writing Lady" has some "fears" for her son. What are some of the fears your parents have had or still have for you? Do you feel these fears were justified? Why or why not?

The Undeclared Major

FROM *A GRAVESTONE MADE OF WHEAT*   Will Weaver

Will Weaver was born in northern Minnesota and grew up on a dairy farm. He is professor emeritus at Bemidji State University in Minnesota.

"Well," Walter said. His mouth went dry. He swallowed twice. "Well," he said, "I think I'm going to major in English."

His father pursed his lips. He pulled off his work gloves one finger at a time. "English," he said.

"English," Walter nodded.

His father squinted. "Son, you already know English."

CRITICAL THINKING POINTS: *As you read*

1. Why is it so difficult for Walter to tell his father about his intended major?
2. Pay attention to the description of the farm and its surroundings. Why might the author offer so many concrete details?
3. Why does it feel to Walter like he's the only "twenty-year-old Undeclared Major on the whole campus"?

I n his gloomy periods Walter Hansen saw himself as one large contradiction. He was still twenty, yet his reddish hair was in full retreat from the white plain of his forehead. He had small and quick-moving blue eyes, eyes that tended skyward, eyes that noted every airplane that passed overhead; his hands and feet were great, heavy shovels. As Walter shambled between his classes at the University of Minnesota in Minneapolis, he sometimes caught unexpected sight of himself in a tall glass doorway or window. He always stopped to stare: there he was, the big farm kid with a small handful of books. Walter Hansen, the only twenty-year-old Undeclared Major on the whole campus.

But even that wasn't true. Walter Hansen had declared a major some time ago; he just hadn't felt up to telling anyone what it was.

At present Walter sat in the last, backward-facing seat of the Greyhound bus, reading *The Collected Stories of John Cheever*. Occasionally he looked up to stare at the blue-tinted fields, which in their passing pulled him, mile by mile, toward home. Toward his twenty-first birthday this very weekend.

By the third hour of the trip Walter had a headache from reading. He put away Cheever and began to watch the passing farms. It was a sunny, wet April in central Minnesota. Farmers were trying to spread manure. Their tractors left black ruts in the yellow corn stubble, and once Walter saw two tractors chained together straining, the big rear wheels spinning, throwing clods in the air, as they tried to pull free a third spreader sunk its hubs beneath an overenthusiastic load of dung.

At the end of the fourth hour Walter's hometown came onto the horizon. It was low and scattered, and soon began to flash by in the windows of the slowing bus like a family slide show that was putting to sleep even the projector operator. A junkyard with a line of shining hubcaps nailed on the fence. A combination deer farm and aquarium with its stuffed black bear wearing a hula skirt, and wheels that stood by the front door. Then the tall and narrow white wooden houses. The square red brick buildings of Main Street, where the bus sighed to a stop at the Shell station. Ducking his head, Walter clambered down the bus steps and stood squinting in the sunlight.

Main Street was three blocks long. Its two-story buildings were fronted with painted tin awnings or cedar shake shingles to disguise the brick and make the buildings look lower and more modern. At the end of Main Street was the taller, dull gray tower of the feed mill. A yellow drift of cornmeal lay on its roof. A blue wheel of pigeons turned overhead. At the stoplight a '57 Chevy chirped its tires, accelerated rapidly for half a block, then braked sharply to turn down Main Street.

Which Walter planned to avoid. On Main Street he would have to speak to people. They would ask him things.

"Walt—so how's the rat race?"

"Walt—where does a person park down there?"

"So Walt, what was it you're going into again? Business? Engineering? Veterinary?"

Carrying his small suitcase, and looking neither left nor right, Walter slipped undetected across Main Street. He walked two blocks to the railroad crossing where he set out east.

The iron rails shone blue. Between the rails, tiny agates glinted red from their bed of gravel, and the flat, sun-warmed railroad ties exhaled a faint breath of creosote. On Walter's right, a robin dug for worms on the sunny south embankment; on the north side, the dirty remnant of a snowbank leaked water downhill. Walter stopped to poke at the snowbank with a stick. Beneath a black crust of mud and leaves, the snow was freshly white and sparkling—but destined, of course, to join the muddy pond water below. Walter thought about that. About destiny. He stood with the chill on his face from the old snowbank and the sun warm on his neck and back. There was a poem buried somewhere in the snowbank. Walter waited, but the first line would not visit him. He walked on.

Walter was soon out of town and into woods and fields. Arms outstretched, suitcase balanced atop his head, he walked one rail for twenty-two ties, certainly a record of some sort. Crows called. A red-headed woodpecker flopped from east to west across the rails. The bird was ridiculously heavy for the length of its wings, a fact which made Walter think of Natural Science, Biology, Veterinary Medicine and other majors with names as solid and normal as fork handles.

Animal Husbandry.

Technical Illustration.

Mechanical Engineering.

Ahead on Walter's left was a twenty-acre field of new oat seeding, brown in the low spots, dusty chartreuse on the higher crowns of the field.

Plant Science.

He could tell people he was developing new wheat strains for Third World countries, like Norman Borlaug.

He walked on, slower now, for around a slight bend he could see, a half mile ahead, the gray dome of his father's silo and the red shine of the dairy barn. He neared the corner post of the west field, where his father's land began. Half the field was gray, the other half was freshly black. He slowed further. A meadowlark called from the fence post. Walter stopped to pitch a rock at the bird.

Then he heard a tractor. From behind a broad swell in the field rose his father's blue cap, tan face, brown shirt, then the red snout of the Massey-Ferguson. The Massey pulled their green four-row corn planter. His father stood upright on the platform of the tractor. He stood that way to sight down the tractor's nose, to keep its front tired on the line scuffed in the dirt by the corn planter's marker on the previous round. Intermittently Walter's father swiveled his neck for a glance back at the planter. He looked, Walter knew, for the flap of a white rag tied around the main shaft; if the white flag waved, the main shaft turned, the planter plates revolved, pink kernels fell—Walter knew all that stuff.

He stopped walking. There were bushes along the fencerow, and he stooped to lower his profile, certain that his father hadn't seen him. First Walter wanted to go home, talk to his mother, have a cup of coffee. Two cups, maybe. A cinnamon roll. A bowl of big cherries in sauce, with cream. Maybe one more splash of coffee. Then. Then he'd come back to the field to speak with his father.

Nearing the field's end, his father trailed back his right arm, found the cord, which he pulled at the same moment as he turned hard to left. Brakes croaked. Tripped, the marker arms rose, the Massey came hard around with its front wheels reaching for their new track, the planter straightened behind, the right arm with its shining disk fell, and his father, back to Walter, headed downfield.

Except that brakes croaked again and the tractor came to a stop. His father turned to Walter and held up a hand.

Walter waved once. He looked briefly behind him to the rails that led back toward town, then crossed the ditch and swung his suitcase over the barbed wire.

His father shut off the tractor. "Hey Walt—" his father called.

Walter waved again.

His father waited by the corn planter. He smiled, his teeth white against the tan skin, the dust. Walter came up to him.

"Walt," his father said.

They stood there grinning at each other. They didn't shake hands. Growing up, Walter believed people shook hands only in the movies or on used-car lots. None of his relatives ever shook hands. Their greeting was to stand and grin at each other and raise their eyebrows up and down. At the university Walter and his friends shook hands coming and going, European style.

"How's it going?" Walter said, touching his boot to the corn planter.

"She's rolling," his father said. He squinted at Walter, looked down at his clean clothes. "What would you do for a stuck disk?" he asked.

"I'd take out the grease zerk and run a piece of wire in there. That failing, I'd take off the whole disk and soak it in a pan of diesel fuel overnight," Walter said.

Father and son grinned at each other.

His father took off his hat. His forehead was white, his hair coppery.

"So how's the rat race, son?"

"Not so bad," Walter said.

His father paused a moment. "Any . . . decisions yet?" his father said.

Walter swallowed. He looked off toward town. "About . . . a major, you mean?" Walter said.

His father waited.

"Well," Walter said. His mouth went dry. He swallowed twice. "Well," he said, "I think I'm going to major in English."

His father pursed his lips. He pulled off his work gloves one finger at a time. "English," he said.

"English," Walter nodded.

His father squinted. "Son, you already know English."

Walter stared. "Well, yessir, that's true. I mean, I'm going to study literature. Books. See how they're written. Maybe write one of my own some day."

His father rubbed his brown neck and stared downfield.

Two white sea gulls floated low over the fresh planting.

"So what do you think?" Walter said.

His father's forehead wrinkled and he turned back to Walter. "What could a person be, I mean with that kind of major? An English major," his father said, testing the phrase on his tongue and his lips.

"Be," Walter said. He fell silent. "Well I don't know, I could be a . . . writer. A teacher maybe, though I don't think I want to teach. At least not for a while. I could be . . ." Then Walter's mind went blank. As blank and empty as the fields around him.

His father was silent. The meadowlark called again.

"I would just be myself, I guess." Walter said.

His father stared a moment at Walter. "Yourself, only smarter," he added.

"Yessir," Walter said quickly, "that's it."

His father squinted downfield at the gulls, then back at Walter. "Nobody talked you into this?"

Walter shook his head no.

"You like it when you are doing it?" his father asked. He glanced across his own field, at what he had planted.

Walter nodded.

His father looked back to Walter and thought another moment. "You think you can make a living at it?"

"Somehow," Walter said.

His father shrugged. "Then I can't see any trouble with it myself," he said. He glanced away, across the field to the next closest set of barns and silos. "Your uncles, your grampa, they're another story, I suppose."

"They wouldn't have to know," Walter said quickly.

His father looked back to Walter and narrowed his eyes. "They ask me, I'll tell them," he said.

Walter smiled at his father. He started to take a step closer, but at that moment his father looked up at the sun. "We better keep rolling here," he said. He tossed his gloves to Walter. "Take her around once or twice while I eat my sandwich."

Walter climbed onto the tractor and brought up the RPMs. In another minute he was headed downfield. He stood upright on the platform and held tightly to the wheel. The leather gloves were still warm and damp from his father's hands. He sighted the Massey's radiator cap on the thin line on the dirt ahead, and held it there. Halfway downfield he remembered to check the planter flag; in one backward glance he saw his father in straight brown silhouette against the chartreuse band of the fencerow bushes, saw the stripe of fresh dirt unrolling behind, the green seed canisters, and below, the white flag waving. He let out a breath.

After two rounds, Walter began to relax. He began to feel the warm thermals from the engine, the cool breath of the earth below. Gulls hovered close over the tractor, their heads cocked earthward as they waited for the disks to turn up yellow cutworms. A red agate passed underneath and was covered by dirt. The corn planter rolled behind, and through the trip rope, a cotton cord gone smoothly black from grease and dusty kernels dropping, the press wheel tamping the seed into four perfect rows.

Well, not entirely perfect rows.

Walter, by round four, had begun to think of other things. That whiteness beneath the old snowbank. The blue shine of the iron rails. The damp warmth of father's gloves. The heavy, chocolate-layer birthday cake that he knew, as certain as he knew the sun would set tonight and rise tomorrow, his mother had hidden in the pantry. Of being twenty-one and the limitless destiny, the endless prospects before him, Walter Hansen, English Major.

As he thought about these and other things, the tractor and its planter drifted a foot to the right, then a foot to the left, centered itself, then drifted again. At field's end his father stood up. He began to wave at Walter first with one hand, then both. But Walter drove on, downfield, smiling slightly to himself, puzzling over why it was he so seldom came home.

1989

CRITICAL THINKING POINTS: *After you've read*

1. What are some of the advantages and disadvantages of being undeclared?
2. Why do you think it takes the author so long to get Walter home? What are some of the things the author hopes to accomplish?
3. Walter is part of the group of students that universities label "first-generation," that is, his parents did not attend college. What risks or difficulties might first-generation students face that others may not?

SOME POSSIBILITIES FOR WRITING

1. Research and present a report to your class on majors. What are the most and least popular? Why do you think this is? What percentage of first-year students are undeclared? How often do students change majors? Why?
2. Have you and your parents ever disagreed on an important decision affecting your life? How and why was it resolved the way it was?
3. Prepare a report on what kinds of services and aid are available to students who are the first in their families to go to college.

STUDENT RESPONSE TO "THE UNDECLARED MAJOR"

I never realized until just now that I didn't really have an identity in my freshman year. I felt like such an outsider and so I never formed into anything. Like the narrator, I too was a first generation college student, and felt that this distanced me even further from everyone. I didn't know that there were so many first generation students. I still find it hard to believe and would like to know where they are all hiding because everyone I know has had parents and even grandparents who graduated from a university! The fact that I was the first to pursue a higher education put much more pressure on me to succeed. I also came from a family of dairy farmers, and I lived on a farm as well. I was ashamed because I feel that farmers are looked down upon by society, whether it is that they aren't intelligent or that they're gross or poor, etc. I basically just hid my identity and that just made it even harder to make friends and feel at home.

It wasn't until my second year that I started to "let go" and tried to find myself. I found some true friends, but I still was having trouble with who I was. After a semester suspended from school, this year I'm doing much better with everything—academically and socially. I'm getting involved, but not too much, and I am getting to know the campus and the area much better as well. I feel that I have a strong grasp of my identity; of course, I know it will always be changing. School has become my "home away from home," and oh how I love that phrase! I've realized many things at college, but one thing that the passage really relates as well is that it's not necessarily where you are, or what the circumstances are, it's who YOU are, and what you are willing to do to overcome obstacles and better yourself.

Homeward Bond

Daisy Nguyen

Daisy Nguyen (b. 1976) was born in Di Linh, Vietnam. She graduated from the University of California at Davis with majors in sociology and French.

This is a new reality, one I did not expect to face when I came "home-home." Still, I call this place home because my family treats me as one of them when I am there. They share their world with me, even when they are sometimes harsh realities. It is something I am not exposed to behind the safe confines of the university.

CRITICAL THINKING POINTS: *As you read*

1. The author uses two home clichés: "Home is where the heart is" and "A house is not a home without love." What are some other sayings or clichés about home?
2. Think of your own definition of "home." What are some details that you associate with "home"?
3. In what ways do the author's home life and university life differ? Make a list.

F or as long as I can recall, perhaps since the day I moved to college, I have had trouble defining the word "home." It is one of those vague terms that lead people to create metaphors or clichés of their own to define. You've heard it all before: "Home is where the heart is," or "A house is not a home without love."

Webster's Dictionary defines it as the region in which something is familiar or native. A friend of mine, when he chooses to visit his family on weekends, always says "I'm going home-home for the weekend." The place he stays at college is simply called "home."

Almost every weekend now, since I have returned to Northern California from a one-year hiatus in France, I go "home-home." After a week of study at school, I go back to visit my family and hang out with friends in San Francisco—basically doing a lot of catching up. Indeed, many things have changed since I've been away and I'm often struck by the oddities that should be familiar to me.

One Saturday, for example, I went over to my cousin May's house to help put together some cards. She rolled to the door, opened it and greeted me. "Daisy! Hurry up and come in here. I've been waiting all week to show you these cards!"

I am now getting used to seeing her look up at me when she opens the door. It didn't use to be that way. May and I used to ride our bikes around Golden Gate Park on Sundays when we were little girls, and as teeny boppers we sashayed through downtown's hippest streets in our best skirts.

Now she stays home more often and she is putting together a small business: selling homemade greeting cards. They include beautiful photos that her father has taken throughout his extensive travels around Asia and North America. We sat in the kitchen pasting photos onto countless cards, while gossiping about family affairs. May also told me her future plans and outlook on life, now that she is in a wheelchair.

This is a new reality, one I did not expect to face when I came "home-home." Still, I call this place home because my family treats me as one of them when I am there. They share their world with me, even when they are sometimes harsh realities. It is something I am not exposed to behind the safe confines of the university.

At home-home, they don't demand me to analyze every problem nor do they demand brilliant response to every question. At home-home, mom just asks me how I have spent my week and how I like her soup. At home-home, I just sit around and listen to the radio with May, recounting stories of our adventures in life and love.

Sometimes, May's mom passes by, in her loud voice, and asks "Is the show on yet?"

"It's time! It's time! Jelly Spring-uh is on! Come and see!"

"Jelly Spring-uh?" I asked myself. "How can she like that awful show?" Here is a woman who has lived in the United States for almost 20 years, who does not understand much English, yet she enjoys the Jerry Springer show. Guess I can't comprehend it all, not everything is familiar to me at home-home.

Andric, the son of my oldest cousin, is the most observant little two-year-old I have ever seen. When May and I sat by the radio chatting, he ran around the kitchen chasing a beach ball and giggling to himself. Occasionally, he came to us and looked inquisitively, wondering what we were doing. When he wanted an apple, he would lift his tiny hand and make a fist, then put it to his cheek, making a sign for "apple." May gave him the apple and lifted him up to her lap. Celine Dion's hit from the "Titanic" soundtrack, "My Heart Will Go On," played on the radio, once again.

"I love this song!" May squealed. We listened to the haunting melodies and May hugged Andric. "I love music," she sighed. "I don't think I can live without it in my life, and when I think about how Andric can't hear music, it makes me love him so much more."

I looked into his smiling eyes and understood even more the reason the whole family adores him, and will do everything to protect him. His big round eyes, with long feathery eyelashes, are so bright you can clearly see life happening inside of him. It was a moment so heartbreaking and so inexplicable, even I couldn't describe it in words.

Now on Sundays, many members of my family go to the Buddhist temple to meditate and pray. There's a nice temple on Van Ness Avenue that my grandma and aunts frequent, so does May and Andric. One rainy morning, I hopped into my aunt's van and tagged along with her and my grandma to the temple.

On the way, grandma told me her worries for everyone in the family and asked about my life. We were driving up Van Ness, a very congested street even on Sunday mornings, when the van stopped at a red light. We waited a moment and my grandma saw a homeless man in crutches standing at the island, asking for money. She quickly grabbed a dollar from her purse and told my aunt, at the drivers' seat, to give the money to him. I looked at the light about to change, the huge distance between the van and the island, and the helpless man who couldn't reach to grab the dollar bill. "No, no, Grandma!" I panicked. "You can't do that! He can't reach for it and we must go."

The light turned green long ago, and cars behind us were honking incessantly. My aunt also panicked and she tossed the bill out the window, hoping he'd catch it. The van sped off. I turned around, and saw through the back window the dollar bill flying away, disappearing in the sea of cars.

To my grandma's dismay, all she could say was "Ay-yah, in America it is even hard to give bums some money when you want to." I knew right then her remark couldn't have been more profound nor appropriate.

When we arrived at the temple, my grandma's face brightened as she saw the crowd sitting there peacefully, chanting ancient songs. Most of all, her daughters, grandchildren and great grandchild, Andric, were there too.

We sat down, I crossed my legs and positioned myself for the upcoming meditation exercise. One of the monks came by, gave me a book and turned to the page where I followed the songs. Of course, I hardly understood the characters on the page, and mimicked to my grandma's singing instead.

After a while, the singing stopped and we sat in a long moment of silence. I was told that during meditation, you're supposed to not think about anything at all. How radical of an idea! It was so strange to me, but I didn't mind. While everyone else were attempting to put this theory into practice, I was happy to listen to the rain drops on the roof and think about how wonderful it was to sit in a room with my family in complete silence.

1998

CRITICAL THINKING POINTS: *After you've read*

1. In what ways is a university life, as the author calls it, "a safe confine"? In what ways is going home often a "safe confine"?

2. Consider the following statement: "Knowledge without compassion is dangerous." How is this statement reflected in the story?

3. What might Nguyen mean when she says, "I'm often struck by the oddities that should be familiar to me"? What are some of these?

SOME POSSIBILITIES FOR WRITING

1. Recall a recent trip home from college. What made you feel most welcomed and at ease, and what made you feel like an outsider?

2. Even if you feel that college has not changed you, imagine ways in which it might. Write a scene that shows rather than tells some of those changes.

3. Compare and contrast this author's experience with that of Walter in "The Undeclared Major." How do the two students balance home differently?

Everyday Use

FROM *IN LOVE AND TROUBLE: STORIES OF BLACK WOMEN*   Alice Walker

Author and poet Alice Walker was the eighth child of Georgia sharecroppers. After a childhood accident blinded her in one eye, she went on to become valedictorian of her local school. She went on to attend Spelman College and Sarah Lawrence College on scholarships. Her first book of poetry was published while she was still a senior at Sarah Lawrence. Walker's writing has won numerous honors, including the National Book Award. In 1983, her acclaimed novel *The Color Purple* won both the National Book Award and the Pulitzer Prize for fiction.

I didn't want to bring up how I had offered Dee (Wangero) a quilt when she went away to college. Then she had told me they were old-fashioned, out of style. "But they're priceless!" she was saying now, furiously; for she has a temper. "Maggie would put them on the bed and in five years they'd be in rags. Less than that!"

CRITICAL THINKING POINTS: *As you read*

1. What kinds of people are each of the characters in this story? What in the story do you base that opinion on?
2. Why do you think the characters act as they do?
3. Every few pages, take a moment to stop and imagine what might happen next.

for your grandmama

I will wait for her in the yard that Maggie and I made so clean and wavy yesterday afternoon. A yard like this is more comfortable than most people know. It is not just a yard. It is like an extended living room. When the hard clay is swept clean as a floor and the fine sand around the edges lined with tiny, irregular grooves, anyone can come and sit and look up into the elm tree and wait for the breezes that never come inside the house.

Maggie will be nervous until after her sister goes: she will stand hopelessly in corners, homely and ashamed of the burn scars down her arms and legs, eying her sister with a mixture of envy and awe. She thinks her sister has held life always in the palm of one hand, that "no" is a word the world never learned to say to her.

You've no doubt seen those TV shows where the child who has "made it" is confronted, as a surprise, by her own mother and father, tottering in weakly from backstage. (A pleasant surprise, of course: What would they do if parent and child came on the show only to curse out and insult each other?) On TV mother and child embrace and smile into each other's faces. Sometimes the mother and father weep, the child wraps them in her arms and leans across the table to tell how she would not have made it without their help. I have seen these programs.

Sometimes I dream a dream in which Dee and I are suddenly brought together on a TV program of this sort. Out of a dark and soft-seated limousine I am ushered into a bright room filled with many people. There I meet a smiling, gray, sporty man like Johnny Carson who shakes my hand and tells me what a fine girl I have. Then we are on the stage and Dee is embracing me with tears in her eyes. She pins on my dress a large orchid, even though she has told me once that she thinks orchids are tacky flowers.

In real life I am a large, big-boned woman with rough, man-working hands. In the winter I wear flannel nightgowns to bed and overalls during the day. I can kill and clean a hog as mercilessly as a man. My fat keeps me hot in zero degree weather. I can work outside all day, breaking ice to get water for washing; I can eat pork liver cooked over the open fire minutes after it comes steaming from the hog. One winter I knocked a bull calf straight in the brain between the eyes with a sledge hammer and had the meat hung up to chill before nightfall. But of course all this does not show on television. I am the way my daughter would want me to be: a hundred pounds lighter, my skin like an uncooked barley pancake. My hair glistens in the hot bright lights. Johnny Carson has much to do to keep up with my quick and witty tongue.

But that is a mistake. I know even before I wake up. Who ever knew a Johnson with a quick tongue? Who can even imagine me looking a strange white man in the eye? It seems to me I have talked to them always with one foot raised in flight, with my head turned in whichever way is farthest from them. Dee, though. She would always look anyone in the eye. Hesitation was no part of her nature.

"How do I look, Mama?" Maggie says, showing just enough of her thin body enveloped in pink skirt and red blouse for me to know she's there, almost hidden by the door.

"Come out into the yard," I say.

Have you ever seen a lame animal, perhaps a dog run over by some careless person rich enough to own a car, sidle up to someone who is ignorant enough to be kind to him? That is the way Maggie walks. She has been like this, chin on chest, eyes on ground, feet in shuffle, ever since the fire that burned the other house to the ground.

Dee is lighter than Maggie, with nicer hair and a fuller figure. She's a woman now, though sometimes I forget. How long ago was it that the other house burned? Ten, twelve years? Sometimes I can still hear the flames and feel Maggie's arms sticking to me, her hair smoking and her dress falling off her in little black papery flakes. Her eyes seemed stretched open, blazes open by the flames reflected in them. And Dee. I see her standing off under the sweet gum tree she used to dig gum out of; a look of concentration on her face as she watched the last dingy gray board of the house fall in toward the red-hot brick chimney. Why don't you do a dance around the ashes? I'd wanted to ask her. She had hated the house that much.

I used to think she hated Maggie, too. But that was before we raised the money, the church and me, to send her to Augusta to school. She used to read to us without pity; forcing words, lies, other folks' habits, whole lives upon us two, sitting trapped and ignorant underneath her voice. She washed us in a river of make-believe, burned us with a lot of knowledge we didn't necessarily need to know. Pressed us to her with the serious way she read, to shove us away at just the moment, like dimwits, we seemed about to understand.

Dee wanted nice things. A yellow organdy dress to wear to her graduation from high school; black pumps to match a green suit she'd made from an old suit somebody gave me. She was determined to stare down any disaster in her efforts. Her eyelids would not flicker for minutes at a time. Often I fought off the temptation to shake her. At sixteen she had a style of her own: and knew what style was.

I never had an education myself. After second grade the school was closed down. Don't ask me why: in 1927 colored asked fewer questions than they do now. Sometimes Maggie reads to me. She stumbles along good-naturedly but can't see well. She knows she is not bright. Like good looks and money, quickness passed her by. She will marry John Thomas (who has mossy teeth in an earnest face) and then I'll be free to sit here and I guess just sing church songs to myself. Although I never was a good singer. Never could carry a tune. I was always better at a man's job. I used to love to milk till I was hooked in the side in '49. Cows are soothing and slow and don't bother you unless you try to milk them the wrong way.

I have deliberately turned my back on the house. It is three rooms, just like the one that burned, except the roof is tin; they don't make shingle roofs any more. There are no real windows, just some holes cut in the sides, like the portholes in a ship, but not round and not square, with rawhide holding the shutters up on the outside. This house is in a pasture, too, like the other one. No doubt when Dee sees it she will want to tear it down. She wrote me once that no matter where we "choose" to live, she will manage to come see us. But she will never bring her friends. Maggie and I thought about this and Maggie asked me, "Mama, when did Dee ever have any friends?"

She had a few. Furtive boys in pink shirts hanging about on washday after school. Nervous girls who never laughed. Impressed with her they worshiped the well-turned phrase, the cute shape, the scalding humor that erupted like bubbles in lye. She read to them.

When she was courting Jimmy T she didn't have much time to pay to us, but turned all her faultfinding power on him. He flew to marry a cheap city girl from a family of ignorant flashy people. She hardly had time to recompose herself.

When she comes I will meet—but there they are!

Maggie attempts to make a dash for the house, in her shuffling way, but I stay her with my hand. "Come back here," I say. And she stops and tries to dig a well in the sand with her toe.

It is hard to see them clearly through the strong sun. But even the first glimpse of leg out of the car tells me it is Dee. Her feet were always neat-looking, as if God himself had shaped them with a certain style. From the other side of the car comes a short, stocky man. Hair is all over his head a foot long and hanging from his chin like a kinky mule tail. I hear Maggie suck in her breath. "Uhnnnh," is what it sounds like. Like when you see the wriggling end of a snake just in front of your foot on the road. "Uhnnnh."

Dee next. A dress down to the ground, in this hot weather. A dress so loud that it hurts my eyes. There are yellows and oranges enough to throw back the light of the sun. I feel my whole face warming from the heat waves it throws out. Earrings gold, too, and hanging down to her shoulders. Bracelets dangling and making noises when she moves her arm up to shake the folds of the dress out of her armpits. The dress is loose and flows, and as she walks closer, I like it. I hear Maggie go, "Uhnnnh" again. It is her sister's hair. It stands straight up like the wool on a sheep. It is black as night and around the edges are two long pigtails that rope about like small lizards disappearing behind her ears.

"Wa-su-zo-Tean-o!" she says, coming on in that gliding way the dress makes her move. The short stocky fellow with the hair to his navel is all grinning and he follows up with "Asalamalakim, my mother and sister!" He moves to hug Maggie but she falls back, right up against the back of my chair. I feel her trembling there and when I look up I see the perspiration falling off her chin.

"Don't get up," says Dee. Since I am stout it takes something of a push. You can see me trying to move a second or two before I make it. She turns, showing white heels through her sandals, and goes back to the car. Out she peeks next with a Polaroid. She stoops down quickly and lines up picture after picture of me sitting there in front of the house with Maggie cowering behind me. She never takes a shot without making sure the house is included. When a cow comes nibbling around the edge of the yard she snaps it and me and Maggie and the house. Then she puts the Polaroid in the back seat of the car, and comes up and kisses me on the forehead.

Meanwhile Asalamalakim is going through motions with Maggie's hand. Maggie's hand is as limp as a fish, and probably as cold, despite the sweat, and she keeps trying to shake hands but wants to do it fancy. Or maybe he don't know how people shake hands. Anyhow, he soon gives up on Maggie.

"Well," I say. "Dee."

"No, Mama," she says. "Not 'Dee,' Wangero Leewanika Kemanjo!"

"What happened to 'Dee'?" I wanted to know.

"She's dead," Wangero said. "I couldn't bear it any longer, being named after the people who oppress me."

"You know as well as me you was named after your aunt Dicie," I said. Dicie is my sister. She named Dee. We called her "Big Dee" after Dee was born.

"But who was she named after?" asked Wangero.

"Her mother," I said, and saw Wangero was getting tired. "That's about as far back as I can trace it," I said. Though, in fact, I probably could have carried it back beyond the Civil War through the branches.

"Well," said Asalamalakim, "there you are."

"Uhnnnd," I heard Maggie say.

"There I was not," I said, "before 'Dicie' cropped up in our family, so why should I try to trace it that far back?"

He just stood there grinning, looking down on me like somebody inspecting a Model A car. Every once in a while he and Wangero sent eye signals over my head.

"How do you pronounce this name?" I asked.

"You don't have to call me by it if you don't want to," said Wangero.

"Why shouldn't I?" I asked. "If that's what you want us to call you, we'll call you."

"I know it might sound awkward at first," said Wangero.

"I'll get used to it," I said. "Ream it out again."

Well, soon we got the name out of the way. Asalamalakim had a name twice as long and three times as hard. After I tripped over it two or three times he told me to just call him Hakim-a-barber. I wanted to ask him was he a barber, but I didn't really think he was, so I didn't ask.

"You must belong to those beef-cattle peoples down the road," I said. They said "Asalamalakim" when they met you, too, but they didn't shake hands. Always too busy: feeding cattle, fixing the fences, putting up salt-lick shelters, throwing down hay. When the white folks poisoned some of the herd the men stayed up all night with rifles in their hands. I walked a mile and a half just to see the sight.

Hakin-a-barber said, "I accept some of their doctrines, but farming and raising cattle is not my style." (They didn't tell me, and I didn't ask, whether Wangero [Dee] had really gone and married him.)

We sat down to eat and right away he said he didn't eat collards and pork was unclean. Wangero, though, went on through the chitlins and corn bread, the greens and everything else. She talked a blue streak over the sweet potatoes. Everything delighted her. Even the fact that we still used the benches her daddy made for the table when we couldn't afford to buy chairs.

"Oh, Mama!" she cried. Then turned to Hakim-a-barber. "I never knew how lovely these benches are. You can feel the rump prints," she said, running her hands underneath her and along the bench. Then she gave a sigh and her hand closed over Grandma Dee's butter dish. "That's it!" she said. "I knew there was something I wanted to ask you if I could have." She jumped up from the table and went over in the corner where the churn stood, the milk in it clabber by now. She looked at the churn and looked at it.

"This churn top is what I need," she said. "Didn't Uncle Buddy whittle it out of a tree you all used to have?"

"Yes," I said.

"Uh huh," she said happily. "And I want the dasher, too."

"Uncle Buddy whittle that, too?" asked the barber.

Dee (Wangero) looked up at me.

"Aunt Dee's first husband whittled the dash," said Maggie so low you almost couldn't hear her. "His name was Henry, but they called him Stash."

"Maggie's brain is like an elephant's," Wangero said, laughing. "I can use the churn top as a centerpiece for the alcove table," she said, sliding a plate over the churn, "and I'll think of something artistic to do with the dasher."

When she finished wrapping the dasher the handle stuck out. I took it for a moment in my hands. You didn't even have to look close to see where hands pushing the dasher up and down to make butter had left a kind of sink in the wood. In fact, there were a lot of small sinks; you could see where thumbs and fingers had sunk into the wood. It was beautiful light yellow wood, from a tree that grew in the yard where Big Dee and Stash had lived.

After dinner Dee (Wangero) went to the trunk at the foot of my bed and started rifling through it. Maggie hung back in the kitchen over the dishpan. Out came Wangero with two quilts. They had been pieced by Grandma Dee and then Big Dee and me had hung them on the quilt frames on the front porch and quilted them. One was in the Lone Star pattern. The other was Walk Around the Mountain. In both of them were scraps of dresses Grandma Dee had worn fifty or more years ago. Bits and pieces of Grandpa Jarrell's Paisley shirts. And one teeny faded blue piece, about the size of a penny matchbox, that was from Great Grandpa Ezra's uniform that he wore in the Civil War.

"Mama," Wangero said sweet as a bird. "Can I have these old quilts?"

I heard something fall in the kitchen, and a minute later the kitchen door slammed.

"Why don't you take one or two of the others?" I asked. "These old things was just done by me and Big Dee from some tops your grandma pieced before she died."

"No," said Wangero. "I don't want those. They are stitched around the borders by machine."

"That'll make them last better," I said.

"That's not the point," said Wangero. "These are all pieces of dresses Grandma used to wear. She did all this stitching by hand. Imagine!" She held the quilts securely in her arms, stroking them.

"Some of the pieces, like those lavender ones, come from old clothes her mother handed down to her," I said, moving up to touch the quilts. Dee (Wangero) moved back just enough so that I couldn't reach the quilts. They already belonged to her.

"Imagine!" she breathed again, clutching them closely to her bosom.

"The truth is," I said, "I promised to give them quilts to Maggie, for when she marries John Thomas."

She gasped like a bee had stung her.

"Maggie can't appreciate these quilts!" she said. "She'd probably be backward enough to put them to everyday use."

"I reckon she would," I said. "God knows I been saving 'em for long enough with nobody using 'em. I hope she will!" I didn't want to bring up how I had offered Dee (Wangero) a quilt when she went away to college. Then she had told me they were old-fashioned, out of style.

"But they're priceless!" she was saying now, furiously; for she has a temper. "Maggie would put them on the bed and in five years they'd be in rags. Less than that!"

"She can always make some more," I said. "Maggie knows how to quilt."

Dee (Wangero) looked at me with hatred. "You just will not understand. The point is these quilts, these quilts!"

"Well," I said, stumped. "What would you do with them?"

"Hang them," she said. As if that was the only thing you could do with quilts.

Maggie by now was standing in the door. I could almost hear the sound her feet made as they scraped over each other.

"She can have them, Mama," she said, like somebody used to never winning anything, or having anything reserved for her. "I can 'member Grandma Dee without the quilts."

I looked at her hard. She had filled her bottom lip with checkerberry snuff and it gave her face a kind of dopey, hangdog look. It was Grandma Dee and Big Dee who taught her how to quilt herself. She stood there with her scarred hands hidden in the folds of her skirt. She looked at her sister with something like fear but she wasn't mad at her. This was Maggie's portion. This was the way she knew God to work.

When I looked at her like that something hit me in the top of my head and ran down to the soles of my feet. Just like when I'm in church and the spirit of God touches me and I get happy and shout. I did something I never had done before: hugged Maggie to me, then dragged her on into the room, snatched the quilts out of Miss Wangero's hands and dumped them into Maggie's lap. Maggie just sat there on my bed with her mouth open.

"Take one or two of the others," I said to Dee.

But she turned without a word and went out to Hakim-a-barber.

"You just don't understand," she said, as Maggie and I came out to the car.

"What don't I understand?" I wanted to know.

"Your heritage," she said. And then she turned to Maggie, kissed her, and said, "You ought to try to make something of yourself, too, Maggie. It's really a new day for us. But from the way you and Mama still live you'd never know it."

She put on some sunglasses that hid everything above the tip of her nose and her chin.

Maggie smiled, maybe at the sunglasses. But a real smile. Not scared. After we watched the car dust settle I asked Maggie to bring me a dip of snuff. And then the two of us sat there just enjoying, until it was time to go in the house and go to bed.

1973

CRITICAL THINKING POINTS: *After you've read*

1. What do the quilts and butter churn seem to mean to Dee (Wangero)? To the narrator and Maggie?

2. How important are the quilts to Maggie? What else seems at least as important if not more so?

3. Why do you think that until recently things like quilts weren't often considered to be art? Can you think of other similar items?

SOME POSSIBILITIES FOR WRITING

1. Does your family have objects like the quilts and butter churn? Write about at least one of them.

2. Choose a scene in the story and write it from a different character's point of view.

3. Choose one of the Critical Thinking Points following the story and develop your original responses further.

This Was the Assignment: Liberating Act

This was the assignment: In the spirit of Gloria Steinem's *Outrageous Acts and Everyday Rebellions*, perform a positive act that represents—for you—something that challenges the way you see the world or how the world sees you. This might include challenging any of the "isms"—sexism, racism, homophobia/heterosexism, classism, ageism, ableism, and so on—or simply examining one "barrier" you have in your life. Prepare a reflection of your act and include the following:

- describe your liberating act and its effect (on you and your audience),
- explain how/why it was "liberating" or "outrageous" for you,
- analyze your feelings afterward and the reactions of people affected by it, and
- write a research paper based on any of the issues surrounding your Liberating Act.

Use examples from the course texts, outside texts (books, essays, zines, movies, advertisements, articles, etc.), films, and/or your own life experience. Grammar, spelling, and organization count toward your grade and affect your ability to communicate your ideas effectively.

The Stages, Struggles and Reliefs of Coming Out

Alicia Merclazo

Alicia Merclazo is a social work major at a Midwestern university.

I have been waiting for the "right moment" to talk to you about this, but I realized with the distance between us and the occasional meeting on holidays without one-on-one time, that there would never be such a thing, hence this letter.

CRITICAL THINKING POINTS: *As you read*

1. Pay attention to how the author weaves together her research and her personal experiences.
2. Do you think a research paper is easier to write if you have a personal connection to the topic? Why or why not?
3. Do you think the author's approach to coming out to her family is a good one? Why or why not?

It is often difficult for people to disclose something very personal about their lives that could lead to lack of acceptance by loved ones. One of the many complex disclosures is coming out, which involves identifying one-self as lesbian, gay, bisexual, transgender, queer, or questioning (LGBTQ). Many LGBTQ individuals who come out are afraid of negative reactions and no support or acceptance. This was a factor for my hesitance to come out to my family and friends. I have been dating the same woman for three years and my relatives did not know. For my liberating act, I chose to write "coming out" letters to my aunts/uncles, my surviving grandparents, and my childhood babysitter (and her husband) who have been like grandparents. They are all very religious, and I was afraid of not being accepted. Although I am confident and comfortable now with who I am and my sexual orientation, it was not an overnight realization. As the website AVERT states in "Coming Out" that "coming out is not a single action, it is a process of coming to terms with being LGBTQ and disclosing this to others." Each person's process of coming out is individualized and unique; however, there are some general common stages to this process.

177

The first stage involves LGBTQ individuals feeling "different" when comparing themselves to others of the same sex. This includes feeling "more-than-friend-attractions" to individuals of the same sex, which commonly occurs in early adolescence ("Coming Out"). I experienced this stage in third grade, when I realized I was attracted to girls more than boys. I wasn't sure what that meant, but I felt as though I was the only one having feelings that way so I didn't tell anyone. This confusion I had about what to label the feelings I was experiencing ties into AVERT's second stage: confusion of one's identity as well as feelings becoming more concrete. Identity confusion is coped with in different ways. One LGBTQ person may deny it, try to force himself/herself to feel differently, or define the feelings as "only a phase." Another LGBTQ person may acknowledge the feelings and accept them as "just who I am." The third Avert stage of coming out is "assuming a lesbian or gay identity." At this stage, reaching out to other LGBTQ individuals and support groups is common. The final stage is being confident in one's sexuality and being open about it with others. This experience of the final stage can be a struggle or a sense of relief to be able to be true to yourself and comfortable with your sexuality. LGBTQ individuals must make sure they are ready for the possible reactions and changes in relationships.

Given the tremendous homophobia in the United States, coming out can also be a personal safety risk. Gregory Herek says in "Hate Crimes Against Lesbians and Gay Men" that *hate crimes* are "words or actions intended to harm or intimidate an individual because of his/her membership in a minority group." These include violent assaults, rape, and even murder (220). These types of crimes are serious because they can victimize an entire class of people. Some have caught the media's attention and spread the news about these types of crimes. One tragedy occurred October 7, 1998 in Laramie, Wyoming, when Matthew Shepard was led by two men, Aaron McKinney and Russell Henderson, to a remote area where he was tied to a fence, severely assaulted, and left to die ("Mathew's Story"). Almost an entire day later, a bicyclist found him. His injuries were deemed too severe for any doctor to operate, and Matthew died on October 12. He was a 21-year-old college student who was killed because he was gay. This tragedy was displayed in the media, which brought national and even international awareness. Matthew's death also generated inspiration for many activists to work toward eliminating hate in all forms, not only towards the LGBTQ community.

Unfortunately, this was only one tragedy out of many. Patrick Corrigan and Alicia Matthews report in "Stigma and Disclosure: Implications for Coming Out of the Closet" that the results of one study showed that 41% of the sampled LGBTQs reported being victims of a hate crime while another 9.5% reported an attempted hate crime against them (237). Another study published in 1998, the same year of Matthew Shepard's death, which attempted to connect economic conditions to hate crimes. Green, Glaser, and Rich write in "From Lynching to Gay Bashing: the Elusive Connection Between Economic Conditions and Hate Crime" that the logic of frustration-aggression "implies that hate crimes directed against target groups such as gay men and lesbians will tend to become more numerous in periods of recession, as the frustrations engendered by economic contracting find expression in attacks against a vulnerable scapegoat" (87). All in all, there have been no solid studies as to what causes homophobia (and thus hate crimes) besides the individual's different religious views and personal values and beliefs. However, people with power in the media show their bias and opinions with the public, which could cause a domino effect in homophobia and hate towards homosexuals.

There are two people with political power who recently made offensive statements against the LGBTQ community. Many Republicans and Conservatives believe that homosexuality is an abomination and a disease that would ruin society. One of these is past Arkansas Governor Mike Huckabee. The Associated Press article "Former Presidential Candidate Mike Huckabee Likens Gay Marriage to Incest, Polygamy" reports that he said, "The effort to allow gays and lesbians to marry is comparable to legalizing incest, polygamy, and drug use." Also, in response to a question asked about gays in the military, he stated that he feels homosexuality is an "aberrant, unnatural, and sinful lifestyle." Sally Kern, an Oklahoma State Legislator, was recorded while speaking to a group of about fifty Republicans, and an audio file of her anti-gay tirade was later posted on You-Tube. She said, "I honestly think it [homosexuality] is the biggest threat our nation has, even more so than terrorism or Islam" (0:58). Over a million people have listened to this posting, and many—myself included—were offended by the things she said. How can loving someone even amount to being compared to bombing our nation? Is there a correlation that I am missing? She continued to state many hurtful things that sparked anger in many of the citizens she claimed to speak for. She said, "No society that has totally embraced homosexuality has lasted more than a few decades" (0:47). Where in her speech are sources that provide proof of societies falling apart solely based on embracing homosexuality? Kern continued this hateful speech for approximately three minutes about how homosexuals are infecting our nation and ruining lives of children by making them think that the homosexual lifestyle is acceptable (1:27). She also provided an example of having cancer in a little toe and if you don't cure it right away, it will spread. She compared this cancer to homosexuals and powerfully argues that "this stuff [homosexuality] is deadly, and it is spreading and it will destroy our young people and it will destroy this nation" (2:45). This quote shows her perspective on the LGBTQ community, comparing us to a cancerous disease that needs to be killed off. If she has the role of a State Legislator and a leader, so how many people will follow her? This certainly does not make it easier to come out because of the fear of being discriminated by everyone around you.

On October 28, 2009 President Obama signed the Matthew Shepard and James Byrd, Jr. Hate Crimes Prevention Act, which expanded existing United States federal hate crime law to include crimes motivated by a victim's actual or perceived gender, sexual orientation, gender identity, or disability. President Obama said, "We must stand against crimes that are meant not only to break bones, but to break spirits—not only to inflict harm, but to instill fear. . . . The rights afforded every citizen under our Constitution mean nothing if we do not protect those rights—both from unjust laws and violent acts." He said that the FBI reported roughly

7,600 hate crimes in the U.S. in 2008, and since 1999 there were more than 12,000 reported hate crimes based on sexual orientation alone. He went on to say that we would never know how many incidents were never reported at all.

Despite the struggles and possible negative consequences that coming out can cause, I decided to write letters to my family about my sexual orientation and disclose my relationship with my girlfriend. On my mother's side, I wrote to my grandparents, my Uncle Paul and his wife Margie, my Uncle Dave, and my Aunt Julie—all in Minnesota. On my father's side, I wrote to my Aunt Eva and her husband Bud, my Uncle Juan and his wife Maria, my Aunt Violet and her husband Pedro—all in Minnesota—and my Aunt Geraldine and her husband Clay in Nevada and my Uncle Early in Hawaii. I also wrote a letter to my childhood babysitter, Hazel and her husband Clem since they have been like grandparents to me since I was born. The letters went generally as follows:

Dear _____,

This letter I'm writing to you is heart-felt, and I ask for you to please read this when you have time. I have been waiting for the "right moment" to talk to you about this, but I realized with the distance between us and the occasional meeting on holidays without one-on-one time, that there would never be such a thing, hence this letter.

I have been dating someone I love for almost 3 years. What you may not have known is that the person I love is a woman. I know it may be a surprise and you may wonder why I have not told you sooner, and I apologize for the wait. I was initially told not to tell anyone in the family about my sexual orientation, but after years of keeping it a secret, I decided that you deserve to know about this large part of who I am and I don't want to try to hide it anymore. I hope for your continued love and compassion, but I would understand other reactions as well.

My girlfriend's name is Tracy, and she is a college freshman majoring in Physical Education. We met in high school through softball and started dating the end of my senior year. I'll tell you a little about her life as well. Her parents divorced when she was young, and she is the youngest of 4 children. Her oldest brother, Alex, is currently serving in the Marines and is engaged to be married in January 2011. Her second oldest brother, Dylan, is 20 and is mentally disabled and also one of the sweetest kids you would ever meet. He enjoys participating in Special Olympics (softball, bowling, and basketball) and loves watching Nascar and the NFL (especially the Packers, but is still a Favre fan). Her third brother, Ethan, is a firefighter and is also engaged to be married.

Tracy was nominated and won Homecoming Queen her senior year in high school. She loves to hunt, and she has two different colored eyes (one green, one half green and half brown). She also recently joined the Army and will be leaving for Basic in Oklahoma 3 days after Krista's wedding, which will be tough on us and our relationship since it cannot be known to the military that we are a couple. However, she will be at the wedding, so you will be able to meet her and talk with her. She is shy at first when meeting someone new, but she has been looking forward to meeting more of my family.

I apologize that I could not talk to you and tell you face-to-face about this because I feel it may come as a shock and you may have questions for me.

I asked for them to respond in some manner, so I would know they received the letter and so I can have the opportunity to hear their honest thoughts and opinions.

This act was very liberating for me because I have kept this from them for years since my mother forbid me to tell anyone in my family about my sexual orientation because I was an "embarrassment to the family." I have still not heard back from two of my relatives, but four out of the eight responses have been positive and supportive. I am still glad that I wrote all of these letters even if the response I received was not the most positive. I believed that it was the best time to tell them given my sister's wedding coming up so they can meet Tracy, also before she leaves for the military. It was most liberating for me because I no longer have to keep my love life a secret and now know my family is aware, whether they accept it or not. I also got to do this on my own without telling my parents which was important to me because I did not get the chance to come out to my parents (they found out about my sexuality by opening a letter from my girlfriend). I know I can live an open and authentic life by completely being myself around my relatives. Even though I'm not supported by everyone in my family, it is a relief to know that everybody now knows the truth, and I don't have to pretend to be something I'm not. I believe it is better to be hated for who I am, than to be loved for who I am not.

Works Cited

"Coming Out." AVERT. June 3, 2010. June 4, 2010. http://www.avert.org/coming-out. htm.

Corrigan, Patrick and Alicia Matthews. "Stigma and Disclosure: Implications for Coming Out of the Closet." *Journal of Mental Health*. 12.3 (2003): 235–248.

"Former Presidential Candidate Mike Huckabee Likens Gay Marriage to Incest, Polygamy." The Associated Press. April 13, 2010. May 15, 2010. http://www.nj. com/news/index.ssf/2010/04/huckabee_likens_gay_marriage_t.html.

Green, Donald, Jack Glaser and Andrew Rich. "From Lynching to Gay Bashing: the Elusive Connection Between Economic Conditions and Hate Crime." *Journal of Personality and Social Psychology*. 75:1 (1998): 82–92.

Herek, Gregory. (1989). "Hate Crimes Against Lesbians and Gay Men. *American Psychologist*, 44.6 (1989): 216–223.

Kern, Sally. "I'm Listening." March 7, 2008. May 14, 2010. http://www.youtube.com/ watch?v=tFxk7glmMbo.

"Matthew's Story." Matthew Shepard Foundation. 1998 to 2006. May 14, 2010. http:// www.matthewshepard.org/site/PageServer?pagename=Our_Story_Main_Page.

Obama, Barack. "Remarks by the President at Reception Commemorating the Enactment of the Matthew Shepard and James Byrd, Jr. Hate Crimes Prevention Act." October 28, 2009 June 4, 2010. http://www.whitehouse.gov/the-press-office/remarks-president-reception-commemorating-enactment-matthew-shepard-and-james-byrd-

2010

CRITICAL THINKING POINTS: *After you've read*

1. How might you make this a better paper with better research?
2. Did any of the hate crime statistics surprise you?
3. Have you kept a secret from your extended family? How does that compare to Merclazo's experience?

SOME POSSIBILITIES FOR WRITING

1. What is your response to Sally Kern's anti-gay message on You-Tube? http://www.youtube.com/watch?v=tFxk7glmMbo.
2. Research Matthew Shepard and Brandon Teena. Write an essay discussing how their tragic murders have prompted more awareness about LGBTQ youth.
3. Research the "Campus Hate Crimes Right to Know Act," which passed in 1997. How might this influence your campus climate? What has been done since then to address the problem?

Further Suggestions for Writing— "Student Relations"

1. What kinds of changes do you think your being away at college will make for your family and/or your friends at home? Write about some of them.

2. Write a letter to your parents titled "Ten Commandments for the Parents of a College Freshman." Include both dos and don'ts.

3. As Shakespeare wrote in *A Midsummer Night's Dream*, "The course of true love never did run smooth." Although this may be true of all people "in love," some pressures are particular to college students involved in romantic relationships. What are some of them, and how do they affect college relationships?

4. Many college students leave behind, or are otherwise separated from, a significant other. What are some of the advantages and disadvantages of being in such a situation? Is it possible to maintain such a relationship? If so, how?

5. Organize a discussion between a group of male and female friends in which the subject is "College Men Are from Mars; College Women Are from Venus." Write a report of the findings of your discussion to present to your class.

6. Working in groups, compare and contrast some aspect of sexual behavior, love, romance, or dating in high school and at college.

7. Evaluate your school's policies on sexual harassment. How well informed about these policies do first-year students seem to be?

8. Find a few recent issues of two different magazines that are popular among college students, one of which is directed primarily at women and the other at men. Compare and contrast the way these two publications reveal attitudes about gender. In what way(s) are gender stereotypes reinforced and/or challenged? What support do you have for your position?

9. As an investigation of how the sexes view each other, compare and contrast some of the metaphors that men use for women at your school and those that some women use for men. What kinds of insights does this lead you to?

10. Many of the pieces in this book depict males in unflattering terms. Working in groups, discuss the issue of "male bashing" on college campuses. Is it acceptable? Why or why not?

11. Recent studies show that more women are attending universities than men and are graduating at much higher rates. Why do you think this is so? Research this relatively new phenomenon and report back to your class on some of the reasons traditional-age women succeed at school more than men.

12. Some young men and women take pride in preserving their virginity until marriage. Write a dialogue between two men or two women in which one of them explains to the other why virginity is valued.

13. What kinds of influences do you think your religious and/or family upbring-ing have had on your attitudes about sex and sexuality and/or love, marriage, and divorce?

14. Some young men and women take pride in preserving their virginity until marriage. Write a dialogue between two men or two women in which one of them explains to the other why virginity is valued.

15. Evaluate your school's program and policies concerning rape education, prevention, and intervention.

16. For an entire day, record the sexual images you see around campus. Watch for images on signs, posters, billboards, books, TV programs, or other private or public places. Did you notice these images without consciously looking for them? Why or why not? Write a composite of the kinds of images you found and the purpose of these images.

17. Argue for or against co-ed dorms.

18. Music played a major part of the sexual revolution of the 1960s and 1970s. Compare and contrast some of those songs to some popular songs in recent years that promote sexuality.

19. Contact your Dean of Students Office or Residence Life Office to find out what types of support are available for lesbian, gay, bisexual, transgender, queer, or questioning students on your campus. Research student organizations that offer an outlet for these students. Deliver a report to your class on your findings.

20. Research and write a paper about the changes, if any, in sexual behavior among college students pre- and post-AIDS. What surprises you about your findings? Why?

21. Interview an adult student. What caused that student to return to school? Are his or her motivations and/or methods for success the same as yours? Why or why not?

22. Compare Robin and Malia's relationship in "50% Chance of Lightning" in Chapter 1 to that of Kate and Carmen in "Carmen" in this chapter.

23. Read *Don't Come Back a Stranger* by James L. Summers (1970), and/or *A Hope in the Unseen: An American Odyssey from the Inner City to the Ivy League* by Ron Suskind (1998), and/or *Black Ice* by Lorene Cary (1992), and/or *Don't Follow Me, I'm Lost: A Memoir of Hampshire College in the Twilight of the '0s* by Richard Rushfield (2009), and/or *How I Survived Three Years at a Two-Year Community College: A Junior Memoir of Epic Proportions* by James Swift (2009), and/or *Race and the University: A Memoir* by George Henderson (2010), and/or some other college-life memoir. How does the college experience portrayed in any or all of these books compare to your experience? Why do you think so?

24. Read *Don't Tell Me What to Do, Just Send Money: The Essential Parenting Guide to the College Years* by Johnson and Schelhas-Miller (2000), and/or *Empty Nest Full Heart: The Journey from Home to College* by Andrea Van Steenhouse (2002), and/or *Letting Go: A Parents' Guide to Understanding the College Years*

by Karen Coburn and Madge Treeger (2009), or a similar guide for parents of college students. After reading these experiences from these points of view, what insights and/or new awareness do you have?

25. Read *I'll Take You There: A Novel* by Joyce Carol Oates (2002), and/or *Move Over, Girl: A Novel* by Brian Peterson (2000), and/or *Better Than I Know Myself* by Donna Grant (2004), and/or *The Rules of Attraction* by Bret Easton Ellis (1998), and/or *Been Down So Long It Looks Like Up to Me* by Richard Farina (1983). How do the college relationships portrayed in any or all of these books compare to yours or those you see around you? Why do you think this is so?

26. Choose at least three films from the list at the end of this chapter. What do they seem to say about student relationships? What support do you have for your position?

27. Choose one of your responses to the "Some possibilities for writing" topics in this chapter and do further research on some aspect of the topic you addressed in your narrative. Write about how and why this new information would have improved your previous effort.

28. Find the original text from which one of the selections in this chapter was taken. What led you to choose this particular text? How does reading more from the text affect your original reading? Is there more you would like to know about the text, its subject, or its author? Where might you find this further information?

Selected Films—"Student Relations"

For more choices, search IMDb.com using such term as College Student or College Life.

American History X (1998, USA). A former neo-Nazi skinhead tries to prevent his younger brother from going down the same wrong path that he did. Drama. 119 min. R.

But I'm a Cheerleader (1999, USA). A naïve teenager is sent to rehab camp when her straitlaced parents and friends suspect her of being a lesbian. Comedy/Romance. 85 min. R.

Creative Nonfiction (2009, USA). College student Ella is completely focused on her ambiguously romantic relationship with her dorm-mate. Drama, 60 min. NR.

Double Happiness (1994, Canada). A young Chinese-Canadian woman has a romance with an Anglo college student, against the wishes of her very traditional father. Comedy/Drama. 87 min. PG-13.

First Love (1977, USA). An idealistic college student finds that neither his classmates nor his girlfriend take sex as seriously as he does. Based on Harold Brodkey's story "Sentimental Education." Romantic drama. 92 min. R.

Ghost World (2000, USA). Best friends Enid and Rebecca graduate from high school and find themselves forced to enter the real world. They fear drifting apart when one considers moving across the country to attend college. Drama. 111 min. R.

Les Cousins (1959, France). Within the milieu of Parisian student life, a decadent city boy and his pure country cousin vie for the affections of the same young woman. Drama. 112 min. N/R.

Lianna (1983, USA). Lianna, a faculty wife and mother in her early thirties, falls in love with Ruth, the visiting professor in a child psychology course she's taking at the college where her husband teaches. Drama. 110 min. R.

Loser (2000, USA). A college student, branded a loser by his roommates and booted from the dorm, falls in love with a coed who has eyes for their professor. Drama. 98 min. PG.

Lost and Delirious (2002, Canada). A newcomer to a girl's boarding school is befriended by her two new roommates and later discovers the others are lovers. Drama. 103 min. R.

Maurice (1987, Great Britain). Two male students feel they have to repress their mutual attraction, given the stifling sexual mores at Cambridge University in the Edwardian era. Based on E.M. Forster's novel of the same name. Drama. 140 min. R.

Mozart and the Whale (2005, USA). Tells the story of two people with Asperger's syndrome, a form of autism, whose emotional dysfunctions threaten to sabotage their budding romance. Romantic comedy. PG-13.

My First Mister (2001, USA). A 17-year-old goth girl has a platonic relationship with a 49-year-old man who has no friends or family. He gives her a job, not to mention a real friendship. Drama. 108 min. R.

Pumpkin (2002, USA). A sorority girl falls in love with a mentally challenged man. Comedy/Drama. 113 min. R.

Requiem (2006, German) A young woman with epilepsy suffers a breakdown during her first year at university. Drama. 90 min. PG-13.

Smoke Signals (1998, USA). After not seeing his father for ten years, Victor hears his dad has died. Thomas, a nerd who tells stories no one wants to hear, offers Victor money for the trip to get his father's remains, but only if Thomas can go along. Comedy/Drama. 88 min. PG-13.

The Sterile Cuckoo (1969, USA). Liza Minnelli plays an aggressive college student pursuing a shy freshman boy. Comedy/Drama. 107 min. PG.

When He's Not a Stranger (1989, USA). Intensely portrayed date-rape story. Made for TV. Drama. 100 min. N/R.

XX/XY (2002, USA). Three college friends begin a dangerous three-way relationship that spirals out of control, leading to dire consequences that haunt them ten years later. Drama/Romance. 91 min. R.

For critical thinking points on these films, see Appendix (p. 277).

Four

Teacher, Teacher

WILL THIS BE ON THE TEST?

A teacher can affect eternity or simply make a class period feel like one. The selections here present teachers in the roles of disciplinarian, mentor, instructor, scholar, and friend, but most of all as people facing many of the same challenges and fears as their students. This chapter will explore the lessons students and teachers give one another, and the inspiration teachers sometimes have on students' lives.

Take This Fish and Look at It

Samuel H. Scudder

Samuel H. Scudder (1837–1911) was a famous entomologist who attended Harvard University.

I was piqued; I was mortified. Still more of that wretched fish! But now I set myself to my task with a will, and discovered one new thing after another, until I saw how just the Professor's criticism had been. The afternoon passed quickly; and when, towards its close, the Professor inquired: "Do you see it yet?"

CRITICAL THINKING POINTS: *As you read*

1. Consider why students need observation skills in order to grow and learn. In what academic situations are these skills most critical? How do you rate yourself as an observer?

2. Consider the type of student Scudder was before his episode with the fish. How might he have changed as a student? As a scientist? As a person?

3. What are some clues to the era in which the essay is set?

I t was more than fifteen years ago that I entered the laboratory of Professor Agassiz, and told him I had enrolled my name in the Scientific School as a student of natural history. He asked me a few questions about my object in coming, my antecedents generally, the mode in which I afterwards proposed to use the knowledge I might acquire, and, finally, whether I wished to study any special branch. To the latter I replied that, while I wished to be well grounded in all departments of zoology, I proposed to devote myself specially to insects.

"When do you wish to begin?" he asked. "Now," I replied.

This seemed to please him, and with an energetic "Very well," he reached from a shelf a huge jar of specimens in yellow alcohol. "Take this fish," he said, "and look at it; we call it a haemulon; by and by I will ask what you have seen."

With that he left me, but in a moment returned with explicit instructions as to the care of the object entrusted to me.

"No man is fit to be a naturalist," said he, "who does not know how to take care of specimens."

I was to keep the fish before me in a tin tray, and occasionally moisten the surface with alcohol from the jar, always taking care to replace the stopper tightly.

188

Those were not the days of ground-glass stoppers and elegantly shaped exhibition jars; all the old students will recall the huge neck-less glass bottles with their leaky, wax-besmeared corks, half eaten by insects, and begrimed with cellar dust. Entomology was a cleaner science than ichthyology, but the example of the Professor, who had unhesitatingly plunged to the bottom of the jar to produce the fish, was infectious; and though this alcohol had a "very ancient and fishlike smell," I really dared not show any aversion within these sacred precincts, and treated the alcohol as though it were pure water. Still I was conscious of a passing feeling of disappointment, for gazing at a fish did not commend itself to an ardent entomologist. My friends at home, too, were annoyed when they discovered that no amount of eau-de-Cologne would drown the perfume which haunted me like a shadow.

In ten minutes I had seen all that could be seen in that fish, and started in search of the Professor—who had, however, left the Museum; and when I returned, after lingering over some of the odd animals stored in the upper apartment, my specimen was dry all over. I dashed the fluid over the fish as if to resuscitate the beast from a fainting fit, and looked with anxiety for a return of the normal sloppy appearance. This little excitement over, nothing was to be done but to return to a steadfast gaze at my mute companion. Half an hour passed—an hour—another hour; the fish began to look loathsome. I turned it over and around; looked it in the face ghastly; from behind, beneath, above, sideways, at a three-quarters' view—just as ghastly. I was in despair; at an early hour I concluded that lunch was necessary; so, with infinite relief, the fish was carefully replaced in the jar, and for an hour I was free.

On my return, I learned that Professor Agassiz had been at the Museum, but had gone, and would not return for several hours. My fellow students were too busy to be disturbed by continued conversation. Slowly I drew forth that hideous fish, and with a feeling of desperation again looked at it. I might not use a magnifying-glass; instruments of all kinds were interdicted. My two hands, my two eyes, and the fish: it seemed a most limited field. I pushed my finger down its throat to feel how sharp the teeth were. I began to count the scales in the different rows, until I was convinced that was nonsense. At last a happy thought struck me—I would draw the fish; and now with surprise I began to discover new features in the creature. Just then the Professor returned.

"That is right," said he; "a pencil is one of the best of eyes. I am glad to notice, too, that you keep your specimen wet, and your bottle corked."

With these encouraging words, he added: "Well, what is it like?"

He listened attentively to my brief rehearsal of the structure of parts whose names were still unknown to me: the fringed gill-arches and movable operculum, the pores of the head, fleshy lips and lidless eyes; the lateral line, the spinous fins and forked tail; the compressed and arched body. When I finished, he waited as if expecting more, and then, with an air of disappointment: "You have not looked very carefully; why," he continued more earnestly, "you haven't even seen one of the most conspicuous features of the animal, which is plainly before your eyes as the fish itself—look again, look again!" and he left me to my misery.

I was piqued; I was mortified. Still more of that wretched fish! But now I set myself to my task with a will, and discovered one new thing after another, until I saw how just the Professor's criticism had been. The afternoon passed quickly; and when, towards its close, the Professor inquired: "Do you see it yet?"

"No," I replied, "I am certain I do not, but I see how little I saw before."

"That is next best," said he, earnestly, "but I won't hear you now; put away your fish and go home; perhaps you will be ready with a better answer in the morning. I will examine you before you look at the fish."

This was disconcerting. Not only must I think of my fish all night, studying, without the object before me, what this unknown but most visible feature might be; but also, without reviewing my discoveries, I must give an exact account of them the next day. I had a bad memory; so I walked home by Charles River in a distracted state, with my two perplexities.

The cordial greeting from the Professor the next morning was reassuring; here was a man who seemed to be quite as anxious as I that I should see for myself what he saw.

"Do you perhaps mean," I asked, "that the fish has symmetrical sides with paired organs?"

His thoroughly pleased "Of course! Of course!" repaid the wakeful hours of the previous night. After he had discoursed most happily and enthusiastically—as he always did—upon the importance of this point, I ventured to ask what I should do next.

"Oh, look at your fish!" he said, and left me again to my own devices. In a little more than an hour he returned, and heard my new catalogue.

"That is good, that is good!" he repeated; "but that is not all; go on"; and so for three long days he placed that fish before my eyes, forbidding me to look at anything else, or to use any artificial aid. "Look, look, look," was his repeated injunction.

This was the best entomological lesson I ever had—a lesson whose influence has extended to the details of every subsequent study; a legacy the Professor had left to me, as he has left it to so many others, of inestimable value, which we could not buy, with which we cannot part.

A year afterward, some of us were amusing ourselves with chalking outlandish beasts on the Museum blackboard. We drew prancing starfishes; frogs in mortal combat; hydra-headed worms; stately crawfishes, standing on their tails, bearing aloft umbrellas; and grotesque fishes with gaping mouths and staring eyes. The Professor came in shortly after, and was as amused as any at our experiments. He looked at the fishes.

"Haemulons, every one of them," he said; "Mr. _____ drew them."

True; and to this day, if I attempt a fish, I can draw nothing but haemulons.

The fourth day, a second fish of the same group was placed beside the first, and I was bidden to point out the resemblances and differences between the two; another and another followed, until the entire family lay before me, and a whole legion of jars covered the table and surrounding shelves; the odor had become a pleasant perfume; and even now, the sight of an old, six-inch, worm-eaten cork brings fragrant memories.

The whole group of haemulons was thus brought in review; and, whether engaged upon the dissection of the internal organs, the preparation and examination of the bony framework, or the description of the various parts, Agassiz's training in the method of observing facts and their orderly arrangement was ever accompanied by the urgent exhortation not to be content with them.

"Facts are stupid things," he would say, "until brought into connection with some general law."

At the end of eight months, it was almost with reluctance that I left these friends and turned to insects; but what I had gained by this outside experience has been of greater value than years of later investigation in my favorite groups.

1874

CRITICAL THINKING POINTS: *After you've read*

1. Professor Agassiz says, "A pencil is one of the best of eyes." What does he mean? How and why might this be true?

2. Scudder says, "I see how little I saw before." Professor Agassiz answers, "That is next best." What does the professor mean? In what ways is this realization a step toward the lesson Scudder learns?

3. What makes this a humorous story? Would it be as effective without the humor? Why or why not?

SOME POSSIBILITIES FOR WRITING

1. Recall a teacher who taught you a lesson you didn't expect to learn. What led to your acquiring that lesson? Write an essay describing your experience.

2. Observation is a skill that is used constantly in social and academic situations. What are some experiences you've had in which your observation skills were absolutely integral to your success? Choose one experience and describe it.

3. Recall a personal experience that turned out poorly because your observation skills failed you. Write about the situation and speculate how it could have turned out differently if you had been more observant.

How Lincoln Learned to Read: Twelve Great Americans and the Educations that Made Them

Daniel Wolff

Daniel Wolff's other work includes *4th of July/Asbury Park: A History of the Promised Land*, Grammy-nominated liner notes for *The Complete Sam Cooke and the Soul Stirrers* CD, and producer credits on the forthcoming Jonathan Demme documentary about New Orleans, *Right to Return*.

The definition of education broadens, opens up to include a whole range of lessons and a lot of different kinds of teachers.

CRITICAL THINKING POINTS: *As you read*

1. Keep track of the types of educations described for each famous American.
2. Which of the "educations" presented in this excerpt is the most like yours? Which the least? Why?
3. Did you learn anything about these famous people you didn't know before?

Abraham Lincoln
February 12, 1809–April 15, 1865
16th president of the United States

. . . Abe's formal schooling ended there. He'd later say all of it "did not amount to one year." But for a pioneer education, five winters of attendance—spanning ages six to sixteen—was considerable. Now he'd spend the equivalent of his high school years testing what he'd learned and adding new skills. Near the crossroads that led down to Rockport, James Gentry ran a local store. Abe got a job there. The store didn't amount to more than a "small stock of goods," but it meant the boy could get his hands on the *Sangamon Journal,* the *Louisville Journal,* and the *St. Louis Republican,* among others. By this time, there were sixteen newspapers being published in Indiana alone.

The lanky teenager reading papers in the local store was only about five years from his first run for office. At twenty-three, he'd campaign on a platform that championed "the public utility of internal improvements." If people were going to stop squirming, were going to develop from pioneer to resident, they'd have to agree on shared goals and pool their resources to accomplish them. Lincoln was heading toward his eventual definition of government: "a combination of the people of a country to affect certain objects by joint effort. The legitimate object of government is to do for a community of people, whatever they need to have done, but cannot do, *at all* or cannot *so well do*, for themselves."

One thing he decided that they couldn't do as well on their own was schooling. Education, he'd declare during his first run for office, is "the most important subject which we as a people can be engaged in." Every man, he thought, ought to receive "at least a moderate [one]" so that "he may duly appreciate the value of our free institutions . . . to say nothing of the advantages and satisfaction to be derived from all being able to read the scriptures." Finally, sounding like a student of Noah Webster, he saw education as a way to make "morality, sobriety, enterprise and industry . . . much more general than at present." He'd done a lot of learning outside school, but he saw a public education system as key to establishing order and civilization.

W. E. B. Du Bois
February 23, 1868–August 27, 1963
U.S. civil rights activist

. . . . Willie was going to become the Negro who went to college. It was an outlandish goal. For one thing, (he'd) . . . have to study a different curriculum from his fellow high school students: Greek and higher levels of algebra and Latin. That meant special textbooks, which he couldn't possibly afford. . . .

And as the teenager socialized with the well-to-do, visited their homes, listened to their plans for the future, he decided he had to try. His given reason undercuts his idyllic description of Great Barrington as a place where everyone was about the same. "In early years," he writes, "a great bitterness entered my life and kindled a great ambition. I wanted to go to college because others did."

It's a pretty stark admission. He doesn't say he wanted to go to college because of what he'd learn there, or even what he might accomplish after going. In fact, he admitted that for "a young and ambitious colored man," there was no telling "what were the possibilities of employment or of any career after such training." No, he wanted to go, as he describes it here anyway, to prove that he could. To prove that Negroes could be not just like other people, but like the most schooled people in the country. While Willie was at Great Barrington High, less than 2 percent of the nation's eighteen-to-twenty-four-year-olds were going to college. And in the history of the nation, only about 650 Negroes had ever graduated from one. . . .

The summer of his third year of high school, he found a different kind of support for his ambition. Willie's 1883 visit to New Bedford was his first extended trip outside Great Barrington, his first time traveling alone, and his first chance to meet anyone from his father's side of the family. He was struck by the landscape at the shore and by a celebration where he got to see thousands of Negroes gathered in one place. But what affected him most was Grandfather Du Bois. The eighty-year-old had never received more than what Willie called "the beginnings of a gentleman's education." Still, here was a model who "held his head high, took no insults made few friends. He was not a 'Negro,'" Willie wrote, "he was a man!"

Helen Adams Keller
June 27, 1880–June 1, 1968
First deaf-blind American to earn a Bachelor of Arts degree

. . . . Helen was almost seven when it happened, the age of a second grader. She'd been born with all her senses, contracted a fever when she was a year and a half, and then, in her words, "Gradually I got used to the silence and darkness that surrounded me." But she never got used to the frustration. "Nothing," as she described it, "was part of anything," Then, Teacher[1] arrived, and a little over a month later, Helen was out by the pump. "Suddenly I felt a misty consciousness as of something forgotten—a thrill of returning thought; and somehow the mystery of language was revealed to me. Everything had a name and each name gave birth to a new thought."

The miracle is language. It lets her name things. And names let her begin to think, to consider how one thing relates to the next. And that connects her to world. "As we returned to the house every object which I touched seemed to quiver with life." Teacher says Helen learned thirty words in the next few hours, had a hundred within ten days, four hundred in less than three months. Knowledge pours in. . . .

Before Teacher arrived, Helen had known a few basic signs: mother, father, ice cream, cake. She could communicate, if crudely. Teacher believed language was in the girl, latent but blocked. That's why she saw the moment by the pump as the *second* step in Helen's education. When Anne Sullivan writes a friend, "A miracle has happened! The light of understanding has shone upon my little pupil's mind, and behold all things are changed!" the letter's dated two weeks before W-A-T-E-R.

What's the earlier miracle? Within a week of arriving, Teacher decided that the first thing Helen needed to know was her place. At dinner, the girl was used to circling the table eating randomly off plates, making a mess. When Sullivan tried to stop her, "She pinched me, and I slapped her every time she did it." While the slapping horrifies the Kellers, Teacher insists their "over-indulgence" is going to make it impossible for Helen to learn. She and her new pupil move into the isolation of the little garden house. Soon, their only other regular contact is with Percy, a black boy, their servant. According to Teacher, Helen's willfulness had to be broken before learning could begin. "[O]bedience is the gateway," Sullivan writes, "through which knowledge and, yes, love, enter the mind of the child."

Rachel Louise Carson
May 27, 1907–April 14, 1964
Writer credited with advancing the global environmental movement

. . . . Carson could "remember no time when I wasn't interested in the out-of-doors and the whole world of nature. Those interests, I know, I inherited from my mother and have always shared with her. I was a rather solitary child and spent a great deal of

---

[1]Anne Sullivan

time in woods and besides streams, learning the birds and the insects and flowers." If she wanted to be a writer, her constant reading made sense. But why did she need to know about nature? And how did she learn?

Her earliest connection to the fields above Springdale, she wrote a friend, had nothing to with facts; it was based on her "sensory impressions of, and emotional response to, the world." Late in life, Carson would write a magazine article that eventually became a slim book called *The Sense of Wonder.* In it, she emphasized exactly this kind of emotional learning. "I sincerely believe that for the child, and for the parent seeking to guide him, it is not half so important to *know* as to *feel.*" She describes walking through the woods with her grandnephew (to whom the book is dedicated): "I have made no conscious effort to name plants or animals nor to explain to him, but have just expressed my own pleasure in what we see . . . just going through the woods in the spirit of two friends on an expedition."

That, Carson argues, is how kids learn best. It seems to be how she learned. "Just going through the woods" sounds a lot like Helen and Teacher wandering the Alabama springtime, and Rachel and her mother brought some of the same educational beliefs to the hills of western Pennsylvania. "If a child is to keep alive his inborn sense of wonder," Carson would write, ". . . he needs the companionship of at least one adult who can share it, rediscovering with him the joy, excitement and mystery of the world we live in."

Elvis Aaron Presley
January 8, 1935–August 16, 1977
One of the most popular U.S. singers of the twentieth century

. . . A photo from that July shows him in a bow tie, white shirt, and country western jacket, his hair in a spiky flattop, a slight smile on his lips. His education is over. In the simplest terms, he's found a voice. "I just landed upon it accidentally." He tells an early interviewer. "More or less. I'm a pretty close follower of religious quarters, and they do a lot of rockin' spirituals. And so that's where I got the idea from, is religious quartets." Religious quartets, blues singers, pop crooners, country-western and gospel starts—all had their influence.

He'd say elsewhere that he relied a lot on indistinct, "going by impulse and just what I feel on the spur of the moment." But he'd been raised to be modest. And haphazard self-education fit in that American tradition of the guy who just stumbles on knowledge. Truth is, he'd worked at it. He'd followed the quartets and then, in his own words, "got an idea."

And isn't that, finally, what he's learned? If his style came partly from groups like the Blackwoods, the idea behind it has to do with the right to have a voice at all. And in that sense, it *is* the sound of someone singing in the spirit. Not singing religious songs and not the Holy Spirit of the Assembly of God. But something related: an inspired, goofy, freed spirit where, suddenly, anything's possible. "Every dream I ever dreamed has come true a hundred times," he'd proclaim late in his life. By then, his sound had brought him staggering amounts of fame and wealth. And though that was part of what he'd been after—the American dream of hitting the jackpot, of buying his parents a Cadillac—they were the results, not the idea itself.

The idea was that he could rock the world, shake clear of the enclosure, go beyond even those electric lines that caged the horizon. The idea was that a person could declare himself in such a way that he stood apart from the landscape of cotton fields and weathered shacks—that he challenged the very notion of being, or not being, "white." People like him were supposed to harden into a category, to disappear. Instead, in an explosion of contradictions, he finds hope. His sudden appearance isn't actually sudden: it rises out of a long history. And so does this idea, this hope: that we can learn what we need to know.

2009

CRITICAL THINKING POINTS: *After you've read*

1. Which of these stories seems the least likely to happen today? Why?
2. Wolff's entire collection asks the question, "How do we learn what we need to know?" What are some of the possible implications of that question?
3. Have you ever had an unexpected teacher? What did you learn and how?

SOME POSSIBILITIES FOR WRITING

1. Write a story about your own education, modeled after these pieces.
2. Read more of Wolff's *How Lincoln Learned to Read: Twelve Great Americans and the Educations that Made Them*. Choose at least one other person from that collection, and prepare an edited summary similar to these readings.
3. Who do you consider to be a current "great American"? Prepare a chapter or part of a chapter similar to those in this collection addressing how that person learned what he or she needed to know.

Teachers: A Primer

FROM *TIME'S FANCY*   **Ron Wallace**

Ron Wallace is Felix Pollak Professor of Poetry and Halls-Bascom Professor of English at the University of Wisconsin–Madison. He is the author of many books of poetry, including *For a Limited Time Only* (2008) and *Long for This World: New and Selected Poems* (2003).

She had a policy: A tattletale
or liar had to face the wall,
a tail pinned to his sorry ass,
and wear the laughter of the class.

CRITICAL THINKING POINTS: *As you read*

1. What is a "primer"?
2. What grades does Wallace cover in the poem? As you read, speculate about the grade level for each teacher and what subject he or she teaches.
3. Why do you think the poet chooses the names he does for the teachers he describes?

MRS. GOLDWASSER
Shimmered like butterscotch; the sun
had nothing on her. She bangled
when she walked. No one
did not love her. She shone,
she glowed, she lit up any room,
her every gesture jewelry.
And O, when she called us all by name
how we all performed!
Her string of little beads,
her pearls, her rough-cut
gemstones, diamonds, we hung
about her neck. And when
the future pressed her flat,
the world unclasped, and tarnished.

MRS. SANDS
Always dressed in tan. Her voice
abrasive as her name. What choice
did a second grader have? You got
what you got. Her room was hot
but she wore wool and heavy sweat
and worked our childhoods, short and sweet.
You didn't sass her or the school or
she'd rap your knuckles with a ruler.
She had a policy: A tattletale
or liar had to face the wall,
a tail pinned to his sorry ass,
and wear the laughter of the class.
So, to this day, my knuckles bent,
I tell the truth (but tell it slant).

MRS. ORTON
The perennial substitute, like some
obnoxious weed, a European interloper
in our native prairie, her instructions
full of nettles, her gestures parsnip
and burdock. Every day at 3:00 P.M.
we'd dig her out of our small lives,
and every morning she'd pop back.
We prayed she'd get the sack.
And to that end we taunted her—
tacks on her chair, a set-back clock—
as, weeping, she plodded through the week
turning, and turning the other cheek.
And every time we thought that we'd
eradicated her, she'd gone to seed.

MISS WILLINGHAM
A Southern Belle, she read *Huck Finn*
aloud to us, dropping her chin
to get the accent right. And me,
for some odd reason, she
singled out to learn the books
of the Bible and recite them back
to her in my high voice
I tried to measure lower. *Nice
boys go to Sunday school,* she said,
and made me promise, when I was grown,

to glorify our heavenly Lord
and take His teaching for my own.
And when she finished that dull story,
she lit out for the territory.

MR. AXT
The basketball coach. Short, tough.
Three days growth on his sharp chin.
Liked to see us all play rough,
and beat up on the stupid, thin,
weak kids who couldn't take it.
He wore white T-shirts, shoes, and slacks,
and taught us all to fake it
if we somehow naturally lacked
the mean competitive spirit.
Once a week he'd have us
bend over and spread our cheeks
for him and old Doc Moffett
who liked to slap us on the butt
and watch as we took leaks.

MRS. REPLOGLE
Her name forbidding, reptilian,
her reputation like a snake
around my expectations.
But then she played *Swan Lake*
and Ferde Grofe's *Grand Canyon Suite,*
a Bach chorale, a Beethoven quartet,
and when we were all back on the street
even the traffic kept a beat.
One day she had us close our eyes
and listen to a symphony
and write whatever image rose
in our small imagination's dark.
And what I saw was poetry,
each note a bird, a flower, a spark.

MR. GLUSENKAMP
His gray face was a trapezoid, his voice
droned on like an ellipse.
He hated students and their noise
and loved the full eclipse
of their faces at the end of the day.

No one could have been squarer,
and nothing could have been plainer
than his geometry.
He didn't go for newfangled
stuff—new math, the open classroom.
And yet he taught us angles
and how lines intersect and bloom,
and how infinity was no escape,
and how to give abstractions shape.

MR. WATTS
Sat cross-legged on his desk,
a pretzel of a man, and grinned
as if chemistry were some cosmic joke
and he'd been dealt a hand
of wild cards, all aces.
He drew for us a "ferrous" wheel
and showed when formic acid reverses
HCOOH becomes HOOCH, a peal
of laughter ringing from his nose.
He gave us Avogadro's number
and in his stained lab clothes
formulas for blowing the world asunder
or splitting genes. God knows
why he died shouting "No!" in thunder.

MISS GOFF
When Zack Pulanski brought the plastic vomit
and slid it slickly to the vinyl floor
and raised his hand, and her tired eyes fell on it
with horror, the heartless classroom lost in laughter
as the custodian slyly tossed his saw dust on it
and pushed it, grinning, through the door,
she reached into her ancient corner closet
and found some Emily Dickinson mimeos there
which she passed out. And then, herself
passed out on the cold circumference of her desk.
And everybody went their merry ways
but me, who chancing on one unexpected phrase
after another, sat transfixed until dusk.
Me and Miss Goff, the top of our heads taken off.

1989

CRITICAL THINKING POINTS: *After you've read*

1. What lessons does Wallace learn from each teacher? Make a list. How does he learn what he does?

2. How do these "lessons" reflect his becoming a poet? Do you think they helped make him a poet, or does his being a poet now simply make these lessons more memorable in retrospect?

3. What stereotypes of teachers are apparent in the poem?

SOME POSSIBILITIES FOR WRITING

1. Recall a teacher who stands out in your memory because of his or her personality, mannerisms, and so on. Write a one-page description of that teacher using specific details.

2. Choose another teacher from a work in this collection and compare him or her to one of Wallace's teachers.

3. Choose a teacher you did not understand or appreciate during the time you were in that teacher's class but learned to appreciate later. What happened to change your mind?

Tales Out of School

AN EXCERPT   **Susan Richards Shreve**

Susan Richards Shreve is the author of many novels, including *A Country of Strangers, The Train Home,* and *Plum and Jaggers.* She is an award-winning children's author and co-editor of *Tales Out of School: Contemporary Writers on Their Student Years.* In her thirty-five years as an educator, she has taught every level, from kindergarten to graduate school.

"Why would you throw your life away?" my mother, the teacher, said to me the first year I taught school. "You could be anything and you choose to be a teacher."

CRITICAL THINKING POINTS: *As you read*

1. Watch for the author's role as student, parent, and teacher. How do her roles impact each tale she tells?
2. What kind of student is the author/narrator? What kind of parent and teacher?
3. Can these tales be grouped or ordered in any way? If so, how?

1. The first day of first grade and I'm sitting in the front row, chewing off the collar of the dress my mother made me, a habit I had of eating the cotton collars of several outfits a year—a condition of general agitation that would be corrected today with regular doses of Ritalin. I'm watching Mrs. Comstock, soft, plump, weary, and very old, write on the blackboard.

"Who reads?" she asks.

I put up my hand. I don't read and wonder as I look around the room whether the other students with their hands up are telling the truth.

"Good," Mrs. Comstock says, satisfied that we're off to a fine start. "I'm going to write down the rules for First Grade, Section A, Mrs. Comstock's class."

1. NO lateness
2. NO impudence
3. NO speaking out in class
4. NO whispering

   5. NO bathroom visits during class
   6. NO morning recess unless classwork is completed
   7. NO food in the classroom
   8. NO temper tantrums
   9. NO pushing or shoving when you line up
 10. NO tears

I'm extremely pleased as I watch the list run down the blackboard. Although I can't read, do not even want to learn if it means, as I'm afraid it will, giving up the hours sitting next to my mother or father in my small bed while they read to me—I do recognize the word NO. I even count the number of NOs filling up the blackboard. There are ten.

"So," Mrs. Comstock says, turning around to face us. "Who can read me the rules?"

I don't raise my hand but there I am sitting directly in front of her and without a second's hesitation, she calls my name. I don't even stop to think.

"No, no, no, no, no, no, no, no, no, no," I say without taking a breath.

2. Checking the obituaries in the *Washington Post* as I have done forever, preferring the story of a whole life, pleased to fill in the missing spaces—I find on page three of the metro section the notice that my fifth grade teacher, age ninety-three, is dead of natural causes. Dead and I didn't know it. She slipped out of the world and I wasn't even aware of the sudden absence of danger when I woke up this morning.

I am a grown-up, forty-two with four children of my own, a responsible job as a teacher. A teacher of course, a teacher of all things.

"Why would you throw your life away?" my mother, the teacher, said to me the first year I taught school. "You could be anything and you choose to be a teacher."

I cut the obit and tape it on the refrigerator.

"My fifth grade teacher," I say when my children ask why the death of a stranger is noted on the fridge.

Friends School, Section 5-B on the first floor next to the library. I sat in the middle of the last row between Harry Slough, who smelled of old bananas, and God's perfect creation, Toni Brewer, with her loopy blond braids and straight A's.

"I never heard you mention your fifth grade teacher to us," one of my children says to me. "Are you *very* upset?"

"Not a bit," I reply. "Only that it took so long to happen."

They look at me in horror, knowing maybe for the first time, the full measure of revenge.

The story of my fifth grade teacher goes like this:

I was going to a Quaker school selective in its choice of students, no blacks, no learning disabilities, but willing to accept the occasional handicapped child that the public schools did not. I wasn't exactly handicapped but I had had polio and when

I was young I wore metal braces and went around on crutches. Children like me used to be taught at home by drop-in tutors, our social lives accommodated by regular deliveries of turkeys and gumdrops and occasional coloring books from the local Kiwanis Club, which did nothing to compensate for the lonely life of home schooling.

It was late autumn before Thanksgiving and I had been in the habit of forgetting my math homework. Maybe I didn't do it and lied about it, maybe I never did my math homework—those details I have forgotten. But this morning the fifth grade teacher noted to the class that once again I had flunked my math test.

"But," she added with a show of enduring patience, folding her arms across her military chest, "we have to be nice to little Suzie Richards because she had polio."

3. In twelfth grade, with little distinction as a student but a belief, not commonly shared, that I was a promising writer, I had Mr. Forsythe as a teacher. We all did. We'd been waiting throughout high school for this extraordinary opportunity to write under his direction. The papers were long, analytic essays in response to questions about our readings in English literature. I had in mind to rescue my academic reputation in Mr. Forsythe's senior English and was stunned as paper after paper came back to me full of red pencil and paragraphs of criticism written in his tiny, crabbed hand with D1 and C2 and D and D and D.

"I suppose you think I'm a terrible writer," I said when I finally went into his office.

He looked up under hooded eyes, an expression of unspeakable boredom on his face. "You make up your answers," he replied.

"These questions require research."

4. I am twenty-two living in England and I'm hired to teach what would be fourth grade at a school in a working-class community across the river from Liverpool. These students are hard-core tough, raised on cowboy movies where they've learned a new vocabulary—*ain't,* for example. There are forty of them and I have never taught school. The only thing I'm told before I walk into the makeshift classroom, two to a desk, is that caning in England is against the law. Of course, I think. I have a Dickensian view of caning, the craggy, long-faced wet-eyed master beating the child to smithereens with a heavy cane.

My despair as a teacher focuses on Lily Diamond, a small, plump, vacant child who has it in mind to drive me crazy. Maybe sixty times a day, she falls off her chair, turns upside down, her legs in the air, screaming, "Ain't, ain't, ain't, ain't," while the rest of the class goes wild with excitement. I have absolutely no control.

It has come to my attention that in the top drawer of my desk there is a small stick, not much longer than a pencil, the same width and hollow like a reed. I have begun to imagine this stick applied to the bottom of Lily Diamond. And one Wednesday during math, right in the middle of a chorus of "ain'ts" from the floor, I take out the stick, walk down the aisle—the children have gone dead silent—and carry out my fantasy. The rest of the school day is bliss. For the first time in weeks I can actually hear my own voice above theirs.

The following morning when I arrive at Birkenhead Elementary the police and the head of the school are standing on the front steps waiting for me. I'm ushered into the principal's office and there facedown on the principal's desk, her dress up, her pink panties pulled down so the full bottom is exposed, is Lily Diamond. Her mother is there with her arms folded across her chest, the officers of the law are examining Lily Diamond's bottom and Lily is screaming.

"I told the American that caning is against the law in England," the head of the school says to the police.

"I had thought a cane was an actual cane," I say, product of the sixties, against all punishment, certainly corporal, now a sudden criminal in my own court.

"A cane is a cane," the head of the school says coolly.

The police make their assessment, give Lily a friendly slap.

"No mark appears to be evident," they say.

Lily hops off the desk, pulls up her pants, shakes herself proudly, giving me a look of complete disdain.

"Ain't you terrible sorry," she says, drawing the word to its full length.

5. It is the summer of my younger son's freshman year in high school and thirty boys are in our living room planning an insurrection. One among them, Danny C, has been dismissed, voted out by the faculty, flunked, they say, unable to return to the Quaker school for his sophomore year.

"How come?" I ask.

"He's an artist," my son says.

"They think he's weird."

"Different."

"Bad."

"Learning disabled." The new catchphrase.

I have known this boy since he was five—a curious, ebullient boy, neither athletic, nor in a conventional sense academic, imaginative, impulsive, fearless.

The boys are examining reasons for his dismissal, studying the school handbook that outlines the rules, looking over Danny's report cards that he has brought to the meeting, as well as the letters the school has sent to his parents that he has slipped out of his mother's file cabinet. They spend all day.

The rules are specific. No drugs, no alcohol, no cheating, no failing grades. There are twenty-six reasons for dismissal and Danny C, as the boys discover, hasn't measured up to any of them.

"Wear coats and ties," my husband says as the boys organize their defense for the head of the school.

The mothers of these boys cannot imagine a reversal of the faculty decision, but cheerleaders always, we drive them to school on the morning of their meeting with Mr. Harrison—thirty adolescent boys with their argument in hand, point by point, all twenty-six reasons for dismissal addressed.

I wasn't at the meeting. The next I knew they were flooding into the house, shedding their ties, a victorious army, organizing their rule of the school for the next three years.

Mr. Harrison had reversed the decision.

"What happened?" I ask my son after everyone has gone home.

"Mr. Harrison is very brave," he says simply.

"How is that?" I ask.

"He listened to us."

6. When I am called to the nursery school where my oldest child is a student, one of twelve in a class of two teachers, Mrs. Nice and Mrs. Something Else, at the school where his father is head of the high school, I have a new baby and a two-year-old and no baby-sitter, so they come along. I have been called in to witness my son in action so I will understand why these two women in a small class are unable to manage him. So I sit in one of those little chairs with my finger in the new baby's mouth so he won't cry and wait for the drama to unfold.

"Po," Mrs. Nice is talking. "Please sit down at the table and get out your crayons."

No one else is sitting down but all around the room the other children turn to look at my son expectantly, a kind of pleasure in their attitude, waiting for something to happen.

My son doesn't sit down.

"Po," Mrs. Nice says again. "What did I tell you?"

He puts his hands over her ears and walks around the periphery of the room very quickly—dum dum dum dum de dum de dum de dum de dum. His hands are in his pockets now and the other children are giggling at him, glancing back and forth at each other. He gives them a knowing collaborator's look.

"You see?" Mrs. Nice says to me. She turns to my son as he passes her on his march.

"Your mother is here watching, Po," she says as if this news will come as a surprise to him. "So you better be good."

"He doesn't ever do what I ask him to do," Mrs. Nice says.

I am beginning to have that mother's sense of a temperature change in my son, an arriving decision, a moment of action. He has stopped his trip around the classroom and is listening to Mrs. Nice, an expression of bemusement on his face.

"Why haven't you told the other children to sit down?" I ask.

"Because they *will* sit down if I ask them to," she says. "So I don't need to ask them to, of course."

I am feeling homicidal.

Suddenly out of the corner of my eye, I see my son running across the room toward me, a maniacal smile on his face, leaping onto the table, racing around the edge of the circle with amazing speed and control, not even falling, his balance so perfect. All around the children are looking at him with something between admiration and envy.

Mrs. Nice is a picture of pure happiness.

"You see the problem, Mrs. Shreve?" she says. "Emotionally disturbed."

I pick up my two-year-old, grab Po by the hand, and we fly out of the room, down the corridor in which my four-year-old son spends hours sitting on a chair, into the parking lot, into the car and home.

"You see, Mom," Po says to me. "Mrs. Nice is crazy."

7. I am probably thirty-five, a teacher and administrator of an alternative school in Philadelphia called Our House for smart children in trouble, attending a conference of teachers in Atlanta where the major speaker will be Margaret Mead. I am sitting with my own children in the lobby of the hotel waiting for the speech when I notice a small, square woman, slightly hassled and bewildered, loaded down with bags and books and papers. I am in her line of vision and she stops.

"Do you know where the speech is?" she asks.

I know who this is, of course. These are the seventies, when Margaret Mead in many circles had the aura of a rock star. She was the mother of us all, accumulating weight from our acclamation.

I tell her this.

She is examining my children playing on the floor with Fisher-Price families and Legos and Matchbox cars.

"Are you coming to the speech?"

"Yes, I am," I reply, adding some compliment that she ignores.

"My speech is about the end of the family as we know it," she looks at me, assessing my role as mother. "Parents have abdicated their role and now the school must take over the family's job. In the next twenty years, they won't have time to educate." She brushes her small hands together, walks between a plastic Fisher-Price family and heads to the lectern.

8. I sit down in the office of the college guidance counselor, relieved that for the fourth and last time I am about to set out on the trip to look at colleges for a child. Especially with this child, this reader of *Anna Karenina* who has told me that she would prefer to be homeschooled or else to go to a fiercely strict Catholic school with nuns who carry rulers peering out of stiff white boards. Either freedom or confinement is what she's after. Not this wishy-washy middle of accommodation and concern and judgment, because no choice a child could possibly make in this atmosphere of freedom of choice will be the right one.

The college guidance counselor and my daughter are already seated and there is decision about the room.

"We are meeting to talk about Kate's college choices, which she should make by the end of her junior year," the counselor says.

Kate has been a good student in spite of her limited attendance, so I'm not worried, in fact almost comfortable this fourth time around.

"So what are you thinking, Kate?" the counselor asks, a conversation I can tell they have already had and are repeating for my benefit.

"I'm actually leaving high school," Kate says.

The counselor, a Quaker and therefore by definition nonconfrontational, looks at me with something close to fury.

"We have never had a student choose to drop out of high school in her junior year," she says.

"I didn't know this was happening," I say, immediately sorry that I hadn't said instead: "Of course. Kate and I discussed the subject last night and decided that high school was absolutely useless for her. Many better things to do with her time."

"I'm very sorry," Kate says, and always polite adds that she is quite fond of the school, admiring the college counselor, respectful of the values, but simply is no longer willing to spend her time there.

In the car coming home, trying to concentrate in order not to run a stop sign or red light or hyperventilate, I ask Kate what she plans to do.

"I haven't decided," she says. "I simply know that I'm not suited to high school."

I am reminded of a conversation I overheard when as a young mother I went to visit a friend whose daughter was in high school.

We were sitting in the living room when her daughter came home from school, dropped her books, her coat, and flopped down on the couch.

"I am miserable in high school," she said crossly to her mother.

"I'm so glad to hear that, darling," my friend said cheerfully. "All of the interesting people I know were miserable in high school."

9. Elizabeth is in fourth grade at a new school and I imagine that she's perfectly happy, since that's what she tells me. She is making new friends, although she doesn't want them to come over and never seems to be invited to their houses. She only misses her old school at night when I turn out the light in her room. So it comes as a terrible surprise when one of the fourth grade mothers asks me do I know about the I Hate Elizabeth Club. The mother has just discovered that her daughter belongs to it. Membership in the club costs a dollar, she tells me, and all the girls in the fourth grade have been asked to join or else to suffer exclusion if they refuse. The rules are simple. No one is allowed to speak to Elizabeth and members are rewarded for an imaginative punishment such as the sticking of straight pins in my daughter's back during Meetings for Worship.

"I thought it was my fault," Elizabeth says when I ask her why she never told me. She doesn't cry. She begs me not to tell the teacher or it will be worse for her.

"I have to," I tell her. "What they have done is terrible and your teacher has the right to know about it. She's in charge."

That night she tells me everything. Day after miserable day of the I Hate Elizabeth Club while I in my stupidity was thinking she was happy.

"What are you going to do then?" she asks me, lying next to me in the dark.

I have made a decision. Already what was done to my child is forming itself into a story in my mind.

"I'm going to write a book about them and call them each by name," I say.

"Maybe you'll be sued," she says.

"I won't be sued," I reply.

Sometime later, maybe three years, I am at lunch with Elizabeth and the former president of the I Hate Elizabeth Club. They aren't friends of course but the former president is trying. I can tell she wants to tell me something, has thought about it for a long time. She has apologized to Elizabeth, once when she had to because she was caught, and recently, just weeks before, when she meant it.

"You used my real name," she says finally.

"Yes I did."

"I read the book," she says. "I didn't realize what I'd done until I read about myself."

2000

CRITICAL THINKING POINTS: *After you've read*

1. Speculate why the narrator doesn't tell any positive stories about her teachers.

2. Does the narrator learn anything as a teacher from even so-called negative experiences with her own teachers or her children's?

3. As a mother, what qualities does the narrator seem to value in her children?

SOME POSSIBILITIES FOR WRITING

1. School rules often begin with "No . . ." Why is that? Research the ideology behind positive and negative rules.

2. Write one of your own "tales out of school."

3. Find and read Kendall Hailey's *The Day I Became an Autodidact* (Delacorte, 1988). How do Shreve's tales compare?

Signed, Grateful

Kate Boyes

Kate Boyes is a multimedia artist whose creative projects include writing (nonfiction, fiction, poetry), weaving, and paper/book arts. She had great fun writing *Paul McCartney*, her biography for young adults of the Beatles musician. She currently serves as writer in residence at Shore Pine Studios, located on the Oregon coast.

But thanks, especially, for not changing my life. Thanks for giving me the chance to talk myself into changing.

CRITICAL THINKING POINTS: *As you read*

1. This essay is written in the form of a letter. How does that form contribute to your reading of the text?
2. Boyes finds a college catalog in a Dumpster, which leads her to apply to college. Why did you apply to and decide to enroll in the college you are currently attending?
3. How does Boyes change throughout the essay? Map the stages of her progress.

D ear Professor,

I didn't belong in college. I should have told you that when we first met. My father had dropped out of school after third grade. My mother had finished high school, but her family thought she was a little uppity for doing that. I clerked parttime nights in a food store and worked days as a baby-sitter. My combined salaries from those two jobs fell far below the poverty level, where I'd lived for much of my life. Statisticians said I didn't belong in college. Who was I to argue?

And I came to college for the wrong reason. My health. I needed health insurance, but neither of my jobs included benefits. Every time one of my kids came down with a cold, every time I felt dizzy with flu, I wondered what would happen to us if we were really sick. How could I tell my kids that they would just have to suffer because I couldn't afford to take them to a doctor? How many extra part-time jobs would I need to take on if the kids or I ever rang up an emergency room bill?

One night when I was emptying the trash at the end of my shift, I noticed a brightly colored catalog in the dumpster behind the store. I fished the catalog out, wiped off the mustard and ketchup drips on the front cover, and took it home. Flipping through the catalog later, I discovered it advertised all the courses available at the local college.

And I discovered something else—taking only one course would make me eligible to sign up for student health insurance. I did some careful calculations. If

I took one course each semester for a year, the cost of tuition, books, and fees would still be far lower than the cost for six months of private insurance. My kids would be covered by the student policy, too. What a deal!

Becoming a student was a great scheme. But I knew, when I took my first course from you, that I was an impostor.

We were both coming to college after a long break. You came from a decade of social work. I came from a decade and a half of post–high school marriage, kids, divorce, and minimum-wage jobs. Neither of us had spoken in a classroom for years.

Perhaps you wondered, that first day you taught, if anything you said affected your students. Well, here's how something you said affected me. You announced that each student must give an oral presentation at the end of the semester. When I came home, my youngest daughter, mimicking my voice and posing the same question I asked her every afternoon, said, "How was school today, Honey?" I couldn't answer. Your announcement of the oral presentation had made me so nervous that I rushed past her to the bathroom, where I lost my lunch.

Weeks passed before I sat through class without nausea. I came early each day to claim the only safe seat—the seat on the aisle in the back row. Close to the door. Just in case. Back with the whisperers and the snoozers. I crouched behind the tall man who always read the student newspaper during class, and I chewed the fingernails on one hand while I took notes with the other hand. I talked myself into going to class each day by telling myself, over and over again, that I was doing this for my kids.

I needed three credits. I didn't need the agony of a presentation. Dropping your course and signing up for something—anything—else made sense. But I stayed, even though I didn't know why. Your lectures certainly weren't polished; you gripped the lectern like a shield and your voice sometimes stopped completely in the middle of a sentence.

I think I stayed because your enthusiasm for the subject left me longing to know more. I looked forward to those few quiet hours each week—those rare times when the store was empty or when the babies were napping—that I spent reading, writing, and thinking about what I'd heard in your class.

And one day, while I was thinking, I recalled a fascinating lecture you gave on the importance of defining terms. I noticed on your syllabus that you hadn't defined "oral presentation." I decided oral meant spoken—in any form—rather than written. When the time came for my presentation at the end of the semester, I carried a tape recorder to the front of the room, pushed "play," and returned to my seat, where I listened with the other students to the oral presentation I'd taped the night before.

When I signed up for the next course you taught—a course on women who had shaped American culture and history—I knew you would require another oral presentation. But I figured a little agony while I started a tape recorder wouldn't be so bad. In this second course, you came out from behind the lectern and paced the aisles as you spoke. You often stood at the back of the room when you made an important point, and all heads turned in your direction. Whispering and sleeping ended when you did that, and newspapers dropped to the floor. Your voice stopped only when you asked a question, and you called on us by name.

I was so caught up in the class that a few weeks passed before I read the syllabus carefully. Then I found your long and precise definition of "oral presentation," a definition that excluded the use of tape recorders. To be sure I understood the definition, you stopped by my desk one day after class and said, "This time, I want it *live!*"

Taking college classes was beginning to sharpen my critical thinking skills, and I put those skills to work when choosing the subject for my presentation. I chose to speak about Lucretia Mott, an early Quaker. Why her? At the end of the semester, when my turn came to present, I walked to the front of the room dressed as Lucretia had dressed, in a long skirt and shawl, and with a black bonnet that covered most of my face. I spoke in the first person. Although I was the person standing in front of the other students and moving my lips, it felt to me as if someone else gave that presentation.

By the time we met again in the classroom, I had had to admit to myself that I was in college for more than my health. I'd scraped together enough credits to be one quarter away from graduation. I had an advisor, a major, and a lean program of study that included no frills, no fluff—just the courses I absolutely needed for my degree. They were all I thought I could afford. Your course didn't fit my program, but I decided to take it anyway, and I skipped lunch for weeks to pay for the extra credits.

When you handed back our first exam, mine had a note scribbled alongside the grade. You said you wanted *me* to give the presentation for this course. Not a tape recorder. Not a persona. The same panic that had gripped me during the first course I took from you returned, and I felt my stomach churn with anxiety. My only comfort came from knowing that by the time I fainted—or worse—during my presentation, the quarter would be over and I would have my degree.

You didn't lecture in this course. You pushed the lectern into a corner and arranged our chairs in a circle. You sat with us, your voice one among many. You gave direction to discussions that we carried on long after class periods officially ended. I came early, not to claim an escape seat but to share ideas with other students. I stayed late to be part of the dialogue.

Three can be a magic number, even in real life. At the end of that third course, I stood in front of the class. I spoke in my own voice, just as I had spoken during our discussion circles. You had erased the distinction between the front of the room and the back, between teacher and student, between those who have knowledge and those who seek to gain knowledge. And I remember thinking, as I walked back to my seat, that I wasn't an impostor in the classroom any more. I had just as much right to be in that room as any of the other students.

I was happy when you stopped to speak with me after class. Happy to belong. Happy to have survived the presentation. Happy to know I never had to do anything like that again. I thought you might congratulate me on surviving the presentation or on finishing course work for my bachelors degree. Instead, you asked where I planned to go to graduate school.

You were doing it again! Every time I crept over the line between the familiar and the fearful, you pushed the line a little farther away. I don't remember how I answered your question, but I remember how I felt when I left the room. Miffed. Okay, angry. I steamed out thinking that you'd already forced me to talk in front of people, to grapple with large concepts, to care about ideas. And now you wanted more?

Weeks later—after graduation, after I'd read all the mindless magazines on the rack at work, after I'd thought about life without the stimulation of classes—I cooled down. And applied to graduate school.

I'm sure you knew the only way I could finance my graduate degree would be by teaching classes as a graduate assistant. You knew I would need to stand in front of a class. Day after day. And speak. I'm also sure—now—that your motives were good and pure when you suggested I continue my education. But for a while, when I couldn't sleep nights before I lectured, when I couldn't eat on days I taught, when I couldn't stand in front of the room without feeling dizzy, I wondered if your motives had something to do with revenge.

Perhaps you wonder now if anything you've done as an instructor has affected your students. Here's how something you did affected me. The first time my voice gave out in the middle of a lecture, I remembered you. I realized then that you had felt as nervous while teaching as I had felt while being taught. Every time you'd pushed me, you were also pushing yourself.

I looked over the lectern at a room full of people who felt, more or less, the same way. Nervous, unsure, but anxious to learn. And I stopped the lecture, arranged the chairs in a circle, and gave everyone the opportunity to speak, to add more voices to the dialogue of education.

So . . . I write this letter to say thanks. My graduate degree opened up a great job for me. Yes, you guessed it—I'm teaching at a university. With health insurance.

But thanks, especially, for not changing my life. Thanks for giving me the chance to talk myself into changing.

1998

CRITICAL THINKING POINTS: *After you've read*

1. How does the narrator, as she says, talk herself into changing?
2. Why does Boyes say, "Statisticians said I didn't belong in college. Who was I to argue?" Who, if anyone, does not "belong" in college? What kinds of statistics might she be talking about?
3. How does the professor's teaching style transform as her student transforms? What evidence in the letter supports this?

SOME POSSIBILITIES FOR WRITING

1. Imagine you are Boyes's professor. Write a response to her in the form of a letter.

2. Read or reread Booker T. Washington's excerpt from *Up from Slavery* in Chapter 1. In what way is Boyes's story similar to Washington's?

3. Imagine Kate Boys is ranking her professor on ratemyprofessors.com. What might she say about him?

STUDENT RESPONSE TO "SIGNED, GRATEFUL"

While reading "Signed, Grateful" I couldn't help but think of my father as he went back to college at the age of 30, while being a single parent with four kids. Kate Boyes was a single parent working two jobs and only enrolled in college to get the cheap health insurance, and in a way it actually relates to the times after the health care bill was just passed. Kate was doing what she felt was best for her and one professor in particular pushed her every step of the way.

It's hard to say how I feel about this reading because of how closely I can relate to it. When my father went back to college he told me he had to meet with the dean, because he just felt as though the dean wanted to meet the guy who was double majoring in math and science as a single parent with four kids. I can completely understand because my father set the curve while he was in school, but I am basically barely getting by.

My father is the only one of his family to go to college, and he has nine brothers and sisters. While I have three brothers and sisters, I am the only one to go to a university. If my dad made it through all that he did to get a degree, in my eyes I would be a failure if I did not complete mine. I may never go on to get the same kind of education my father did, considering he has a master's degree, but it is not out of the question. I just need to take care of this semester and next semester and then I can think about where to go from there. So by the end of my college, I just won't have completed it for myself but for my father. I have never let my dad down, and there is no way I am going to start now.

What Teachers Make

Taylor Mali

Taylor Mali is the author of two books of poetry, *The Last Time As We Are* (2009) and *What Learning Leaves* (2002), and four CDs of spoken word. He received a New York Foundation for the Arts grant in 2001 to develop *Teacher! Teacher!* The one-man show about poetry, teaching, and math won the jury prize for best solo performance at the 2001 Comedy Arts Festival. View more of his work at www.taylormali.com.

I make kids work harder than they ever thought they could.
I can make a C+ feel like a Congressional medal of honor
and an A− feel like a slap in the face.

CRITICAL THINKING POINTS: *As you read*

1. Which statements about teachers seem unrealistic and/or overly idealistic? Why?
2. What parts of this poem seem like thing teachers shouldn't make? Why?
3. What parts of this poem would your parents particularly admire or be troubled by? Why?

He says the problem with teachers is, "What's a kid going to learn
from someone who decided his best option in life was to become a
teacher?"
He reminds the other dinner guests that it's true what they say about
teachers:
Those who can, do; those who can't, teach.

I decide to bite my tongue instead of his
and resist the temptation to remind the dinner guests
that it's also true what they say about lawyers.

Because we're eating, after all, and this is polite company.

"I mean, you're a teacher, Taylor," he says.
"Be honest. What do you make?"

And I wish he hadn't done that
(asked me to be honest)
because, you see, I have a policy

about honesty and ass-kicking:
if you ask for it, I have to let you have it.

You want to know what I make?

I make kids work harder than they ever thought they could.
I can make a C+ feel like a Congressional medal of honor
and an A− feel like a slap in the face.
How dare you waste my time with anything less than your very best.

I make kids sit through 40 minutes of study hall
in absolute silence. No, you may not work in groups.
No, you may not ask a question.
Why won't I let you get a drink of water?
Because you're not thirsty, you're bored, that's why.

I make parents tremble in fear when I call home:
I hope I haven't called at a bad time,
I just wanted to talk to you about something Billy said today.
Billy said, "Leave the kid alone. I still cry sometimes, don't you?"
And it was the noblest act of courage I have ever seen.

I make parents see their children for who they are
and what they can be.

You want to know what I make?

I make kids wonder,
I make them question.
I make them criticize.
I make them apologize and mean it.
I make them write.
I make them read, read, read.
I make them spell definitely beautiful, definitely beautiful,
definitely beautiful
over and over and over again until they will never misspell
either one of those words again.
I make them show all their work in math.
And hide it on their final drafts in English.
I make them understand that if you got this (brains)
then you follow this (heart) and if someone ever tries to judge you
by what you make, you give them this (the finger).

Let me break it down for you, so you know what I say is true:
I make a goddamn difference! What about you?

2002

CRITICAL THINKING POINTS: *After you've read*

1. This poem was meant primarily to be read out loud. What elements would contribute to it being presented that way? Why?

2. Read this poem out loud, and then find a video of Taylor Mali reading his poem on YouTube. What are some of the differences between the two readings?

3. What might be some answers to, "What's a kid going to learn from someone who decided his best option in life was to become a teacher?"

SOME POSSIBILITIES FOR WRITING

1. Write your own poem, perhaps "What Lawyers Make." Or chose a profession you are considering.

2. Given the often relatively low pay and social status, why would someone want to become a teacher?

3. What kinds of "differences," both good and bad, have teachers made in your own life?

This Was the Assignment: Teacher Observation

This Was the assignment: Choose one of your current teachers and write an analysis of him or her based on some of the following items:

- The course syllabus might tell a student if the teacher is organized, approachable, rigid, and so on.
- The way a teacher dresses often says a lot about that teacher's personality and personal style.
- Stance and body language may help determine how comfortable the teacher feels in front of the class. For instance, whether a teacher stands behind a podium, paces when she lectures, or sits among her students in a circle.
- Amount of dialogue between teacher and students or among students. Is the teacher the "expert" or "guide?" Does student input help shape the process and context of the class?
- Is lecturing the primary teaching mode? Are multiple modes of teaching used? Finally, determine if your teacher employs a liberal or traditional teaching style or a combination of both. How does that style affect the dynamics of the class?

Jon Anderson is a biology major who wrote this piece for a Student Success Seminar.

She has always been a wonderful, caring person, but now that wonderful person is also a wonderful professor. I think she deserves to hear that.

CRITICAL THINKING POINTS: *As you read*

1. What is the value in carefully observing a professor?
2. Watch for how the teacher evolves throughout the time Anderson observes her in the classroom.
3. Do you think Anderson would react differently to his professor if she didn't undergo her own transformation as a teacher? Why or why not?

Since I'm repeating my Genetics class, actually for a third time since I withdrew the first two times, I've had the opportunity to observe the same professor over a period of time. Interestingly, it was her first time teaching when I took her course the first time around. Much like Kate Boyes and her professor in "Signed, Grateful," I was nervous to be taking such an intimidating course, and I could tell that my professor was nervous to be in charge of one.

218

I remember how difficult it was to follow her during lectures as she stood in one place, delivering her thoughts in a monotone, hesitant voice. She would often stutter or completely stop speaking and, overall, it was almost impossible to practice active listening in such a situation. It certainly didn't help that she used PowerPoint presentations that consisted, mostly, of the exact phrases that she used in class. It was especially hard to pay attention since I knew that those slides, in their entirety, would be available online.

I must say, even though I was a bit angry that all of this was affecting my ability to learn, I could understand her situation as well. I felt bad for her. Some students would make inappropriate comments when she would stutter, and I know that she could likely hear at least some of those comments. I could see the pain in her face, on occasion, as she would look at her sea of students and notice that it was speckled with disappointed looks. She, even to this day, has always made it quite easy to read her feelings, and I have always found this to be beneficial. It's too bad that she had to be sad as a result of what she went through though. However, I feel that this has played a vital role in shaping the professor that stands before me this semester.

Although I was hesitant to attempt her class again, I sure am glad that I decided to. One of the best things about it is seeing how well she is doing and knowing how quickly that change happened. I'm really happy for her and I'm also really happy that it's much easier and much more fun to learn from her now. Yet again though, I can't wait until the end of the semester! This time, however, it's not because I dislike the learning experience. This time I just can't wait to see my good grades, but more importantly, I can't wait to tell her how great she has become. I don't want to be thought of as a suck-up, so I will wait until the time is right. Still, after seeing her struggle in front of a cruel class day after day that first semester, she deserves to be told that I've noticed her achievements and that all of her hard work is very much appreciated. After all, she is human, and every human deserves a nice compliment from time to time. She has always been a wonderful, caring person, but now that wonderful person is also a wonderful professor. I think she deserves to hear that.

The biggest thing that I noticed, right off the bat this semester, is how comfortable she has become in front of the class. She basically befriends everyone on the first day! She gets the class talking immediately, asks everyone what they expect from the course, etc. We frequently discuss our weekends and what we've done in our free time. We do this, both, in lecture as a large group and in lab, where she enjoys talking with us individually. She truly loves being a part of her students' lives. I believe there are about sixty people in the class, and she knows all of us by name! Hearing chatter and negative comments during her lectures has completely ceased. Instead, I overheard, just the other day, two girls talking behind me about how sweet our professor is. It kind of choked me up when I realized that she's been that way since I've known her. I'm so happy that her new teaching skills have let that shine through. She moves about the room more, gets the class involved, loves getting questions from students, and has a voice of sincere excitement when she speaks.

As for the syllabus, for both lecture and lab, we have stayed on track. She is very organized, yet flexible. She let us vote to determine the days of the exams once we knew the rest of our schedules. As far as her clothing, she is always very well dressed, usually in a dressy yet casual way. It is professional and modern. Overall, I would say that she is a happy moderate when it comes to the scale of liberal vs. conservative teaching. Watching her become this way has made me very happy. The professor who once stood like a statue and delivered boring lectures, I now consider to be my very smart, enthusiastic, and caring friend. She has made me look at learning in a whole new way. I now especially love learning about the field of Genetics. She and I are both very happy with how well I'm doing now. She gives me a big smile when I turn in my exams and I smile right back, both of us knowing that we have done well. I guess the only sad thing is that I won't get to take the class again, although something tells me that I'll still see my friend from time to time. I'll see her in the halls of Phillips, I'll see her at her office when I go there to chat, and, ultimately, she will be with me in my thoughts when I nail the interview that sparks my career.

2009

CRITICAL THINKING POINTS: *After you've read*

1. Why do you think it is difficult for students to tell teachers even the positive comments they have about them?
2. How does this teacher affect Anderson?
3. How does Anderson's experience compare to Kate Boyes's in "Signed, Grateful"?

SOME POSSIBILITIES FOR WRITING

1. Write your own response to this assignment.
2. Consider the benefits of keenly observing people around you (teachers, bosses, partners, etc.). Write an observation of someone who holds some power in your life.
3. Spend some time reviewing students' ratings of professors on www.ratemyprofessors.com (what could be considered "teacher observations"). Compare your observations about your current teachers to what their former students wrote about them.

Further Suggestions for Writing— "Teacher, Teacher"

1. Write an essay about "How to impress a professor."

2. Recall a time when you were entranced by a teacher. Write about the qualities you found attractive and why you respected or liked that teacher.

3. Write about a teacher you thought represented a lifestyle or ideal but who turned out to be much different—for example, the health teacher who is a smoker, or the dull math teacher who is funny outside of class.

4. Do you expect your relationships with your college teachers to be similar to or different from your earlier relationships with teachers? Why or why not? In what ways?

5. Argue for or against a policy at your school banning or regulating romantic/sexual relationships between teachers and students.

6. Interview your advisor about what he or she feels to be the advisor's role. How much does your advisor feel he or she can and/or should do for advisees? How much are students expected to do for themselves?

7. Do you think that students are in the best position to be able to evaluate their teachers? Defend your answer.

8. Visit your college Learning Center and interview tutors or staff about the causes of test anxiety. Research some ways to alleviate test anxiety.

9. One of the objectives of a university education is to challenge your beliefs and perhaps even change your mind about some of those beliefs. Briefly explain one thing that you are sure you will never change your mind about and why you think so. Then choose something you might be likely to reconsider, or perhaps have already begun to reconsider. Again, be sure to include why you think so.

10. Interview your current teachers and ask them who their greatest or most important teachers were. After a number of interviews, write an essay on what makes a successful teacher.

11. Interview faculty about the success stories of some of their students whom they have mentored. Can you come up with and support some generalizations about what teachers remember about their students?

12. Taking into consideration all the inherent problems and shortcomings of the lecture format, what kinds of alternative teaching methods do you think could be put into place in the classroom? Use classes you are taking now, or have taken in the past, as examples.

13. Research and define the terms "passive learning" and "active learning." Which of these seems to be the way you have learned previously? Which seems to be the dominant learning style you have encountered so far at your current school? Why do you think that is so?

14. What are "open admissions" programs? What is the history of such programs? What schools offer them? Write an essay in which you argue for or against such programs.

15. Describe an incident or a pattern of gender discrimination that you have noticed in connection with faculty, staff, or students since you arrived at college.

16. Research your university's policy on faculty and staff dating students. Do you agree with this policy? Why or why not?

17. Read either *College Life Through the Eyes of Students* by Mary Grigsby (2009) or *How to Survive Your Freshman Year: By Hundreds of College Sophomores, Juniors, and Seniors Who Did (Hundreds of Heads Survival Guides) by Hundreds of Heads Books,* Mark W. Bernstein, Yadin Kaufmann, and Frances Northcutt (2008). Compare your choice to either *Lecture Notes: A Professor's Inside Guide to College Success* by Philip Freeman (2010) or *All A's All Ways: A Professor Reveals the Secrets to Success* by Benjamin Bloch (2005). What have you learned by doing this comparison?

18. Determine the number of faculty and staff of color at your university. How does your university compare to other campuses in your state? How does it compare nationally? Why do you think that is so? Are there any policies in place at your school to recruit more professionals of color?

19. Given the generally low pay and social status, why would anyone want to teach at the college level? At any other level? Write an analysis of what might cause or inspire someone to become a teacher.

20. Many colleges have an honor system that requires students to sign a pledge not to cheat and to report others whom they observe cheating. Does your college have a similar system? Working in groups, consider the issue of an honor system at your college.

21. Students are often uncertain about what constitutes academic dishonesty and especially what qualifies as plagiarism. On what issues of academic dishonesty (definitions, policies, sanctions) do you think there is confusion or ambiguity?

22. Why do students cheat?

23. Can or should professors set out to change the minds of students? Why or why not?

24. Argue for or against tenure for professors.

25. Read *What the Best College Teachers Do* by Ken Bain (2004), and/or *Clueless in Academe: How Schooling Obscures the Life of the Mind* by Gerald Graff (2003), and/or *The Effective, Efficient Professor: Teaching Scholarship and Service* by Philip C. Wankat (2002), or some other examination of college teaching. What insights and/or new awareness have you gained regarding college teaching after considering these points of view?

26. Argue for or against Web sites like www.ratemyprofessors.com.

27. Read *Accidental Lessons: A Memoir of a Rookie Teacher and a Life Renewed* by David W. Berner (2009), or *Teacher Man: A Memoir* by Frank McCourt (2005), or *Finding Mrs. Warnecke: The Difference Teachers Make (A Memoir)* by Cindi Rigsbee (2010), or *Hands Up!: A Year in the Life of an Inner City School Teacher* by Oenone Crossley-Holland (2010), or some other memoir of a teacher. What insights or surprises do you find about the profession?

28. Choose at least three films from the list at the end of this chapter. What do they seem to say about college teachers? What support do you have for your position?

29. Choose one of your responses to "Some possibilities for writing" in this chapter and do further research on some aspect of the topic you addressed. Write about how and why this new information would have improved your previous effort.

30. Find the original text from which one of the selections in this chapter was taken. What led you to choose the text you did? How does further reading from the text affect your original reading? Is there more you would like to know about the text, its subject, or its author? Where might you find this further information?

Selected Films—"Teacher, Teacher"

The Blackboard (1999, Iran). Set along the Iran–Iraq border in the mountainous area of Kurdistan, *The Blackboard* follows two teachers in search of students Drama. 84 min. N/R.

The Blackboard Jungle (1955, USA). A middle-aged school teacher takes on inner-city kids and street thugs in this 1950s classic. Drama. 101 min. N/R.

Chalk (2006, USA). An improvisational take on the high school experience, told from the educators' point-of-view. 85 min. PG.

Children of a Lesser God (1986, USA). A speech teacher at a school for the deaf finds himself drawn to a tough, headstrong, beautiful janitor. Adapted from the play by Mark Medoff. Romantic drama. 119 min. R.

Conrack (1974, USA). When Pat Conroy arrives on a small South Carolina island to take on his new teaching post, he finds that his students are illiterate and developmentally disabled. He takes matters into his own hands and turns his students' lives around. Drama. 106 min. PG.

The Corn Is Green (1945, USA). Schoolteacher Lilly Moffat (Bette Davis) is dismayed by conditions in a Welsh mining town. She sets up a school to teach basic education to the villagers. Drama. 115 min. N/R.

Dangerous Minds (1995, USA). A former marine takes a teaching position in an inner-city school and struggles to reach her intelligent but socially defiant students. Drama. 99 min. R.

Dead Poets Society (1989, USA). Unorthodox prep-school English teacher John Keating (Robin Williams) inspires his 1950s-era students to love literature. The film received an Oscar for best original screenplay. Drama. 128 min. PG.

Doubt (2008, USA). In a Bronx Catholic school in 1964 a popular priest's ambiguous relationship with a troubled 12 year old black student is questioned by the school's principal. Drama. 102 min. PG.

Educating Rita (1983, Great Britain). A bright but unschooled hairdresser hires a dissolute, alcoholic tutor (Michael Caine) to expand her literary horizons. Drama. 110 min. PG-13.

Emperor's Club (2002, USA). An idealistic prep-school teacher attempts to redeem an incorrigible student. 108 min. PG-13.

The First Year (2001, USA). Follows five teachers in California through the first year of their teaching careers. Documentary series. N/R.

Freedom Writers (2007, USA). A young teacher inspires her class of at-risk students to learn tolerance, apply themselves, and pursue education beyond high school. Drama. 123 min. PG-13.

Front of the Class (USA, 2008). Based on the true story of Brad Cohen, a young man with Tourette's Syndrome who defies the odds to become a teacher. Drama. 90 min. N/R.

Goodbye, Mr. Chips (1939, Great Britain). A retired headmaster of a boys' boarding school reminisces about his career and personal life. Drama. 114 min. N/R.

Half Nelson (2006, USA). An inner-city junior high school teacher with a drug habit forms an unlikely friendship with one of his students after she discovers his secret. Drama. 106 min. R.

High School High (1996, USA). An over-the-top parody of the "High School Movie." Comedy. 86 min. PG-13.

Lean on Me (1989, USA). Morgan Freeman plays Joe Clark, an unorthodox, demanding, and sometimes overbearing principal who is devoted to the students of his inner-city high school—sometimes at the expense of his own job security and personal safety. Drama. 104 min. PG-13.

Lianna (1983, USA). Returning adult student Lianna falls for her visiting professor. Drama. 110 min. R.

Lucky Jim (1957, Great Britain). A lowly college lecturer bungles his attempts to impress his department head. Comedy. 95 min. N/R.

The Man Without a Face (1993, USA). The story of a relationship between a teacher and his troubled pupil. Mel Gibson stars and directs. Drama. 113. PG-13.

The Mirror Has Two Faces (1996, USA). A college math professor tired of sexual politics makes a deal with a dowdy colleague (Barbra Streisand) that they provide companionship for one another. Romantic comedy. 126 min. PG-13.

Mona Lisa Smile (2003, USA). A free-thinking art professor (Julia Roberts) teaches conservative 1950s Wellesley students to question their traditional societal roles as women. Drama/Comedy/Romance 103 min. PG-13.

Mr. Holland's Opus (1995, USA). Follows the career of Glen Holland, a frustrated composer who becomes a high school music teacher. He writes music and struggles to reach certain students, while neglecting to communicate with his deaf son. Drama. 143 min. PG.

Music of the Heart (1999, USA). A music teacher struggles to keep her violin program alive in a Harlem school. Drama. 124 min. PG.

Oleanna (1994, USA). David Mamet wrote and directed this adaptation of his controversial play about collegiate sexual harassment and sexual politics. Drama. 89 min. R.

The Paper Chase (1973, USA). First-year law students toughen up to survive the acid wit of their intimidating professor (John Houseman). Comedy/Drama. 111 min. PG.

Pay It Forward (2000, USA). Kevin Spacey plays a seventh-grade teacher whose class assignment puts into action an idea that could change the world. Drama. 123 min. PG-13.

The Prime of Miss Jean Brodie (1969, Great Britain). Based on the play by Jay Presson Allen. Between the two world wars, the unconventional Jean Brodie teaches her group of female students about love, life, and the rights and responsibilities of liberated women. Drama. 116 min. NR.

The Principal (1987, USA). A principal assigned to a crime-ridden high school struggles to turn things around. Drama/Crime. 109 min. R.

Remember the Titans (2000, USA). Denzel Washington stars as an African American coach hired to take a high school football team through their first racially integrated season. Based on actual events in 1971 at Virginia's T. C. Williams High School. Drama. 113 min. PG.

Renaissance Man (1994, USA). A down-and-out ad executive is hired to teach "thinking skills" to Army recruits. Comedy. 128 min. PG.

Sarafina! (1992, USA). In a world where truth is forbidden, an inspiring teacher (Whoopi Goldberg) dares to instill in her students lessons not found in schoolbooks. In doing so, she challenges their freedom and hers. Drama. 119 min. PG-13.

Schooled (2007, USA). An earthy character study about a teacher in crisis who discovers an alternative school that teaches him to connect with kids as people. Drama. 121 min. NR.

A Single Man (2009, USA). A story that centers on an English professor who, after the sudden death of his partner, tries to go about his typical day in Los Angeles. Drama. 101 min. R.

Songcatcher (2000, USA). After being denied a promotion at the university where she teaches, Dr. Lily Penleric, a brilliant musicologist, impulsively visits her sister who runs a struggling rural school in Appalachia. There she stumbles upon the discovery of her life: a treasure trove of ancient Scots–Irish ballads, preserved intact by the seclusion of the mountains. Drama. 109 min. PG-13.

Stand and Deliver (1988, USA). A class from an East L.A. barrio commits to taking the Advance Placement Test in calculus, inspired by their dedicated, tough-love teacher (Edward James Olmos). Drama. 105 min. PG.

Surviving Desire (1991, USA). A neurotic English professor falls for his student, who, for her part, is using the affair as fuel for her writing. Romantic comedy. 86 min. N/R.

Teachers (1984, USA). A high school teacher, frustrated by class after class of "flunkies," goes to extremes to help his students and ends up in trouble with the school board. Comedy/Drama. 106 min. R.

To Sir, with Love (1967, Great Britain). An inexperienced teacher takes matters into his own hands in order to teach his upstart, adolescent students. Drama. 105 min. N/R.

Up the Down Staircase (1967, USA). A young, naïve schoolteacher faces the reality of teaching young, not so naïve students at New York City's Calvin Coolidge High School. Based on the novel by Bel Kaufman. Drama. 124 min. N/R.

Wit (2001, USA). A fiercely demanding English literature professor deals with her cancer treatment. Drama. 98 min. PG-13.

Wonder Boys (2001, USA). A pot-smoking, aging writing teacher and his bizarre and brilliant student embark on a lost weekend that changes them both. Comedy/Drama. 120 min. R.

For Critical Thinking Points on these films, see Appendix (p. 277).

Five

Been There, Done That

LOOKING FORWARD, LOOKING BACK

Education can change some people or help them recognize how they have stayed the same. This chapter proves it is never too soon to look ahead, offering pieces that explore life after graduation and providing the advantage of hindsight when offered by those who have survived challenges similar to those that today's students face.

READING SELECTIONS

Bricklayer's Boy

When I Heard the Learn'd Astronomer

The Art of Regret

Raising My Hand

It's Electric: Fragments of My Life as an Epileptic

Reunion

Scarlet Ribbons

Passion

On the Radio

Only Connect: The Goals of a Liberal Education

This Was the Assignment: Instructions for Life

Bricklayer's Boy

Alfred Lubrano

Alfred Lubrano is a reporter for the *Philadelphia Inquirer* and the author of *Limbo: Blue-Collar Roots, White-Collar Dreams* (2004).

> *"I envy you," he said quietly.*
> *"For a man to do something he likes and get paid for it—*
> *that's fantastic."*

CRITICAL THINKING POINTS: *As you read*

1. What do you associate with the phrase "blue-collar"? Why?
2. How is Lubrano's young-professional life different from his father's working-class life?
3. Lubrano is a second-generation American. How might his family's immigrant history affect his father's perspective on success?

When he was my age, my father was already dug in with a trade, a wife, two sons and a house in a neighborhood in Brooklyn not far from where he was born. His workaday, family-centered life has been very much in step with his immigrant father's. I sublet what the real-estate people call a junior one-bedroom in a dormlike condo in Cleveland suburb. Unmarried and unconnected in an insouciant, perpetual-student kind of way, I rent movies during the week and feed single woman in restaurants on Saturday nights. My dad asks me about my dates, but he goes crazy over the word "woman." "A girl," he corrects. "You went out with a girl. Don't say 'woman.' It sounds like you're takin' out your grandmother."

I've often believed blue-collaring is the more genuine of lives, in greater proximity to primordial manhood. My father is provider and protector, concerned only with the basics: food and home, love and progeny. He's also a generation closer to the heritage, a warmer spot nearer the fire that forged and defined us. Does heat dissipate and light fade further from the source? I live for my career, and frequently feel lost and codeless, devoid of the blue-collar rules my father grew up with. With no baby-boomer groomer to show me the way, I've been choreographing my own tentative shuffle across the wax-shined dance floor on the edge of the Great Middle Class, a different rhythm in a whole new ballroom.

I'm sure it's tough on my father, too, because I don't know much about brick-laying, either, except that it's hell on the body, a daily sacrifice. I idealized my dad as a kind of dawn-rising priest of labor, engaged in holy ritual. Up at five every day, my father has made a religion of responsibility. My younger brother, a Wall Street white-collar guy with the sense to make a decent salary, says he always felt safe when he heard Dad stir before him, as if Pop were taming the day for us. My father, fifty-five years old, but expected to put out as if he were decades stronger, slips on machine-washable vestments of khaki cotton without waking my mother. He goes into the kitchen and turns on the radio to catch the temperature. Bricklayers have an occupational need to know the weather. And because I am my father's son, I can recite the five-day forecast at any given moment.

My father isn't crazy about this life. He wanted to be a singer and actor when he was young, but that was frivolous doodling to his Italian family, who expected money to be coming in, stoking the stove that kept hearth fires ablaze. Dreams simply were not energy-efficient. My dad learned a trade, as he was supposed to, and settled into a life of pre-scripted routine. He says he can't find the black-and-white publicity glossies he once had made.

Although I see my dad infrequently, my brother, who lives at home, is with the old man every day. Chris has a lot more blue-collar in him than I do, despite his management-level career; for a short time, he wanted to be a construction worker, but my parents persuaded him to go to Columbia. Once in a while he'll bag a lunch and, in a nice wool suit, meet my father at a construction site and share sandwiches of egg salad and semolina bread.

It was Chris who helped my dad most when my father tried to change his life several months ago. My dad wanted a civil-service bricklayer foreman's job that wouldn't be so physically demanding. There was a written test that included essay questions about construction work. My father hadn't done anything like it in forty years. Why the hell they needed bricklayers to write essays I have no idea, but my father sweated it out. Every morning before sunrise, Chris would be ironing a shirt, bleary-eyed, and my father would sit at the kitchen table and read aloud his practice essays on how to wash down a wall, or how to build a tricky corner. Chris would suggest words and approaches.

It was also hard for my dad. He had to take a Stanley Kaplan-like prep course in a junior high school three nights a week after work for six weeks. At class time, the outside men would come in, twenty-five construction workers squeezing themselves into little desks. Tough blue-collar guys armed with No. 2 pencils leaning over and scratching out their practice essays, cement in their hair, tar on their pants, their work boots too big and clumsy to fit under the desks.

"Is this what finals felt like?" my father would ask me on the phone when I pitched in to help long-distance. "Were you always this nervous?" I told him yes. I told him writing's always difficult. He thanked Chris and me for the coaching, for putting him through school this time. My father thinks he did okay, but he's still awaiting the test results. In the meantime, he takes life the blue-collar way, one brick at a time.

When we see each other these days, my father still asks how the money is. Sometimes he reads my stories; usually he likes them, although he recently criticized one piece as being a bit sentimental: "Too schmaltzy," he said. Some psychologists say that the blue-white-collar gap between fathers and sons leads to alienation, but I tend to agree with Dr. Al Baraff, a clinical psychologist and director of the Men-Center in Washington, D.C. "The core of the relationship is based on emotional and hereditary traits," Baraff says. "Class [distinctions] just get added on. If it's a healthful relationship from when you're a kid, there's a respect back and forth that'll continue."

Nice of the doctor to explain, but I suppose I already knew that. Whatever is between my father and me, whatever keeps us talking and keeps us close, has nothing to do with work and economic class.

During one of my visits to Brooklyn not long ago, he and I were in the car, on our way to buy toiletries, as one of my father's weekly routines. "You know, you're not as successful as you could be," he began, blue-collar-blunt as usual. "You paid your dues in school. You deserve better restaurants, better clothes." Here we go, I thought, the same old stuff. I'm sure every family has five or six similar big issues that are replayed like well-worn videotapes. I wanted to fast-forward this thing when we stopped at a red light.

Just then my father turned to me, solemn and intense. His knees were aching and his back muscles were throbbing in clockable intervals that registered in his eyes. It was the end of a week of lifting fifty-pound blocks. "I envy you," he said quietly. "For a man to do something he likes and get paid for it—that's fantastic." He smiled at me before the light changed, and we drove on. To thank him for the understanding, I sprang for the deodorant and shampoo. For once, my father let me pay.

1989

CRITICAL THINKING POINTS: *After you've read*

1. Lubrano discusses the differences between himself as a white-collar worker and his dad as a blue-collar worker. What are other differences between the two men?

2. Do you think Lubrano's father would have reacted differently to a daughter's—rather than a son's—professional success? Why or why not?

3. Lubrano writes, "I've often believed blue-collaring is the more genuine of lives, in greater proximity to primordial manhood. My father is provider and protector, concerned only with the basics: food and home, love and progeny." Do you agree with his statement? Why or why not?

SOME POSSIBILITIES FOR WRITING

1. Lubrano writes, "Some psychologists say that the blue-white-collar gap between fathers and sons leads to alienation." Research this gap between parents and children.

2. Interview a father, uncle, or grandfather about his job. Try to discover whether he is doing something he likes or working just for pay.
3. In the last decade, boys and men have lagged behind girls and women in just about every educational category. Research some of the causes of this diminished success.

When I Heard the Learn'd Astronomer

Walt Whitman

In 1855, Walt Whitman (1819–1892) published the first of many editions of *Leaves of Grass*, a volume of poetry indisputably ranked among the greatest in American literature. Today, Whitman's poetry has been translated into every major language. It is widely recognized as a formative influence on the work of such American writers as Hart Crane, William Carlos Williams, Wallace Stevens, and Allen Ginsberg.

When I sitting heard the astronomer where he lectured with
  much applause in the lecture room,
How soon unaccountable I became tired and sick

CRITICAL THINKING POINTS: *As you read*

1. Exactly what is an "astronomer"? What kinds of people might be attracted to or successful in the field of astronomy?
2. Walt Whitman is famous for the sounds his poems make. As you read, write down phrases that strike you as particularly wonderful or odd arrangements of words. What makes these phrases "poetic"?
3. What makes the astronomer "learn'd"? In what ways is he or is he not "learn'd"?

When I heard the learn'd astronomer,
When the proofs, the figures, were ranged in columns before me,
When I was shown the charts and diagrams, to add, divide,
    and measure them,
When I sitting heard the astronomer where he lectured with
    much applause in the lecture room,
How soon unaccountable I became tired and sick,
Till rising and gliding out I wander'd off by myself,
In the mystical moist night-air, and from time to time,
Look'd up in perfect silence at the stars.

1892

CRITICAL THINKING POINTS: *After you've read*

1. Read or reread Antler's "Raising My Hand," later in this chapter. What common themes do the poems share?

2. What kinds of statements might the poet be making about formal education? What in the poem leads you to your opinions?

3. The poet Jack Gilbert wrote, "We must unlearn the constellations to see the stars." How is his statement a reflection of Whitman's poem?

SOME POSSIBILITIES FOR WRITING

1. Why might the speaker in this poem, at the very end, look up "in perfect silence at the stars"? Explore at least two different reasons.

2. Find Walt Whitman's "Song of Myself" and read Section 6, which begins "A child said, What is the grass?" The speaker of that poem, the poet, seems to be the teacher in that situation. How does reading this poem change your reading of "When I Heard the Learn'd Astronomer," if at all?

3. Write a scene in which Antler, the author of "Raising My Hand," meets Walt Whitman. What do they talk about? How is each conversation a reflection of what you know about the author?

The Art of Regret

Jonathan Ritz

Jonathan Ritz's essays and stories have appeared in *Cimarron Review, Passages North,* The *Chicago Tribune,* and other publications. His work has been nominated for two Pushcart Prizes. He teaches writing at Michigan State.

When I look back at the fall of 1989—the semester I started at Pitt after failing out of Penn State—I think of it as the first step up I took from the bleak years of high school and early college. It wasn't that I changed myself or my life drastically; I simply made a few small but precise turns of some inner emotional screw.

CRITICAL THINKING POINTS: *As you read*

1. What regrets does the narrator have? What regrets does he think his mother has?
2. Why do people sometimes contemplate "what if," or, as Ritz says, its remorseful cousin "if only"? Have you ever done this? About what?
3. How can negative experiences motivate a person?

AMANDA: You are the only young man I know who ignores the fact that the future becomes the present, the present the past, and the past turns into everlasting regret . . .

TOM: I will think that over and see what I can make of it.

—Tennessee Williams, *The Glass Menagerie*

In the summer of 1989 my mom and I made a car trip from her father's house in Florida back to our home in Pittsburgh. We took turns driving, and the first night of our trip we stayed in a Motel Six in Savannah, Georgia. It was early evening and we were still a little wound up from the road, but neither of us felt much like swimming or watching cable TV, so I talked her into buying us a bottle of wine at a nearby gas station. It took a bit of coaxing, though, because I was currently on a run of bad luck in which drinking had had some part, and my mom felt a little guilty about her complicity.

I was not quite twenty years old and had just failed out of Penn State, the All-American college of my father's salad days. A week later I'd gotten busted for underage drinking at a friend's party, which resulted in a two-hundred dollar fine and a ninety-day suspension of my driver's license, due to start the day we returned home. The suspension would last the entire summer, ending just in time for me to begin commuting to classes at the University of Pittsburgh in the fall.

We sat at the table in our motel room and drank the wine, with ice, out of plastic cups. We talked some about the car and the trip. In two days we would be back home, back in Pittsburgh, and it would be time for mom to return to work. My mother had graduated from college with a triple major in art history, English, and French (the world's three most practical disciplines, she'd joke), then gone on to teach high school in Detroit. A few years later she met and married my father, and when my older brother was born she left her teaching job to stay home full time. When she re-entered the working world with two kids and twenty years later, what was awaiting her was a secretarial job in a suburban financial planning firm. Her boss was a homely, humorless man who condescended to her, even as she was fixing up his incompetently written correspondences before mailing them.

I was listening to her familiar complaints sympathetically, when suddenly we were talking, for some reason, about Charleston, West Virginia, a city we'd be passing through the next day.

"You know we almost lived in Charleston," she told me.

We'd moved several times as I was growing up, and I had some dim recollection of Charleston being a possible destination at one time. "When was that?"

"When we were living in Cincinnati. Your father was in the running for a job in Charleston. We even went down one weekend to price houses."

"I guess I remember that."

"That was a good job," my mother said, somewhat dreamily. "Partner in charge of the Charleston office." At the time my father was an accountant working for a national firm.

"Charleston," I said. "I wonder what that would have been like."

"Well, we would have been . . . wealthy." She laughed a little at the word, like it was some kind of happy accident that might have befallen our family. "It was quite a good job. And it's a small city, Charleston," she continued. "It's where Governor Rockefeller and his wife live. There's probably only one good private school and country club. I imagine we would have gotten to know the Rockefellers eventually." She stirred the ice in her glass with a finger. "They might have become friends."

It was unusual to hear this kind of talk coming from my mom. A running source of amusement for our family was the bourgeois pretensions of our fellow suburbanites: the neighbors across the street with a mailbox which was a bronze replica of their house; the family next door with the $2,000 pure-bred German husky my mother described as "Aryan;" the neighbors who each Christmas put up an array of lights so vast and blinding that it was inadvisable to look directly at it. I had seen my mother look at all these people with ridicule, even scorn, and yet here she was, waxing wistfully about lost chances for big money, missed opportunities to befriend the aristocracy.

But I knew what she was doing. She had just visited her eighty-year-old father, my grandfather, who looked healthy, but eighty. His home was full of reminders of her mother, who had died the year before. And here she was drinking wine from a gas station with her twenty-year-old son, who was basically a good kid but seemed to be going nowhere fast. And on Monday it was back to work, back to the job where no one cared that she was a triple-major in college, or that she spoke French pretty well, or that she had a racy sense of humor. This was her life, her reality, so she was, for a few minutes, allowing herself to imagine another one.

I poured the last of the wine into our glasses. "So, I would have gone to a private school, you said?" I wanted to hear more about it. I thought of the factory-like high school I'd attended in suburban Pittsburgh. My graduating class had been almost 700 kids; my name was misspelled on my diploma.

"If you'd wanted. It would be your choice." She touched me on the shoulder. "You would have been a lot happier there."

I was quiet a moment, thinking about there. After all, my current situation was this: I had failed out of college after two semesters, and soon I'd be back home to spend the summer working some mindless job, some mindless job my parents would have to drive me to. And there was more. The girl I'd been seeing at Penn State had moved back to New Jersey for the summer, and out of my picture for good, and I had more or less decided that it was impossible I'd be meeting anyone new for awhile. Of course, you could also add to that list that I was a white, middle-class American male, with two parents who invariably put my needs before their own, but this, needless to say, didn't seem to count for much at the time. My disappointments and failures seemed much more significant.

So we sat there together, mother and son, both of us indulging in the same thoughts, both of us, I knew, speaking silently to ourselves the same words. Different. Wealthy. What if . . .

What if my family had made that move? What if we'd joined a country club with an Olympic-sized swimming pool, where all summer I was given privileged access to the tanned daughters of the town's elite? What if I'd gone to a private high school where I simply wasn't permitted to be an anonymous under-achiever?

What if, Charleston?

The memoir of adolescence generally narrates the author's passage into self-understanding; in contemporary memoirs, this understanding often involves a coming-to-terms with a bizarrely dysfunctional family, with parents and other relations in the throes of dramatic maladies. As a memoirist, I have no such luck; I have only that most pedestrian of human proclivities to explore: regret. Like most kids, I grew up assuming that my family was normal, so I figured that regret was a common indulgence, a sort of benign national pastime. It was a given that the reality of our lives was something we viewed with disappointment, always weighing it against some expansive, unrealized alternative. For my mother and me, this took the form of reveries like our Charleston one: What if things had been done differently?

For my father, it manifested itself in his professional wanderlust. By the time I was seventeen and preparing to go to college, my family had moved four times in order for my father to change jobs. My dad seemed to be in a constant state of dissatisfaction with his current occupation; by the time we had relocated and he'd settled into a new job, he was already starting to assemble a list of grievances, already starting to plan the possibility and occasion of his escape. It was certainly not the principle of work he had a problem with—he held religiously to the Protestant ethos that hard work is by its very nature virtuous. Instead, it was the type of work that it had become his lot to do—answering to bosses who were deceitful and political, dealing in abstract financial principles that seemed to have no relevance to anything truly useful. Surely, he must have figured, there is a better alternative. And every few years our family would pack up and pursue one.

In contrast to my dad's grocery list of complaints—the alcoholic co-worker, the carping client—my mom composed lyrical ballads of regret. Dad's sorrows were generally aired at the evening meal, as we dispatched the family pot roast, but mom tended to wax wistfully before dinner, as she was out in the kitchen preparing the roast. With a glass of wine in one hand and an oven thermometer in the other, she'd sing along with a weepy Sinatra album playing a bit too loudly in the living room (last night, when we were young). Some nights I'd wander in and she'd tell me about different moments from her past, things which only later in life did I come to recognize as her touchstones of regret. She talked about boys she had dated in high school, a journalism contest she won as a teenager, her acceptance (eventually declined) to Bennington, the teaching she had done in Detroit before getting married. When I was little I would listen in awe as my mother described the rich potential of her past. Then my father would get home, and we'd eat.

As for me, I exhibited my parents' tendencies in equal measure. I was certainly my father's son, losing interest in my various adolescent pursuits with impressive swiftness. In sports, I went from rabid interest in baseball to obsession with soccer in one season. In school, I would spend the fall quarter enchanted with history, only to be fully out of love with it by Christmas (in just about every subject I'd run the entire spectrum of grades over the course of a year, finishing with my inevitable C+). Even with friends I jumped around a lot, moving between whichever social cliques would have me like some kind of high school double agent.

But I was also—probably even more so—my mother's son. Even at fifteen I had racked up an impressive list of regrets, and figured that I had already made several irreparably wrong turns on the road of life. Friday nights I would gather with my friends at a hang out spot in the woods and pass along pilfered bottles of beer. For awhile I would joke and gossip with everyone else, but soon the booze would soak in and I would start indulging in the joys of "what if," and its remorseful cousin, "if only." Even surrounded by friends, reeling pleasantly from an illicit buzz, I was deeply dissatisfied. I longed for things I didn't have. I wanted new friends to hang out with on Friday nights. I wanted a girlfriend. I wanted to be recognized as extraordinary, or at least special, for something. As a teenager, I could drink and get as morose as a balding middle-age divorced guy.

One day in late spring, during my final semester of high school, my dad took the day off work and the two of us drove up to the "Happy Valley" of State College, Pennsylvania, so I could see the campus. There was a certain absurdity to the trip because I was currently failing Senior English, a class required for graduation, and I was undecided about college in general, but I could tell my dad was looking forward to it, so I tried to act interested. At the time, the only thing I had any real interest in was writing self-absorbed songs on a cheap electric guitar laden with heavy, wet distortion (a style of music Seattle would make popular, but not for another few years). My parents understood that writing and playing music was my dream, but they also wanted me to go to college, so we made a deal: I would go to Penn State to study classical guitar, an instrumental style I didn't know the first thing about, but I could also join a rock band and play in bars at night instead of getting a part-time job.

We began our visit with a brief sweep around the campus, my dad animatedly describing his alma mater's various attractions: Beaver Stadium (where he only missed three home games in four years); the ivy-covered brick building where most of his business courses met; the diner (now a bar) on College Avenue where he'd worked as a short order cook. It was unusual for the two of us to take a trip together, even more unusual to see my dad so excited, and I tried to muster some enthusiasm on his behalf.

"Sounds like you really loved college," I said.

"Well," he started, and paused. We were at an intersection, and he watched as a group of students crossed in front of us. "I guess I did."

"It's supposed to be the best years of your life."

My dad looked over at me and smiled, which surprised me; he was generally distrustful of such overblown statements.

Later we met with a music professor, who shook my dad's hand and gave us a pile of forms to fill out. Paunchy and non-descript, the professor looked depressingly like the band teacher at my high school. He asked me what my instrument was, and when I said "guitar" he looked briefly to my dad, who nodded.

By the time we left the building I was already depressed, my adolescent hopes already meeting head on with the unappealing realities. I pictured myself on the first day of class, walking into a room full of other music students. They would all be warming up their polished acoustic guitars, running expertly through arpeggio scales, and I would get out my dented electric and start banging out the opening bar chords of "Cinnamon Girl," slightly out of tune.

"Wrong room," they would all say at once. "Wrong room."

We left the music building and walked the several blocks into downtown. The day was clear and cool; the students were wearing shorts and heavier tops, mostly sweatshirts turned inside out. We must have been instantly recognizable as a father and son prospecting the campus, and that transparency made me uncomfortable as it would any teenager, but I was still glad to have him with me. Not only because he knew his way around, but because this was really his day, and I was glad to have the attention off me, glad to be excused from the obligation of acting ambitious and optimistic. We ate lunch at a fast food restaurant right across from the diner-turned-bar, where 30 years earlier my father had wielded lard and spatula to earn money for his undoubtedly modest living expenses.

Maybe ghosts aren't just the spirits of the dead, but also the traces of ourselves that we leave in the past. About a year later, as I was completing the fiery descent of my final semester at Penn State, I'd have this strange notion that the ghost of my dad as a young man, a shadow from his best years long past, was with me, watching, helplessly.

Many of us, I think, try to make sense of our lives by constructing them as narratives: we're the protagonist in a story we read by living through it. There are supporting characters, conflicts and tension, recurring themes and motifs, and, if we're lucky, occasional periods of climax and resolution. When I look back at the fall of 1989—the semester I started at Pitt after failing out of Penn State—I think of it as the first step up I took from the bleak years of high school and early college. It wasn't that I changed myself or my life drastically; I simply made a few small but precise turns of some inner emotional screw. Part of this was a result of a creative writing course I took, the first class I signed up for at Pitt.

The class was called "Introduction to Fiction," and I wasn't sure if it was a writing course or a literature one; I took it because it met in the late afternoon and it filled a general Humanities requirement (unnerving, sometimes, to consider how many of my life's paths were decided arbitrarily). Our first assignment was to complete a short story. My mind turned quickly to the most clearly identifiable "short stories" I could think of—the half-hour Twilight Zone episodes I had collected on video as a kid. The day the story was due I sat down and typed out eight-pages: one Christmas Eve a hopeless drunken man who has squandered all his life's possibilities is given a gift-wrapped box by a mysterious Santa on a street corner. The man unwraps the box and is instantly transported into an alternate version of his life, all sober and shining, complete with house, wife, kids. The story was titled, inscrutably, "The Present," and I thought it had a certain eerie redemptive quality to it, but the day it was workshopped the other students called it "unbeliev-able" and "predictable." Then the instructor, pronouncing the final judgment, called my story "genre."

The mass rejection stung, but I caught on quickly. The other students—most of them English majors—were handing in stories that seemed to me simply typed pages from their diaries, but those stories met with steady praise from the other students and the professor. There were stories about smoking pot and drinking in bars and having sex on seedy futons, all of them in first-person. After workshopping several of these stories the class seemed to arrive at the conclusion that the writers were their narrator–protagonists, which everyone found exciting. It was certainly a new experience for me, looking around at my classmates and thinking, "there's the one who was molested by his uncle," and, "there's the one whose boyfriend is probably gay." I still couldn't remember most of their first names.

By the time I began working on my second story I was determined to gain admittance to the fold. The problem was, I didn't have the same things the others did to draw upon; my defeats and failures were significant, but hardly interesting. I began a draft—switching to the de rigueur first-person—about a college student who is failing out after his first year. I put him in his spartan dorm room on the last day of the semester, his roommate and friends already packed and gone for the summer. I had him gather together his "few lonely possessions": Kerouac paperbacks and Grateful Dead bootlegs, his journals. I had him smoke a joint and listen to Dylan's Blood on the Tracks and reflect on the seemingly inevitable nature of his failures. I was on page three.

Now what? I couldn't keep the character (his name was Jake, a pseudonym I assumed in many daydreams) in the dorm room, sitting on his bed, the entire story. Should I have him move back home, only to get an underage drinking citation and lose his driver's license? Should I have him confront his father, who sees in Jake's failures an extension of his own? Should I have his mother show up, and have the two of them move to West Virginia? I was hacking away at the story, trying out different possibilities, when it came to me.

I would let Jake escape—not only his immediate circumstances, but himself.

He finishes his joint and throws the Dylan CD into his traveling bag. He walks a mile to the Greyhound station and buys a ticket. No one knows anything about his plans (doesn't Jake have a family? Parents who will be worried sick when they don't hear from him?). He travels two days and arrives in a city where an old buddy lives. The friend gives Jake a place to live, sets him up with a job, introduces him to girls who see Jake as the beguilingly formless creature that he is. The friend becomes a brother—all the family Jake needs. I titled the story, "Homeward, and then Home."

The day it was workshopped the other students interrupted each other with praise. They looked at me as if for the first time, as if they hadn't before noticed me sitting at the table with them. At the bottom of the professor's typed comments— just above his signed name—he'd written, You've shown some real talent here. It was the first time in ten years I had received any kind of praise from a teacher. I left class with my head spinning. The acclaim had flushed my face, and made me so grateful I almost felt guilty.

For close to an hour I walked dreamily up and down Forbes Avenue, thinking about the possibilities. I thought about the thousand episodes from my own life that I was going to rewrite; the thousand different daydreams I was going to flesh out in words and step right into. After lunch I went over and signed the forms to declare myself an English major, then went to my professor to share the news of my conversion.

I knocked lightly on his open door and stepped in. He was sitting back in his chair, feet up on his desk, reading a book called Dreams of Distant Lives. I thought, yes, exactly.

Later that evening—the one we spent at the Motel Six during our trip back from Florida—my mother and I finished up our wine, then walked to a diner across the street. We didn't say much as we ate, both of us sliding deeper into our what-might-have-been, Charleston lives. I started thinking about how high school could have been different for me there. Perhaps I would have been a better student and a more disciplined athlete. Editor of the literary magazine and, say, captain of the soccer team. I saw myself saying heartfelt and final farewells to teachers and friends at the end of my senior year. After a stellar high school career I'd been accepted to Yale University, where I'd be starting classes in the fall.

The waitress refills my water glass, and I look up at my mother, who is quietly finishing a chicken salad sandwich. I know the look on her face; she is also elsewhere. Maybe she is having dinner with Jay Rockefeller, the Governor of West Virginia and a friend of the family.

Julie, he's saying between bites of pheasant, *I was wondering if you'd be interested in running the local wing of my re-election campaign.*

My mother considers this for a moment and asks a few pointed questions.

Oh, yes, one thing, the Governor interjects, *the job will require someone with a good command of French.*

They discuss details for a moment. Then my mom makes a slightly off-color but very funny joke, and it's a done deal.

1999

CRITICAL THINKING POINTS: *After you've read*

1. Why does praise for his second story affect the narrator so greatly? Have you experienced anything like this? Is this internal or external motivation?
2. What does the narrator learn from his parents' regrets?
3. How might this essay have been different if it had been written the semester after Ritz failed out of college rather than ten years afterward?

SOME POSSIBILITIES FOR WRITING

1. Ritz says, "Maybe ghosts aren't just the spirits of the dead, but also the traces of ourselves that we leave in the past." What prompts him to say this? Do you agree? Why or why not?
2. How do the narrator's parents' regrets differ from his? From each other's? Why do you think this is?
3. The narrator writes that it's "unnerving, sometimes, to consider how many of my life's paths were decided arbitrarily." Is this true for you? For people you know? How?

Raising My Hand

FROM *LAST WORDS*   Antler

Antler (his penname) is the author of *Factory* (City Lights) and *Last Words* (Ballantine), winner of the Walt Whitman Award and a Pushcart Prize. His poems appear in more than eighty anthologies, including *Earth Prayers, A New Geography of Poets; Reclaiming the Heartland: Lesbian & Gay Voices from the Midwest;* and *American Poets Say Goodbye to the Twentieth Century.*

> *How often I knew the answer*
> *And the teacher (knowing I knew)*
> *Called on others I knew (and she knew)*
> *had it wrong!*

CRITICAL THINKING POINTS: *As you read*

1. Think of a time when you knew the answer and the teacher called on someone else. How did you feel? Did this situation affect you differently when you were younger?
2. How would you characterize this teacher's attitude toward her students? What details in the poem led you to think this?
3. In what ways does this piece work as a poem? Could it have been written as a story? What changes would have to be made?

One of the first things we learn in school is
if we know the answer to a question
We must raise our hand and be called on
before we can speak.
How strange it seemed to me then,
raising my hand to be called on,
How at first I just blurted out,
but that was not permitted.
How often I knew the answer
and the teacher (knowing I knew)
Called on others I knew (and she knew)
had it wrong!

How I'd stretch my arm
as if it would break free
and shoot through the roof
like a rocket!
How I'd wave and groan and sigh,
Even hold up my aching arm
with my other hand
Begging to be called on,
Please, me, I know the answer!
Almost leaping from my seat
hoping to hear my name.

Twenty-nine now, alone in the wilds,
Seated on some rocky outcrop
under all the stars,
I find myself raising my hand
as I did in first grade
Mimicking the excitement
and expectancy felt then,
No one calls on me
but the wind.

1990

CRITICAL THINKING POINTS: *After you've read*

1. Have you ever known a student like the narrator? What were some of your reactions to him or her? Were you ever such a student? How did your classmates react to you?

2. What are some of the reasons a teacher might not call on a student with a raised hand? Have you ever known the answer to a question but did not raise your hand? What were some of the reasons you didn't?

3. Antler talks about one of the basic "rules" of formal education—raising one's hand to speak. Make a list of other rules you've learned, from elementary school through high school or college. What rules now seem silly and outdated?

SOME POSSIBILITIES FOR WRITING

1. Speculate about what questions the narrator is thinking of answering when he raises his hand at the end of the poem.

2. Choose one of the rules you've listed above. Write at least a page about how you continue to use that rule or how you never use that rule now.

For instance, in fourth grade you had to ask to use the bathroom, but you don't usually need to do that as an adult.

3. Read or reread Walt Whitman's "When I Heard the Learn'd Astronomer," earlier in this chapter. Compare and contrast it to Antler's poem. What does each seem to be suggesting about teaching? What does each seem to be suggesting about learning?

It's Electric: Fragments of My Life as an Epileptic

Amanda Schaefer

Amanda Schaefer earned a degree in literature and religious studies. She lives, works, writes, and reads voraciously in Eau Claire, Wisconsin.

She says, "You're epileptic? Me too, when I was younger,"
and smiles.

I'm electric/epileptic/electric/epileptic/alive/able/capable

CRITICAL THINKING POINTS: *As you read*

1. Schaefer creates a version of herself by drawing from a variety of "texts" (literature, music, cinema, television, family narratives, etc.). Pay attention to the kinds of texts she uses.
2. How might this be considered a "research paper"?
3. Pay attention to the way this essay looks on the page. How does that influence you as a reader?

"I sing the body electric."

—Walt Whitman

And then again, anybody whose mouth is cut crossways is given to lying, unconsciously as well as knowingly. So pay my few scattering remarks no mind . . . I know only my part.

—Zora Neale Hurston, *Dust Tracks on a Road*

No matter what my Mom does in her life, she's not going to hell when she dies. She tells me that she's already been there—nine months pregnant, Wichita, Kansas, mid-August. The memories I have of Kansas are not my own. I was only two when we moved, so I have to borrow memories from my mom. She was born there, but grew up in the foothills of the Rocky Mountains. She never really liked Kansas around the time I was born—too hot, too sticky, too flat. Yellow. I always think

245

yellow when I think of Kansas in August. Wheat fields, heat. I was born to the sound of cicadas buzzing like live wires in the trees. Or not. I certainly can't be trusted with these things.

I sing the body electric.

Cap'n Crunch and Schoolhouse Rock on a Saturday morning. Katie had the blue feet-in pajamas; I had the pink ones. As I tongued the cuts on the roof of my mouth (Cap'n Crunch is *dangerous*) and watch the electricity montage, I think of dad. They're singing about my dad.

How did it feel, Dad, when the current paralyzed you, sticking you to the floor? What did it *feel* like?

"I hadn't slept all night, and the base needed power. I was so groggy that I forgot to flip it off before I <insert technical jargon I'll never understand>. Someone had to knock me off before I got electrocuted."

Wow dad. I can't even imagine.

Wait a few years. Sleep deprivation leads to electric current for more than one generation of Schaefer.

I sing the body electric.

Then something bent down and took hold of me and shook me like
the end of the world. Whee-ee-ee-ee, it shrilled, through the air crackling
with blue light, and with each flash a great jolt drubbed through me till
I thought my bones would break and the sap fly out of me like a split
plant. I wondered what terrible thing it was that I had done.

— Sylvia Plath, *The Bell Jar*

If Kansas is yellow, my seizures are blue.

—It's ok, dad. I just dropped my fork. Your eyes are scaring me. Is this the way you looked when you saw Uncle Ray seize? Uncle Tim? I can't control my arms now. I'm so tired. Why'd you wake me up, mom? I'm getting dizzy. Dad, what's going——

I sing the body electric.

She calls it her inheritance. You can't get from one side of the room to
the other without cracking your head on it.

—Toni Morrison, *Song of Solomon*

Electricity is my inheritance. Grampa, Wild Bill. He would climb a utility pole in a storm to fix something that had gone wrong. While he was up there, something crossed, something touched, something went wrong, the back of his shoulder was blown out by a rogue current. Grampa, how did it feel? Grampa, what's going—

I sing the body electric.

I'm sorry I got the white gurney dirty. I don't remember walking outside with no shoes. I don't remember anything.

> The only people for me are the mad ones, the ones who are mad to live, mad to talk, mad to be saved, desirous of everything at the same time, the ones who never yawn or say a commonplace thing, but burn, burn, burn like fabulous yellow roman candles exploding like spiders across the stars.
>
> —Jack Kerouac, *On the Road*

"You look like the type."

I didn't honestly think he was saying I was the Jack Kerouac type—likening my abundance of extra electricity to an abundance of spirit, creativity and charisma. But I was surprised at the scornful laugh. I had honestly not thought there was a "type." I realized that he was implying a stereotype—wearing a helmet, that stigma of mental disability. Retarded, to use his word for it.

I can't drive like other kids at my high school. I have to be excused from class to take medication. My grades are good, though. But what if that's not enough? What if I can't do the things I want because of these rogue currents in my brain?

I sing the body electric.

> She chewed things. As a baby, as a very young girl, she kept things in her mouth.
>
> —Toni Morrison, *Song of Solomon*

I had become defensive after that. I wanted to make my epilepsy something for other people to be scared of, not just me. If I act tough about it, it makes it harder for them to make fun of me.

"I have an oral fixation."

"Oh reeeeealy."

"Yeah. Thumb sucker. It's why I smoke."

"Girls only tell guys they have oral fixations for one reason."

"Yeah? Well, I got to tell you, I have epilepsy. Anything you put in my mouth I'm liable to bite off."

"Jesus. I should have known from your haircut you were a man-hater. Dyke." The static crackled as he brushed past me.

I sing the body electric.

> Listening to him, I decided that I must be an English teacher and lean over my desk and discourse on the eighteenth-century poets and explain the roots of the modern novel.
>
> —Zora Neale Hurston, *Dust Tracks on a Road*

Well, it was actually a woman. She helped me realize that what I want to do is teach English, to teach literature.

> What if I can't?
> > you look like the type
> What if I have a seizure during class?
> > look like the type
> What if my brain is fried?
> > look like the type
> What if my medication makes me unable?
> > look like the type
> what
> > look
> if
> > like
> I'm
> > the
> too
> > type
> *electric?*

She says, "You're epileptic? Me too, when I was younger," and smiles. I'm electric/epileptic/electric/epileptic/alive/able/capable

I sing the body electric.

2004

CRITICAL THINKING POINTS: *After you've read*

1. How does the recurring Walt Whitman line "I sing the body electric" tie the entire piece together?
2. Schaefer's essay is written without a linear plotline. How does this affect you as a reader?
3. How do each of the people in Schaefer's essay influence her?

SOME POSSIBILITIES FOR WRITING

1. Using Schaefer's essay as a model, write your own "mystory" by creating a fragmented representational version of yourself by drawing from a variety of "texts" (literature, music, cinema, television, family narratives, etc.).
2. Research literary theorist Robert Scholes and metafiction. Argue for or against Schaefer's essay being considered an example of metafiction.
3. Research the causes and cures of epilepsy.

Reunion

Dawn Karima Pettigrew

Reverend Dawn Karima Pettigrew holds a degree in social studies, with a focus on popular culture and media, from Harvard University, as well as a Master of Fine Arts in creative writing from Ohio State University. An ordained minister of Cherokee, Creek, Chickasaw, Choctaw, and other Native American descent, she is the author of *The Way We Make Sense* (2002) and *The Marriage of Saints* (2006).

> *I see Ollie Panther in the grandmother's cheekbones,*
> *and that young guy might as well be Thomas Crow.*
> *Probably could see the whole Cherokee nation,*
> *if I sit here and study them all long enough.*

CRITICAL THINKING POINTS: *As you read*

1. Why might the title be read as ironic? Is it sarcastic? If so, to whom is it addressed?
2. How does Jane Gisgi "reinvest," if at all, in Qualla Boundary Reservation?
3. What are some details that represent the narrator's past life on the Qualla Boundary Reservation? What are some details that represent her current life as an Ivy League student?

*Jane Gisgi, Ivy League student, reinvests in
    Qualla Boundary Reservation*

I endure the air-kisses,
avoid the cellular phones,
wend my way through the basil and hypocrisy
in the brunch-hour air.

Painted and powdered,
white-washed and well-read,
I slide into my seat
boy-girl-boy-girl.
Three pairs of sky-colored eyes
blink back at me.

I forget to remember to thank the waiter.
My eyes find,
at one table made from two,
earthen hands, clay-colored faces.
Men swing hair they can sit on.
Women balance babies between their knees and the table.

I see Ollie Panther in the grandmother's cheekbones,
and that young guy might as well be Thomas Crow.
Probably could see the whole Cherokee nation,
if I sit here and study them all long enough.

Higher education might hurt less if I know them,
it's no threat to my diploma if I wave.

"Look at that."
My undecided boyfriend sounds like anthro stirred with psych.
I was born in the dark, but it wasn't last night.
I've read enough textbooks to know what's coming.
"Looks like they brought the whole tribe with them."
He might love me, he's so mean without malice.

I should shout,
make a scene,
right out of drama class,
chant or cry,
"We do bring everyone with us.
No one is left behind.
We do not warehouse old people for profit,
or eat without children or raise them in boxes."
That's not what comes out.
After all, I left the mountains.
Tired of tourists, bored with bears,
embarrassed everytime Cousin Jess went chiefing,
I ran to college,
ran from drums,
ran from dulcimers.
It's amazing what'll make you go foolish.

I lift my head,
meet each pair of eyes in pale faces,
"Those people are my family."
My smile is wet sugar.

The eyes across the table drop,
fingers pinch the hearts from artichokes.
Soft "sorry" mixing with talk of Sartre
makes everything in me miss the mountains.

1998

CRITICAL THINKING POINTS: *After you've read*

1. How does the narrator's life in the mountains conflict with the life she adapted to at college? What details in the poem lead you to your conclusions?
2. In what ways do Native American students often leave a way of life behind when they go to college? How might this be similar to or different from the kinds of changes other students go through?
3. What might Pettigrew be feeling when she says, "Higher education might hurt less if I know them, / it's no threat to my diploma if I wave"?

SOME POSSIBILITIES FOR WRITING

1. Write about a time when you were with a group of peers and you were embarrassed to see someone from your past, such as an ex-boyfriend or ex-girlfriend, a friend from elementary school, or a family member.
2. Create the next scene for Jane and her boyfriend as they leave the restaurant. What might their conversation be like? How might the episode in the restaurant affect their future relationship?
3. Why does the narrator say, "Those people are my family"? Support your conclusions with details from the poem.

Scarlet Ribbons

Michael Perry

Michael Perry is the author of three memoirs: *Population 485* (2003), *Truck: A Love Story* (2007), and *Coop* (2010). He has released two albums with his band, the Long Beds. He lives online at www. sneezingcow.com.

> *It's one thing to speak of the heart as a center of emotion, quite another to see it lurching between the lungs like a spasmodic grey slug.*

CRITICAL THINKING POINTS: *As you read*

1. What makes a "liberal arts" education?
2. What skills do writers and nurses share?
3. Would you prefer to have a nurse or doctor who was also knowledgeable and interested in fields such as music, art, and literature? Why or not?

The man in the small room with me is a convicted murderer. He is immense and simple, looks as if he was raised on potatoes and homemade biscuits. I'd lay money that before he wound up here, his clothes smelled of bacon grease. He knows I am uneasy. I know he knows, because he looked me square in the eye, grinned, and told me so. Still, *The New York Times Magazine* has given me an assignment, and although I may be edgy in this prison, in this room with concrete blocks close all around, with this bulky killer two feet away, I must complete it.

I am to determine if the prisoner is happy.

The first person to whom I ever administered an intramuscular injection was a cheery wee granny. I see her still, seated on a hospital chair, flannel gown hiked up to expose her left quadriceps, head fluffed with a blessing of fine white curls, smile as sweet and warm as a batch of sugar cookies. The steel needle is cocked an inch from her skin, and she chirps: "Have you ever done this before?"

"Oh yes," I lie. Brightly. Smoothly. Never breaking eye contact.

Heraclitus said you can never step in the same river twice. Jorge Luis Borges said time is forever dividing itself toward innumerable futures—that we choose one alternative at the expense of all others. We can never be who we set out to be, but will always be who we were. I went to college to become a nurse. I became a writer.

We spring from a thicket of tangents. I remember the exact moment I decided to become a nurse. I was reading *Sports Illustrated* in the high school library. I was supposed to be in World Literature, but the university recruiter was in town, and we were allowed to skip class to catch her pitch. I signed up, but once in the library, headed straight for the magazine rack, lolling through *People* and *Newsweek* while the rest of the students joined the recruiter at a long table. Late in her presentation, I overheard her reciting a list of majors: "Biology. Business. Economics. History. Nursing."

"Nursing," I thought. "That sounds interesting."

I filled out the necessary paperwork, and reported for class in the fall.

Nursing is so easily caricatured by white skirts and chilly bed pans. Pills and needles. Shots. But this is like saying painting is about paint. Practiced at its best, nursing is humane art, arisen from intimate observation and expressed through care. Again and again our instructors reminded us that every patient is a point of convergence, an intersection of body, mind and spirit. We were trained to obtain quantifiable data with stethoscopes and sphygmomanometers, but we were also warned not to ignore intuition. We learned to change sheets without removing a bedridden patient, we learned how to prevent decubitus ulcers by monitoring pressure points, we learned to stick lubricated feeding tubes up noses, but we also learned to seek eye contact, percept nonverbal communication, and establish trust so rapidly that within five minutes of meeting a stranger we could quite comfortably inquire after his bowel habits. Facilitate, reflect, and clarify. Employ empathic response. These are the interviewing tools of the nurse. Also eminently functional, as it turns out, in the service of interviewing murderers for *The New York Times*. Every time I filled a syringe, I was filling my writer's pen with ink.

Heraclitus also said we are never being, but becoming, and in between clinical rotations and classes on skin disease, all nursing students were required to enroll in humanity courses. This rankled me. I have never been taken with the concept of a liberal arts education. The idea of lounging around dissecting Tom Jones when I should have been dissecting piglets always struck me as mark-time dawdling along the road to employability. I'd change out of surgical scrubs and hustle off to badminton class, Econ 110, or The United States Since 1877, or Introduction to Film, or Introduction to Creative Writing, or Folk Music in America. I expected the Chemistry 210, the General Zoology, the Developmental Psych and the Survey of Biochemistry, and willingly submitted to the Minnesota Multiphasic Personality Inventory assessment designed to reassure the beehived matron at the helm of the nursing school that I was unlikely to bite my patients or develop perverse affections for iodine swabs, but a .5 credit course in relaxation? What did these things have to do with nursing? Peering into the thicket of tangents, I saw nothing but obstruction.

Early one morning during a summer O.R. rotation, long before most people had finished their first cup of coffee, a surgeon inflated and deflated a lung for me. It pressed out of the patient's bisected chest like a greasy trick balloon, then shrunk back and retreated into a cheesy lump beside the patient's writhing heart.

The mechanics were fascinating. Here was the corporeal gristle revealed. We tote our organs around not even knowing them. There is nothing abstract about a glistening length of intestine. But by drawing back the curtain, the surgeon managed to reframe the mystery. Now that I had peeked behind the liver, eyed the discrete lumps of organ, I wondered where the spirit might lie. It's one thing to speak of the heart as a center of emotion, quite another to see it lurching between the lungs like a spasmodic grey slug. We were as deep in the body as you can get—exactly where did they keep the soul? The finite, meaty nature of it all blunted my ability to imagine the body as a place for spirits.

When I was a child, my father, a quietly eccentric farmer, would sometimes come in the house after the evening milking, rustle up his blighted trumpet, and play "A Trumpeter's Lullaby." We sat at his feet, and he swayed above us, an overalled gnome, eyes closed, gently triple-tonguing the wistful passages. The notes twined from the brass bell in liquescent amber, settling over our hearts and shoulders, wreathing us in warm, golden light. Many years later I found myself standing at a meds cart in a surgical ward, sorting pills into cups, chafing in my polyester student nurse smock, short of sleep and overwhelmed by my patient care assignments, desperately trying to sort out the drug interactions before my instructor arrived to grill me on the same, when "A Trumpeter's Lullaby" came seeping from the speaker in the ceiling. I was swept with a desperate melancholy. I have never been so lonely. And try as I might, I could not see how the path on which I stood could be backtracked to the feet of my trumpeting father. In more dramatic circumstances, I might have stripped off my smock, gobbled the meds, and run off to join an agrarian brass band, but my instructor appeared and began to ask me if there was any danger in administering Diazepam and Clonidine in tandem. I fidgeted, answered hopefully, and resumed forward motion.

After four years, I took my nursing boards, convinced I'd fail, and passed just fine. Worked as a nurse for a while and liked it. But I kept having trouble remembering all the numbers, and how Demerol interacted with Elavil, and just what it was phagocytes did, and yet I could remember the poem the stunted guy behind me in creative writing wrote about electrical highlines, and what the professor said it lacked, and how I believed the highline guy could have done better, and how I remembered the way the folk music professor crossed his legs and fingered his guitar when he explained that the scarlet ribbons in "Scarlet Ribbons" weren't ribbons at all, but bright blood on a child's fractured head, and I thought of the lung puffing and falling, and I said if I can conjure these things so easily while I stumble over drug interactions and hematocrits, perhaps I ought to write instead. I took to talking about this. Over-frequently, apparently, because one day my girlfriend said, "Why don't you stop talking about it and do it?"

And so I did.

There was much to learn, but much less to unlearn.

I wonder if Heraclitus would dare tell the prisoner he was not stepping in the same river twice. A lifetime of days between those tan concrete blocks? Sounds like the same old river to me. Still, our little visit must have been a diversion. I imagine he chuckled with his roomie later when he described catching me in my unease. It was a fair cop. But as he leaned in and grinned, I slid the needle in and drew out what I needed. When I stepped out of the prison, it was cold and windy, but the waning light seemed to propose an answer.

1999

CRITICAL THINKING POINTS: *After you've read*

1. Why do you think humanities courses are required of nursing or other technical majors?
2. What might Perry mean when he says about changing careers, "There was much to learn, but much less to unlearn"?
3. The last few words seem to leave the essay quite open ended. Why do you think Perry chose to close his essay this way? What answer do you think is proposed?

SOME POSSIBILITIES FOR WRITING

1. Do you know people who are employed in jobs or careers that they hate? Speculate about what might make them stay.
2. Many college faculty and administrators would like to think that the first year of college is one of exploration. Argue for or against first-year students declaring a major.
3. Which type of degree do you think is more valuable, a technical degree that teaches a specific skill or a liberal arts degree that offers exposure to many different areas of education? Why do you answer the way you do?

STUDENT RESPONSE TO "SCARLET RIBBONS"

I thought that the reading made some good observations about what a liberal education is and spoke to its importance. In my opinion, the connection was made in the reading between a liberal arts education and something we are passionate about that touches us or interests us at a deeper, more meaningful level. When the writer wrote about his time as a nurse, he described it all as being very mechanical, about facts, numbers, interactions between medications, etc. Although he was interested in it and found the work to be important, his heart wasn't really in it. When he first decided to be a nurse and started his education, I don't think this mattered to him as much. He didn't even understand why they wanted him to take general education course, which reminds me a lot of how people at this school often think. I must admit that when I have to take upper level math classes or classes that I don't feel I need, I feel the same way. But as time went on, he started to be ripped away from the nursing profession by the connections he felt with other things that he was more passionate about. I think he felt almost lost in the nursing profession because it did not speak to his heart. This illustrates a very important thing we face in college. Some majors you can choose will pay a lot and have a lot of job advancement, but many of those do not appeal to me as much. However, ones that do are often ones with a very unclear career path (like philosophy!) and possibly very low pay. It's basically a trade-off for a lot of us students between picking something we are passionate about and choosing something that has a more secure future. But he makes a good point, that being a nurse is just as important of a job as writing about a prisoner. Although some people would not agree that they are of equal importance, every job needs a willing participant to carry it out, and society learns and grows because of every person and role. Overall, I do think that it is important for people like doctors and nurses to still have to take general education classes in college. It broadens your knowledge and understanding of the world, as well as shows you possible alternative paths that might better suit you.

Passion

Monica Coleman

Rev. Monica A. Coleman, PhD, is an ordained elder of the African Methodist Episcopal Church and the author of *The Dinah Project: A Handbook for Congregational Response to Sexual Violence* (2010) and *Making a Way Out of No Way: A Womanist Theology* (2008). Coleman is associate professor of constructive theology and African American religions at Claremont School of Theology and co-director of the Center for Process Studies. Read more about her at http://monicaacoleman.com.

Sometimes I think it was easier before I surrendered . . . accepted.

CRITICAL THINKING POINTS: *As you read*

1. What is Coleman's definition of a "calling"? Can it be solely religious in nature?
2. Do you typically think of the word "passion" when you think of a career? Why or why not?
3. What kinds of "callings" have you experienced or do you know that others have experienced?

Passion. Something in your heart that you can't let go of. Or more importantly, that won't let go of you. Something that makes your eyes sparkle and the pace of your words increase whenever someone asks you about it. That thing that keeps you up at night. Thinking and wrestling. That thing you do senseless activities for—like turn down good-paying jobs. That thing, that without, you are convinced you will die.

For me, that passion has always been books. I can not remember my life without books. My mother was a reading teacher, so I grew up believing that every room in a house was supposed to have a bookshelf, and every book on it should have been read . . . a couple times. I have been punished for reading—when I stayed up late with a flashlight under the covers instead of going to sleep—but I was usually rewarded. Summer book clubs at the local library, book reviews for the elementary school paper, payment of five dollars for every book I read during the summer—and ten dollars if my father chose the book. When my classmates spent the last weeks of their senior year traveling, gardening, building cars and robots, I read a book and made my first attempt at literary criticism by comparing the folk legend of the flying Africans to Toni Morrison's *Song of Solomon*. In trudging through the stacks at the local university library and sitting for hours in the PS 153 section, I discovered my passion—books.

257

My craving quickly became particular. After spending an entire high school summer reading through the works of James Baldwin and finding myself depressed, angry, and still inspired, I found my first heroines: Alice Walker, Toni Morrison, Zora Neale Hurston. I read quickly, and absorbed their stories like they were my own. I lived in the bodies of several women, I cursed at my blond-haired dolls, and I walked down the streets of Eatonville, Florida [home of Zora Neale Hurston]. Soon, my literary journeys became my committed cause: I berated my high school teachers for teaching only the "major works." I demanded more reading of literary criticism. I wanted course credit for writing on Gloria Naylor. I instituted a book club.

So it was like going to heaven the day I changed my economics and mathematics major to African American Studies. No one had ever told me that I could major in that which I loved. I had discovered that I could spend four years of my time and energy reading more, writing about reading, reading more, and writing about reading. The day I met Henry Louis Gates, Jr. was like finding the pot of gold at the end of my rainbow. Not only could I major in African American Studies (focusing on literature), but I could study with the man whose criticisms I read in my spare time. I could learn directly from the mind of someone who had previously been a name I had seen in everyone's bibliography. It's the same feeling I got when I met Nellie McKay, Toni Morrison, Hazel Carby, Deborah McDowell and Arnold Rampersad. They would never remember me, but I put their faces with their names, and my world had suddenly and swiftly become not only real, but attainable. I fell in love with books, their authors, their critics, and I fell in love with academia.

Of course I wanted to write. Don't all lovers of literature secretly want to write?! But the deeper passion was for teaching. I wanted less to become a Nella [Larsen], Jessie [Fauset], Gloria [Naylor], Gayl [Jones], Ntozake [Shange] or Octavia [Butler], than I wanted to nurture others into the love affair I had found with them. I had no desire to write a novel. In fact, I am still certain that I would fail if I tried. I just wanted to see the light in someone else's eyes. I wanted to see the marked up books in the hands of my students. I wanted to be the harsh midwife that Maryemma, Thadious and Jamaica were to me as they watched me labor through thirty-page papers, and still insisted I could do better. Most importantly, I wanted to be paid to spend hours in the libraries, at the computer and know that I was not crazy.

I remember trying to explain to my parents that academia is a career, a job, a joy, even. They sat blank-eyed, as do all from the generation that believes you go to school to get a job. Wanting to be a professor is like never leaving school. It is like never graduating. To them, it was some quirky license I had invented to become "a professional student." I won numerous grants that allowed me to research full time during my summers. I found fellowships that supported term-time research. I bonded with the stacks on campus, in small public libraries and in The Library of Congress. The more I researched without affecting my parents' checkbooks, and the more I convinced them that people do this—that Black people do this—the more supportive they became. So I was just as surprised as my parents when I found another passion. One I tried to ignore, but could not. One that I tried to escape, but could not. One that meant death, if I did not. It was ministry.

Unlike my passion for books, I had no role models. In my hometown, I had never seen a preacher under the age of 35, let alone a female minister. I didn't even know that there were young ministers or female ministers until I went to college. I came to know many as surrogate mothers and sisters. I simply assumed that I had my passion and they had theirs. I lived for Black women's books, and their authors, while they lived for "The Book" and its Author. I had prayed, and considered academia my calling.

Yet there was another calling on my life. When I had stopped paying attention, the time I once spent reading Barbara Christian and Mary Helen Washington, became time I spent on the train to church. The nights that were reserved for reading yet-another-unassigned novel, were spent on my knees, praying for the members of the Bible Study I now led. The courses that I once took in the Department of English, became graduate courses in the Divinity School. My friends were still the aspiring politicians and professors, but some were now aspiring preachers. These things made me a devoted Christian, I told myself, not a minister.

I knew it immediately, and I was outraged. One day my Bible opened to the book of Amos and I read, "But neither was I a prophet, nor was I a prophet's son, but I was a herdsman and a gatherer of sycamore fruit, and the Lord took me as I followed the flock and said, 'Go prophesy unto my people.'" I immediately called my best friend, and said to her, "Guess what God had the nerve to tell me!" I knew what it meant because I had read it, "But I was not a preacher, nor a preacher's kid, but a student, a scholar-in-training, and the Lord took me . . ." Instantly I knew it was a calling to preach—a calling towards ordained ministry—and I didn't want it. I was perfectly happy on my life plan to B.A. by twenty, Ph.D. by twenty-five, book by twenty-nine, tenure by thirty-two—and sometime fall in love, get married, have children. Everyone has dreams. This was mine.

Quiet as it's kept, I didn't want the hassle of being a young woman in the ministry in the Black church. My new exposure to seminaries, young preachers, and female preachers had quickly informed me of the disbelief and disrespect I would encounter if I woke up one day and said, "I've been called to preach." I didn't want to fight a system that seemed to respect age and male ego just as much as, if not more than, the calling itself. I didn't want to wear the tired look of carrying the burdens of your family, friends and congregation. I didn't want to stand behind a pulpit and be expected to say something important or holy. My disdain quickly became fear when I declared to myself that I would not do this "preaching thing." I heard wrong. I was called to academia. Period.

I soon learned that fighting the culture of ministry, and fighting God were two very different things. They both seemed impossible. I didn't want to do the former, even though victory was possible; and I consistently did the latter when defeat was inevitable. I didn't consciously hear myself asking other ministers about their callings. I didn't really even notice when I applied for scholarships and listed "ministry" as an interest. I didn't realize that I was writing sermons in my head. I was completely caught off guard the morning I prayed, "Okay God, I give up. I'll do this because I love You."

Sometimes I think it was easier before I surrendered . . . accepted. I was happy leading seminars, teaching Bible Study, receiving calls in the middle of the night by friends who would say, "I thought you could get a prayer through." No one really noticed me, and there were no expectations on my personal life—what kind of men I should date, what length of skirts I must wear, what style of hair I must choose. Now, two months before my senior year, I was entering a world about which I knew nothing except "Christ and Him crucified." That didn't seem like enough when I had three months to apply to seminaries, pursue ordination, explain to my professors, mentors, family and friends that "the plan had changed." I barely left time to do my own personal mourning over the dismantling of the dream.

I began to feel how it was actually harder to live without my passion. Everytime I heard a sermon, I secretly wanted to preach—even though I didn't know what to do. Everytime I prayed, something seemed to be blocking communication between God and myself. Everytime I tried to find a Ph.D. program that would fit my needs, something didn't work out. The day I preached my first sermon, I found a comfort in sitting in the pulpit that I had previously only known when sitting down in the African American Studies section of Harvard Book Store. Once again, I was in love.

With the clarity of hindsight, I recognize ministry as a life-long passion as well. I remember the things that I said to family members about my interest in studying the Bible. I recall the times that I spent more time in church than at home or in school. I reminisce about the summer workshops I held for the children at my home church. It was all so natural, I didn't even notice it. I didn't know the passion was there, until it bubbled up inside me and threatened to erupt if I did not acknowledge it.

I went to seminary at Vanderbilt Divinity School. Attending seminary is known as a painful process because it causes one to consider your faith under the microscope of your professors. Sometimes it seems like they take their tools and try to chisel away at your inner core of beliefs. Everything that isn't stone, will fall away. I have discovered the parts of me that are stone, and the parts that are not. I feel a mixture of joy and anguish when I walk into a bookstore. I am reminded that I have left the plan that so quickly became part of my soul. I see the new books, and yearn to buy and read them all. I realize that I am out of the academic loop that once sustained me—I haven't been to conferences, I haven't read the Op-Ed page of *The New York Times*, I haven't seen a "Call for Papers" since I graduated from undergrad. In my core, I ache for Octavia and J. California—or sometimes, just the thrill of library research and the anticipation of instruction. In the height of those painful moments, I found that both my passions are true. I have discovered a way to have my cake and eat it too.

I first tasted the cake the year I convinced the director of field education at Vanderbilt that teaching can be considered ministry. I arranged to perform a grossly underpaid internship at a local university. As a "teaching assistant" in the department of Africana Studies, I returned to my first love. Every week, I taught twenty-five students about Martin Luther King, Malcolm X and contemporary issues in

Black manhood. The class content was more political and sociological than literary, but the educational process was the same. I used excerpts from my favorite poets. I taught my students how to improve their writing and research techniques. I learned that religious questions arose no matter the official nature of the topic. Much to my surprise, I could respond to their inquiries. When their eyes lit up with recognition and understanding after class discussion, I did not feel like a thorough scholar. I felt like a successful minister.

I learned to change "the plan." I still intend to apply to Ph.D. programs, and I make more time to read and write between preaching engagements and seminary assignments. In the delay of one passion, I found joy in another. I have come to enjoy preaching, and the way the spoken word can reach another person. I have fallen in love with my denomination's liturgy, and I revel in small opportunities to read scripture, pray, or line a hymn. I bring my three years of theological education into every church Bible study I attend. I also believe that teaching college students is a valid branch of ministry. After all, it was my professors who ministered to me.

I also found ministry in being a graduate student. My friends in other graduate schools often asked me to pray for them, to find scriptures for them, to tell them something about God, and everything about my calling. The joy comes in telling them about both my callings, and saying, "Well, there are plans and passions. Sometimes they diverge, but sometimes they come together too."

1997

CRITICAL THINKING POINTS: *After you've read*

1. What books or movies have inspired you in the same way Coleman was inspired by African American writers?
2. Are there some careers for which passion is a requirement more than others? What makes that so?
3. College students are often pressured into an area of study by their parents or even their peers. How is Coleman's struggle different from that situation?

SOME POSSIBILITIES FOR WRITING

1. Write a definition of "passion" as it pertains to a career. Use concrete details to describe this abstract concept.
2. Coleman says, "Well, there are plans and passions. Sometimes they diverge, but sometimes they come together too." Write about a time when a plan you made came together perfectly with one of your passions. Now describe a time when the two did not merge.
3. Recall a time when your life plans changed significantly. What led to that change? Was the outcome positive because of, or in spite of, that change? Was the outcome negative? What made it so?

On the Radio

FROM *COMING LATE TO RACHMANINOFF*   **Richard Terrill**

Richard Terrill is the author of *Coming Late to Rachmaninoff*, winner of the Minnesota Book Award for poetry; *Almost Dark*; and several books of creative nonfiction, including *Fakebook: Improvisations on a Journey Back to Jazz* and *Saturday Night in Baoding: A China Memoir*. He teaches creative writing in the MFA program at Minnesota State University, Mankato.

In eighty years or less, describe
one unimaginable sorrow.

CRITICAL THINKING POINTS: *As you read*

1. What is a GED? Who generally gets one?
2. How does the speaker of the poem feel about the interviewer? How do you know that?
3. What makes a good test question?

> *"I wrote my answer about my parents dying in the same year,*
> *one in the spring and one in the fall."*
>   —Cecil Smith, age 94, oldest known recipient of a GED

I wonder what the question was,
and what those in charge,
suits and ties in Central Office,
those who studied education hard but hated
to teach and couldn't say so,
what they expected the young people to answer;

1. In 500 words, why did you quit school?
2. What is the worst thing that can happen to someone?
3. What did you learn from experience
you could not have learned in school?

The inflection of the interviewer rises and falls,
peaks and valleys of condescension.
She talks as if he understood
a different language
(he does, though not the one she speaks).

It was the kind of feature they run ten minutes
before the news, public radio
finding novelty, reaching
beyond New York to the provinces.
Her voice climbs the ladder of the slide
then starts down the waxed way

"What's next for you, Mr. Smith, a dorm room at UCLA?"
"Well, keeping good health, I imagine."

*4. In eighty years or less, describe
one unimaginable sorrow. Be vague,
general, and philosophical. Cite examples
only from your own experience, feeling free
to ignore the reading selections from your test packet.
5. Have you ever felt bad about an experience
and later realized you shouldn't have?
If not, explain.*

2003

CRITICAL THINKING POINTS: *After you've read*

1. What are some other answers Mr. Smith might have given to the interviewer?
2. Why do you think the narrator might have come up with questions four and five? Are they good questions?
3. Why does the interviewer come up with the questions she does? Are they good questions?

SOME POSSIBILITIES FOR WRITING

1. Attempt to answer one of the questions in the poem.
2. Write this same scene from the point of view of Mr. Smith.
3. Choose one of the Critical Thinking Points from above and develop your original responses further.

"Only Connect": The Goals of a Liberal Education

William Cronon

William Cronon is the Frederick Jackson Turner and Vilas Research Professor of history, geography, and environmental studies at the University of Wisconsin-Madison. He has been a Rhodes Scholar, Danforth Fellow, Guggenheim Fellow, and MacArthur Fellow, and he has won prizes for his teaching at both Yale and University of Wisconsin.

My list consists not of required courses but of personal qualities: the ten qualities I most admire in the people I know who seem to embody the values of a liberal education.

CRITICAL THINKING POINTS: *As you read*

1. What do you associate with the phrase "liberal education"? Where do your associations come from?
2. Cronon writes about liberal education as "an educational tradition that celebrates and nurtures human freedom." Consider how his ten qualities might do this.
3. Do you believe that it is possible to become a liberally educated person even if you are not attending a liberal arts school? If so, how might one attain these ten qualities?

W hat does it mean to be a liberally educated person? Many of us continue to place great stock in these words, believing them to describe one of the ultimate goods that a college or university should serve. So what exactly do we mean by liberal education, and why do we care so much about it?

In speaking of "liberal" education, we certainly do not mean an education that indoctrinates students in the values of political liberalism, at least not in the most obvious sense of the latter phrase. Rather, we use these words to describe an educational tradition that celebrates and nurtures human freedom. These days liberal and liberty have become words so mired in controversy, embraced and reviled as they have been by the far ends of the political spectrum, that we scarcely know how to use them without turning them into slogans—but they can hardly be separated from this educational tradition. Liberal derives from the Latin *liberalis*, meaning "of or relating to the liberal arts," which in turn derives from the Latin word *liber*, meaning "free." But the word actually has much deeper roots, being akin to the Old English word *leodan*, meaning "to grow," and *leod*, meaning "people." It is also related to the Greek word *eleutheros*, meaning "free," and goes all the way back to the Sanskrit word *rodhati*, meaning "one climbs," "one grows." Freedom and growth: here, surely, are values that lie at the very core of what we mean when we speak of a liberal education.

All the required courses in the world will fail to give us a liberal education if, in the act of requiring them, we forget that their purpose is to nurture human freedom and growth.

I would therefore like to return to my opening question and try to answer it (since I too find lists irresistible) with a list of my own. My list consists not of required courses but of personal qualities: the ten qualities I most admire in the people I know who seem to embody the values of a liberal education. How does one recognize liberally educated people?

Ten Qualities

1. They listen and they hear.

This is so simple that it may not seem worth saying, but in our distracted and over-busy age, I think it's worth declaring that educated people know how to pay attention—to others and to the world around them. They work hard to hear what other people say. They can follow an argument, track logical reasoning, detect illogic, hear the emotions that lie behind both the logic and the illogic, and ultimately empathize with the person who is feeling those emotions.

2. They read and they understand.

This too is ridiculously simple to say but very difficult to achieve, since there are so many ways of reading in our world. An educated person is literate across a wide range of genres and media. Educated people can appreciate not only the front page of the *New York Times* but also the arts section, the sports section, the business section, the science section, and the editorials. They can gain insight from not only *The American Scholar* and the *New York Review of Books* but also from *Scientific American, The Economist, The National Enquirer, Vogue,* and *Reader's Digest.* They can enjoy John Milton and John Grisham. But skilled readers know how to read far more than just words. They are moved by what they see in a great art museum and what they hear in a concert hall. They recognize extraordinary athletic achievements; they are engaged by classic and contemporary works of theater and cinema; they find in television a valuable window on popular culture. When they wander through a forest or a wetland or a desert, they can identify the wildlife and interpret the lay of the land. They can glance at a farmer's field and tell the difference between soy beans and alfalfa. They recognize fine craftsmanship, whether by a cabinetmaker or an auto mechanic. And they can surf the World Wide Web. All of these are special forms of reading, profound ways in which the eyes and the ears and the other senses are attuned to the wonders that make up the human and the natural worlds. None of us can possibly master all these forms of "reading," but the mark of an educated person is to be competent in many of them and curious about all of them.

3. They can talk with anyone.
Educated people know how to talk. They can give a speech, ask thoughtful questions, and make people laugh. They can hold a conversation with a high school dropout or a Nobel laureate, a child or a nursing-home resident, a factory worker, or a corporate president. Moreover, they participate in such conversations not because they like to talk about themselves but because they are genuinely interested in others. A friend of mine says one of the most important things his father ever told him was that whenever he had a conversation, his job was "to figure out what's so neat about what the other person does." I cannot imagine a more succinct description of this critically important quality.

4. They can write clearly and persuasively and movingly.
What goes for talking goes for writing as well: Educated people know the craft of putting words on paper. I'm not talking about parsing a sentence or composing a paragraph, but about expressing what is in their minds and hearts so as to teach, persuade, and move the person who reads their words. I am talking about writing as a form of touching, akin to the touching that happens in an exhilarating conversation.

5. They can solve a wide variety of puzzles and problems.
The ability to solve puzzles requires many skills, including a basic comfort with numbers, a familiarity with computers, and the recognition that many problems that appear to turn on questions of quality can in fact be reinterpreted as subtle problems of quantity. These are the skills of the analyst, the manager, the engineer, the critic: the ability to look at a complicated reality, break it into pieces, and figure out how it works in order to do practical things in the real world. Part of the challenge in this, of course, is the ability to put reality back together again after having broken it into pieces—for only by so doing can we accomplish practical goals without violating the integrity of the world we are trying to change.

6. They respect rigor not so much for its own sake but as a way of seeking truth.
Truly educated people love learning, but they love wisdom more. They can appreciate a closely reasoned argument without being unduly impressed by mere logic. They understand that knowledge serves values, and they strive to put these two—knowledge and values—into constant dialogue with each other. The ability to recognize true rigor is one of the most important achievements in any education, but it is worthless, even dangerous, if it is not placed in the service of some larger vision that also renders it humane.

7. They practice humility, tolerance, and self-criticism.
This is another way of saying that they can understand the power of other people's dreams and nightmares as well as their own. They have the intellectual range and emotional generosity to step outside their own experiences and prejudices, thereby opening themselves to perspectives different from their own. From this commitment to tolerance flow all those aspects of a liberal education that oppose parochialism and celebrate the wider world: studying foreign languages, learning about the cultures of distant peoples, exploring the history of long-ago times, discovering the many ways in which men and women have known the sacred and given names to their gods. Without such encounters, we cannot learn how much people differ—and how much they have in common.

8. They understand how to get things done in the world.
In describing the goal of his Rhodes Scholarships, Cecil Rhodes spoke of trying to identify young people who would spend their lives engaged in what he called "the world's fight," by which he meant the struggle to leave the world a better place than they had found it. Learning how to get things done in the world in order to leave it a better place is surely one of the most practical and important lessons we can take from our education. It is fraught with peril because the power to act in the world can so easily be abused—but we fool ourselves if we think we can avoid acting, avoid exercising power, avoid joining the world's fight. And so we study power and struggle to use it wisely and well.

9. They nurture and empower the people around them.
Nothing is more important in tempering the exercise of power and shaping right action than the recognition that no one ever acts alone. Liberally educated people understand that they belong to a community whose prosperity and well-being are crucial to their own, and they help that community flourish by making the success of others possible. If we speak of education for freedom, then one of the crucial insights of a liberal education must be that the freedom of the individual is possible only in a free community, and vice versa. It is the community that empowers the free individual, just as it is free individuals who lead and empower the community. The fulfillment of high talent, the just exercise of power, the celebration of human diversity: Nothing so redeems these things as the recognition that what seem like personal triumphs are in fact the achievements of our common humanity.

10. They follow E. M. Forster's injunction from *Howards End*: "Only connect . . .".
More than anything else, being an educated person means being able to see connections that allow one to make sense of the world and act within it in creative ways. Every one of the qualities I have described here—listening, reading, talking, writing, puzzle solving, truth seeking, seeing through other people's eyes, leading, working in a community—is finally about connecting. A liberal education is about gaining the power and the wisdom, the generosity and the freedom to connect.

1998

CRITICAL THINKING POINTS: *After you've read*

1. Choose what you think are the most important qualities from Cronon's list. Why are those important to you? What do they say about your chosen major or future?

2. Are there any qualities that you would add to Cronon's list? Try to come up with two more qualities of a liberally educated person.

3. Which of the qualities on Cronon's list may be most difficult for you to develop? Why those?

SOME POSSIBILITIES FOR WRITING

1. Research the benefits of a liberal education. Are employers more likely to choose a candidate who has a liberal education or a more technical education?

2. Consider your university's general education requirements. Argue for or against making general education truly general so all majors would have the same options for fulfilling university requirements.

3. What role does technology play in becoming a liberally educated person?

This Was the Assignment: Instructions for Life

THE FOLLOWING FIFTY "INSTRUCTIONS" WERE GATHERED FROM A VARIETY OF FIRST-YEAR STUDENTS

This Was the Assignment: Read "Instructions for Life" (http://www.a-silver-lining.org/instructions4life.html), and then write your own list. Try to come up with fifteen to twenty maxims that describe how you want to live your life.

CRITICAL THINKING POINTS: *As you read*

1. Which of these instructions for life seems to speak to your strengths as a person, and which to your weaknesses? Why?

2. Try to categorize the instructions. Which of them have to do with work, romance, or friendship? Which of them might pertain to all categories?

3. Do you think most people have a set of instructions they live by? If so, are they their own or adopted from someplace else (religious doctrine, self-help book, etc.)?

Learn the rules, and then break some.

1. 90% of success is just showing up (so Woody Allen says). For the next 10%: show up and do what they tell you.

2. Energy in, energy out: when you give energy to anyone or anything, you get energy back.

3. Think before any words leave your mouth: how might this affect my audience?

4. Never repeat anything negative you hear; only repeat positive statements.

5. Pay attention to the details. What brand of coffee does your friend drink? What's your mom's favorite book? People notice when you pay attention: love lives in the details.

6. Listen twice as much as you talk.

7. Do something physical every day.

8. Mean what you say: relationships—with loved ones, co-workers or acquaintances—go much more smoothly if you're straightforward about what's on your mind. Life is difficult enough without people wondering if you mean what you say.

9. Phrases for life: "Please" opens nearly every door, "Thank you" means it will open again soon, "I'm sorry" is absolutely necessary.

10. People are sometimes mean or rude or nasty for no reason; kill them with kindness.

11. Join the "real" club: when you want to reach out to someone but you're afraid they'll think you're hokey or sentimental or sucking up, do it anyway. People instinctively recognize when you're being real.

12. Less clutter makes you feel more content in any surroundings.

13. You always have a choice, even if it's how you react to someone or to a situation.

14. Be grateful for 5 things each day. Keep a "gratitude journal" or spend time at the end of each day considering 5 things you're grateful for that day.

15. Be a good friend to everyone who wants you to be a friend; you know very little about how much of an asset you are to other people's lives.

16. Trust in few but be trustworthy to all.

17. Learn the rules, and then break some.

18. Remember that silence is sometimes the best answer.

19. Mind your own business.

20. Give more than people expect; you never know what you might get back.

21. Live life through music, it can be a source of inspiration when you have none.

22. Don't judge on first impressions, you could miss a golden opportunity.

23. Be yourself no matter the situation and stand up for what you believe in.

24. Lend a helping hand and a loving heart. Helping people in need or someone less fortunate is such a wonderful thing . . . it will brighten up your day too!

25. Everyday take time for yourself to relax and gather your thoughts of the day.

26. Pour your heart and soul into someone or something—you might get hurt, but there is someone for everyone or something to help everyone.

27. "Pay it forward." When someone does something nice for you, you return the favor by doing something good for someone else.

28. Don't judge others. Get to know them first and you might be shocked.

29. Laugh as much as possible. It will make you and the people around you feel better.

30. Make and keep as many friends as possible.

31. Marry your best friend.

32. Don't follow your dreams, lead them.

33. Sometimes the questions are hard and the answers are simple.

34. Don't let what you can't do stop you from doing what you can do.

35. It's better to be alone than in bad company.

36. Nobody can go back and start a new beginning, but anyone can start today and make a new ending.

37. Do not eat so much that you get a stomach ache.

38. Bring an umbrella with you everywhere.

39. Explore the world a bit before settling down.

40. Follow your heart at all times, but never forget your brain along the way.

41. Be involved with your community, family, friends, and faith.

42. Once a month think about something you want and work your ass off for it. Then stop and think how much somebody less fortunate would want this and give it to them. You will actually get the better end of the deal.

43. Happiness is a choice not a guarantee. Make the choice to share it.

44. Good friends are cheaper than therapy so hold on to them with all you have. When you realize you've made a mistake, take immediate steps to correct it.

45. Trust in God but lock your car.

46. If you make a lot of money, put it to use helping others while you are living. That is wealth's greatest satisfaction.

47. Get mad and then get over it.

48. Learn the rules so you know how to break them properly.

49. Love is everything it's cracked up to be. That's why people are so cynical about it. It really is worth fighting for, being brave for, risking everything for. And the trouble is, if you don't risk anything, you risk even more.

50. Talk slowly but think quickly.

2010

CRITICAL THINKING POINTS: *After you've read*

1. Which are the most memorable instructions from this reading for you? Why?

2. Which would you have a hard time believing in? Why?

3. Which of these instructions seem too trite and common place to be valuable? Why?

SOME POSSIBILITIES FOR WRITING

1. Do an Internet search for *Mahatma Gandhi's "Seven Deadly Social Sins,"* and compare and contrast these to "Instructions for Life" (those written by students). What can you learn from such a comparison and contrast?

2. Choose a quote that you have tried to live your life by. Write something that illustrates putting this quote into action in your life.

3. Research other "Instructions for Life" on the Internet. Compare and contrast the kinds of lists you find.

Further Suggestions for Writing—
"Been There, Done That"

1. Write an essay titled "Looking Forward/Looking Back," no matter where you are in your college career.

2. Compare and contrast the life you know as a college student to the life you might have had if you had made some other choice.

3. Compare and contrast some aspect of your school—for example, graduation requirements, football, dating—now to how it was twenty or forty years ago or more. Research your material.

4. Education, or what it means to be educated, means different things to different people. Choose two or three people from your life—parents, teachers, siblings, friends—for whom education means something quite different from what it means to you and examine some of these differences.

5. Human nature is constantly puzzling. Explore your thoughts on some apparently contradictory aspect of human behavior that you find particularly on a college campus: for instance, students pay tuition but often choose to miss class; most college students are legally adults but are often treated like children.

6. Does your school offer distance-education courses? Argue for or against these courses.

7. Argue for or against a topic such as speech codes at your university, the Greek system at your school, intramural athletics, or exploitation of student athletes.

8. Argue that college should or should not prepare students for specific careers.

9. Argue that universities do too much or too little for students.

10. Argue that too much has been made of technology at your university.

11. Argue that student athletes at major universities are or are not exploited.

12. Many people feel student organizations that endorse political and/or religious beliefs should not be supported by student fees. Argue for or against that proposition.

13. Write a paper titled "A History of Recent Affirmative Action Policies on College Campuses."

14. Do you believe that men and women communicate differently from one another? Research this subject to find support for your opinion.

15. What do you make of the fact that college grades do not seem to correlate very well with success after graduation? What might be some of the causes and/or implications of this lack of correlation?

16. Evaluate your high school's ability to prepare a student for college. Go beyond just your own experience.

17. Compare and contrast the university system in the United States to that in some other country.

18. Compare and contrast two-year institutions and four-year colleges or universities.

19. Interview someone you know who has a "job" and someone who has a "career." Compare the two concepts of work, using their specific examples. What are some generalizations you can make about the differences between a job and a career?

20. Working in groups, read and discuss the mission statement and rationale for general studies requirements in your college catalogue. What values do these statements express? Do you agree with them? Why or why not? Do you feel that a person who enrolls in your college has an obligation to endorse and uphold these values? Compare your reactions with those of the other groups in your class.

21. Why do students care what other students think? Write an essay called "Peer Pressure among College Students."

22. Research shows that current college graduates will change careers about six times throughout a lifetime. Visit your campus Career Center to gather information about at least three potential careers for yourself. What about your life now makes you believe that each of these careers might be appropriate for you? What education and/or skills do you need to acquire for each profession?

23. Why do some students drop out of college?

24. Read or reread Samuel H. Scudder's "Take This Fish and Look at It," in Chapter 4, and compare it to Walt Whitman's "When I Heard the Learn'd Astronomer." What theories of education and knowledge do the two pieces share? How are they different?

25. Write a scene in which Will Weaver's character, Walt, has a conversation with Alfred Lubrano ("Bricklayer's Boy"). What might the two men say about their fathers?

26. Imagine a dialogue between the narrators of "Signed, Grateful" (Chapter 4) and "Passion." What might they talk about? What might they say? What support do you have for your position?

27. Read *Shakespeare, Einstein, and the Bottom Line: The Marketing of Higher Education* by David L. Kirp (2003), and/or *Brainwashed: How Universities Indoctrinate America's Youth* by Ben Shapiro (2004), and/or *The Uses of the University* by Clark Kerr (2001), and/or any other broad examination of higher education. After considering these points of view, what insights and/or new awareness have you come to concerning your own education?

28. Choose at least three films from the list at the end of this chapter. What do they seem to say about life after college? What support do you have for your position?

29. Choose one of your responses to "Some possibilities for writing" in this chapter and do further research on some aspect of the topic. Write about how and why this new information would have improved your previous effort.

30. Find the original text from which one of the selections in this chapter was taken. What led you to choose the text you did? How does reading more from the text affect your original reading? Is there more you would like to know about the text, its subject, or its author? Where might you find this further information?

Selected Films—"Been There, Done That"

Amongst Friends (1993, USA). Three wealthy suburban childhood friends turn to crime as young adults. Written and directed by 26-year-old Rob Weiss. Drama/Crime. 86 min. R.

Art School Confidential (2006, USA). Starting from childhood attempts at illustration, the protagonist pursues his true obsession to art school. But as he learns how the art world really works, he finds that he must adapt his vision to the reality that confronts him. Drama, 102 min. R.

A Beautiful Mind (2001, USA). A biopic of the meteoric rise of John Forbes Nash Jr., a math prodigy who was able to solve problems that baffled the greatest of minds. He overcame years of suffering from schizophrenia to win the Nobel Prize. Drama. 135 min. PG-13.

The Big Chill (1983, USA). An ensemble cast of baby boomers reunite for a long weekend after the suicide of an old college friend. Drama. 103 min. R.

Carnal Knowledge (1971, USA). A gritty look at the seedy sex lives of two college pals (Jack Nicholson and Art Garfunkel) through the filter of their partners (among them Candice Bergen and Ann-Margret). Drama. 96 min. R.

Dark Matter (2007 USA). Based on actual events, a Chinese university student responds violently when his chances for a Nobel Prize are dashed by school politics Drama, 88 min. R.

Fight Club (1999, USA). A 30-something-year-old man disillusioned by what his life has become encounters an exciting stranger who introduces him to a new way of life. Drama/Thriller. 139 min. R.

Forrest Gump (1994, USA). Chronicles Forrest Gump's accidental experiences with some of the most important people and events in the United States from the late 1950s through the 1970s including meeting with Elvis Presley, President Kennedy, Lyndon Johnson, and Richard Nixon; fighting in Vietnam; and so on. Comedy/Drama. 132 min. PG-13.

Four Friends (1981, USA). Three men who love the same woman find their entwined lives fractured by college, drug abuse, and the Vietnam War. Drama. 115 min. R.

Girl, Interrupted (1999, USA). Feeling adrift since graduation, Susanna "accidentally" overdoses on pills and booze and is accused of trying to commit suicide. Based on

Susanna Kayson's autobiographical account of her stay in a mental hospital in the 1960s. Drama. 127 min. R.

The Graduate (1967, USA). Director Mike Nichols's watershed portrait of an aimless college graduate (Dustin Hoffman) whose progression from sex to love finally defines him. Drama/Comedy. 105 min. R.

The Heidi Chronicles (1995, USA). Adapted by Wendy Wasserman from her Pulitzer Prize–winning play, the film follows a woman from prep school to Vassar College and on through her adult life and loves. Made for cable. Drama. 94 min. N/R.

How to Make an American Quilt (1995, USA). Finn is a graduate student finishing a master's thesis and preparing for marriage when she returns to her grandmother's home for the summer and records her elders' tales of romance and sorrow as they construct a quilt. Drama. 109 min. PG-13.

Kicking and Screaming (1995, USA). Four recent college graduates don't want to face the realities of life on the outside. Comedy. 96 min. R.

Lions for Lambs (2007, USA). Injuries sustained by two Army rangers behind enemy lines in Afghanistan set off a sequence of events involving a congressman, a journalist, and a professor. Drama, 92 min. R.

Marie (1985, USA). The true story of a single mother (divorced after her husband battered her) who works her way through school and finally rises to the head of the Tennessee parole board. Sissy Spacek stars. 113 min. PG-13.

No Sleep 'til Madison (2002, USA). One by one, 30-year-old Owen Fenby's friends are deserting his annual pilgrimage to the Wisconsin State High School Hockey Tournament, forcing him to confront some harsh truths about his hockey obsession. Comedy. 85 min. N/R.

Old School (2003, USA). Three men are disenchanted with life and try to recapture their college days. Comedy. 90 min. R.

Reality Bites (1994, USA). A bright young cast (Winona Ryder, Ethan Hawke, Ben Stiller, Janeane Garofalo) stumbles into the real world after college. Romantic drama. 94 min. PG-13.

Reign Over Me (2007, USA). A man who lost his family in the September 11 attack on New York City runs into his old college roommate. This renewed friendship helps the man recover from his grief. Drama. 124 min. R.

Riding in Cars with Boys (2001, USA). Beverly Donofrio's best-selling memoir spans 20 years, from Bev's pregnancy at 15 in 1963, through parenthood on welfare with a heroin-addicted husband, and some resentment as an adult as her teenaged son takes priority over her ultimate goal of finishing college and publishing her memoir. Drama/Comedy. 132 min. PG-13.

Romy and Michele's High School Reunion (1997, USA). Lisa Kudrow and Mira Sorvino play ditzy best friends who attend their ten-year high school reunion, but first they completely remake their styles and identities in order to impress the people who tormented them in school. Comedy. 92 min. R.

St. Elmo's Fire (1985, USA). A loose-knit group of college friends finds that each of them bears a unique burden in facing adulthood. Drama. 108 min. R.

Tao of Steve (2000, USA). Underachieving, overweight kindergarten teacher Dex rediscovers a woman at his ten-year college reunion who forces him to re-examine his Zen-like system of seduction. Comedy. 87 min. R.

When Harry Met Sally (1989, USA). After graduating from college, Sally (Meg Ryan) carpools with her friend's boyfriend, Harry (Billy Crystal), to New York City. They meet by chance several times over the years and form a bond. Romantic comedy. 96 min. R.

For Critical Thinking Points on these films, see Appendix (p. 277).

Appendix

Thinking and Writing About Film

AS YOU WATCH

1. How is film, as a genre, different from written genres such as poetry, essays, novels, and short stories? Which are you more likely to interpret: a film or one of the other genres? Why?

2. Some people say the book has been replaced by the film. Do you believe this is true? Why or why not?

3. How are films more accessible than books by a general audience? Is this positive or negative? In what ways?

4. What stereotypes are apparent in the film you are watching? In what ways, if any, does the movie attempt to break out of stereotypes?

5. Take note of the soundtrack. How does it affect your emotions?

6. How does the film's narrative move along (action and frames)? Is the film chronological, backwards, futuristic? Why is it arranged this way?

AFTER YOU'VE WATCHED

1. With which character in the film do you most identify? Which character do you identify with the least? Why?

2. In your opinion, does this film offer a realistic depiction of high school or college? Why or why not?

3. In what ways is this film a reflection of its time? If the film's action takes place before its release date, do you think the era in which it was made affects the way the story is told?

4. What, specifically, in the film makes this a "coming of age" movie? Could it fall into another category? Can you create a category for this film?

5. Do you believe this film promotes a positive or negative image of students or teachers, men or women? How? Why?

6. Through whose eyes (whose perspective) do you see most of the action? Does the perspective change during the course of the film? Does this character change during the course of the film? If so, why?

SOME POSSIBILITIES FOR WRITING

1. In their credits, films often cite an original source text. Is this film based on a play, novel, or short story? If so, read the original and determine what has been added and/or deleted in the transition from print to film. Speculate as to why those aspects were added and/or deleted. Which did you prefer, the original text or the film version? Why?

2. Choose at least two characters from the film and imagine, then write, a page of original dialogue between them. Extend an existing scene in the film or create your own.

3. Read at least three reviews of this film and compare and contrast them. Which do you agree/disagree with? Why?

4. Imagine you have been asked to film "A Day in the Life of a Freshman" on your campus. What elements of your life would you include? If you have access to a video camera (many university libraries rent them), film some of your scenes.

5. Choose one piece in this collection and write a proposal to a film studio about why this piece would make an excellent film.

6. Watch at least three films from three different decades, and write a response about how each depicts high school and/or college students or teachers. What do these films seem to be saying about education/learning? In what ways are these films a representation of the times in which the stories take place and/or the times in which they were made?